MW00332080

SOUL WINNERS

The Ascent of America's Evangelical Entrepreneurs

DAVID CLARY

Prometheus Books

Guilford, Connecticut

(PB) **Prometheus Books**

An imprint of Globe Pequot, the trade division of
The Rowman & Littlefield Publishing Group, Inc.
4501 Forbes Boulevard, Suite 200, Lanham, Maryland 20706
www.rowman.com

Distributed by NATIONAL BOOK NETWORK

Copyright © 2022 by David Clary

All rights reserved. No part of this book may be reproduced in any form or
by any electronic or mechanical means, including information storage and
retrieval systems, without written permission from the publisher, except by
a reviewer who may quote passages in a review.

British Library Cataloguing in Publication Information Available

Library of Congress Cataloging-in-Publication Data

Names: Clary, David, 1974– author.
Title: Soul winners : the ascent of America's evangelical entrepreneurs /
  David Clary.
Description: Lanham, MD : Prometheus, an imprint of Globe Pequot, the trade
  division of the Rowman & Littlefield Publishing Group, Inc., [2022] |
  Includes bibliographical references. | Summary: "Soul Winners is a
  thoughtful and informative history that reveals the longstanding
  connections between business, politics, and religion in America, and the
  profound effect that evangelism has had on the country"—Provided by
  publisher.
Identifiers: LCCN 2021059253 (print) | LCCN 2021059254 (ebook) | ISBN
  9781633887824 (cloth) | ISBN 9781633887831 (epub)
Subjects: LCSH: Evangelists—United States—Biography. |
  Evangelicalism—United States—History. | Christianity—Economic
  aspects—United States—History. | Christianity and politics—United
  States—History. | United States—Religious life and customs.
Classification: LCC BV3780 .C575 2022 (print) | LCC BV3780 (ebook) |
  DDC 269/.20922—dc23/eng/20220331
LC record available at https://lccn.loc.gov/2021059253
LC ebook record available at https://lccn.loc.gov/2021059254

(∞)™ The paper used in this publication meets the minimum requirements of
American National Standard for Information Sciences—Permanence of Paper
for Printed Library Materials, ANSI/NISO Z39.48-1992.

For Jackie

There is but one rule—win souls for Jesus. Any tactics that produce the general result are good tactics. A good is wrought; therefore, the methods employed cannot be wrong.

—Evangelist Billy Sunday[1]

CONTENTS

PROLOGUE

The Plague

Evangelical Defiance and the Coronavirus Pandemic

> This is not about a virus. This is about shutting down the
> gospel of Jesus Christ. . . . And all these pastors that say, "Well,
> we should just roll over and comply," you don't understand.
>
> —Rodney Howard-Browne, addressing his Florida
> megachurch congregation, Easter 2020[1]

Days after the first case of a mysterious virus was confirmed in the
United States, President Donald Trump went on TV to downplay the
threat. "We have it totally under control. It's one person coming in from
China, and we have it under control. It's going to be just fine," Trump said
on CNBC on January 22, 2020.[2] The novel coronavirus that caused the
disease COVID-19 soon spread unchecked in dozens of countries. Trump
continued to tell Americans not to worry. "It's going to disappear. One
day—it's like a miracle—it will disappear. And from our shores, we—you
know, it could get worse before it gets better. It could maybe go away.
We'll see what happens. Nobody really knows," he said at a White House
event on February 27.[3]

The World Health Organization declared it a pandemic on March
11, and Trump proclaimed a national emergency two days later. By then,
the nation had reported two thousand cases and fifty deaths. Americans
were told to thoroughly wash their hands and follow such social-distancing
practices as keeping at least six feet apart from others in public settings. In-
fectious disease experts concluded that respiratory droplets primarily spread
the virus. They said that made indoor gatherings particularly dangerous.

In the absence of a national stay-at-home order, state and local governments imposed shutdowns that upended everyday life. In some areas, only
essential businesses like grocery stores, gas stations, banks, and pharmacies

were open. Sporting events, concerts, conventions, and fairs were canceled. Movie theaters, restaurants, and theme parks were closed. Such milestones as weddings, birthdays, and graduations were postponed or converted into virtual events. Without an effective treatment or vaccine, no one knew how long it would take for life to get back to normal.

The restrictions on public activities applied to houses of worship, and religious groups agreed that the emergency warranted canceling in-person services. The Church of Jesus Christ of Latter-day Saints suspended public gatherings worldwide on March 12. Roman Catholic dioceses dispensed the faithful from the obligation to attend Sunday Mass. The most notable exceptions to compliance were some evangelical churches and leaders.

At a service on March 15, Florida megachurch leader Guillermo Maldonado railed against government recommendations to avoid gatherings of more than 250 people. He urged his congregants to show up in person. "Do you believe God would bring his people to his house to be contagious with the virus? Of course not," said Maldonado, cofounder and "apostle" of the King Jesus International Ministry near Miami. "Fear is a demonic spirit."[4]

On the same day, fellow Floridian Rodney Howard-Browne told his congregants he would not close his church until the rapture "because we are raising up revivalists, not pansies."[5] Two weeks later, his River at Tampa Bay Church held two large services in defiance of county stay-at-home orders. Sheriff's deputies arrested Howard-Browne, who was charged with unlawful assembly and violating public-health emergency rules, both second-degree misdemeanors. "His reckless disregard for human life put hundreds of people in his congregation at risk and thousands of residents who may interact with them this week in danger," said Chad Chronister, the Hillsborough County sheriff.[6] (Prosecutors later dropped the charges.)

Meanwhile, Jerry Falwell Jr., then the president and chancellor of Liberty University in Lynchburg, Virginia, was pushing for his school to remain open. Falwell, the son of Liberty's late founder, Jerry Falwell Sr., insisted that new campus protocols were sufficient to let students live in dorms while taking classes online. "We think Liberty's practices will become the model for all colleges to follow in the fall, if coronavirus is still an issue," Falwell said on March 23.[7] His move to allow thousands of students, faculty, and staff on campus infuriated local officials. Within days, students fell ill with COVID-19 symptoms, with the first positive case confirmed on March 29. By mid-April, Liberty and the surrounding community reported seventy-eight cases and one death.[8] Falwell continued to reject orders to social distance and wear masks. (Falwell resigned several months later after a series of embarrassing personal scandals.)

All three evangelical leaders were fervid Trump supporters and shared the president's cavalier attitude toward the virus, or the "plague," as he sometimes called it. All were also running large enterprises that relied on a constant flow of people and donations. As the nation's unemployment rate soared to levels not seen since the Great Depression, a frustrated Trump erroneously claimed on April 13 that he had "total" authority to decide when to lift stay-at-home orders. Daily deaths related to COVID-19 spiked into the thousands in mid-April.

Trump and his Republican allies fed into the evangelical resistance.[9] After Howard-Browne's arrest, Governor Ron DeSantis issued a statewide order in Florida deeming houses of worship essential and clearing them to host gatherings of any size. Rich Vera, who runs a healing ministry in Orlando, told his crowd of in-person worshippers on April 5—Palm Sunday—that "this is not a time to hide, this is not a time to chicken out and this not a time to listen to online services only."[10] Trump tweeted that he would be watching the Palm Sunday service conducted online by Greg Laurie, a Southern California megachurch pastor.

The president wanted restrictions to be waived to allow in-person church services for Easter. Tony Spell, leader of a Pentecostal megachurch in Baton Rouge, Louisiana, refused to comply with a state ban on gatherings of more than fifty people and hosted hundreds of people indoors for each of his two services. Spell, pastor of Life Tabernacle Church, attacked the governor's order as an unconstitutional attack on religious liberty. When Spell went to court months later to answer misdemeanor charges for violating the order, he was denied entry for not wearing a mask. He claimed that masks are the "precursor" to the Antichrist and that a vaccine would "have the ability to track all of humankind."[11]

Trump continued to stoke tensions between churches and states by claiming on May 22 that governors needed to open houses of worship immediately. "If they don't do it, I will override the governors. In America, we need more prayer, not less," he said.[12] His statement did not have the force of law, but it signaled to his religious conservative base that he was with them. "We feel vindicated in the fact that this is what we have said all along, that churches are essential to our communities," said Jim Franklin, pastor of Cornerstone Church in Fresno.[13] Pastors argued that churches needed to be open to help people struggling with mental health problems and addiction relapses triggered by the shutdowns.

Franklin was among the more than twelve hundred pastors who signed a declaration against California's plan to allow businesses like shopping malls and restaurants to reopen at a greater capacity than worship services, claiming it discriminated against religion. The South Bay United Pentecostal Church in Chula Vista sued Governor Gavin Newsom on that basis, but the U.S. Supreme Court declined on May 29 to lift the state's restrictions.[14] Hundreds of churches, including Franklin's, reopened for Pentecost Sunday services on May 31 anyway.

Spotty contact tracing and testing made it difficult to track community transmission of the virus, but the noncompliance of churches harmed public health: Lighthouse Pentecostal Church in Oregon was deemed the epicenter of the state's largest outbreak in June 2020; at least fifty-one cases were tied to Graystone Baptist Church in West Virginia that the pastor attributed to "the attack of the devil on my church" rather than the lack of mask wearing; and a *New York Times* database in July linked 650 coronavirus cases to nearly forty churches.[15]

In June and July, new cases of COVID-19 surged across the Sun Belt, prompting some state and local governments to revive restrictions on public activities and mandate face coverings in public. With the virus spreading fast in Arizona, Trump spoke June 23 at a Phoenix megachurch that installed air purifiers claiming they could "kill 99.9 percent of COVID in ten minutes."[16] Trump's audience inside Dream City Church consisted of thousands of young supporters who were largely maskless and sat shoulder to shoulder.[17]

By the fall of 2020, overall cases topped 7 million and the White House itself felt the impact of the coronavirus. On September 26, Trump announced at a large social occasion that Judge Amy Coney Barrett would be nominated to replace the late Justice Ruth Bader Ginsburg on the Supreme Court. About two hundred mostly maskless dignitaries attended the event, with some hugging each other and speaking at close quarters both in the Rose Garden and inside the White House. Among those who tested positive in the following days were the president, the first lady, two senators, and Laurie, the megachurch pastor.[18]

The president received antiviral treatments and spent four days at a hospital. He then continued hosting large rallies with dense, maskless crowds as if the pandemic was a thing of the past. But the virus was again spreading out of control, setting records for new daily cases into the fall and straining hospital systems in the Upper Midwest and Mountain West. The nation's death toll surpassed four hundred thousand on January 19, 2021, as the one-year anniversary of the first recorded death approached.[19]

Signs of hope glimmered on the horizon as the Biden administration took control. Regulators granted emergency authorization to coronavirus vaccines, which were administered beginning in mid-December. The inoculations were effective—cases, deaths, and hospitalizations all fell sharply in January, February, and March—and they produced vanishingly few serious side effects. Many evangelicals distrusted the vaccines just as they had resisted scientific and government guidance throughout the pandemic. Some claimed that the vaccines contained aborted fetal cell tissue and that the true extent of vaccine-related deaths and injuries was not being reported. Others did not speak against vaccination, but they also did not encourage their followers to get their shots.

These attitudes had a direct effect on community response. A poll in late February 2021 found that about 45 percent of white evangelical adults said they would not get vaccinated against COVID-19, a far higher percentage than all other demographic groups.[20] Public health experts worried that the pandemic could be prolonged if tens of millions of evangelicals refused vaccination. They were proven right when the highly contagious Delta variant drove a surge in infections during the summer of 2021. Deaths and hospitalizations overwhelmingly consisted of unvaccinated people. A Pew Research Center poll in August 2021 reported that only 57 percent of white evangelical adults had received at least one coronavirus shot—far behind other religious groups and well below the overall figure of 73 percent. (The poll also revealed a sharp partisan divide: 60 percent of Republicans and people who lean Republican had received at least one dose compared to 86 percent of Democrats and Democratic leaners.)[21]

The push for vaccine mandates by governments and employers spurred a new round of evangelical outrage. Some churches, such as Skyline Church near San Diego, provided information to people seeking religious exemptions to the shots. "We've actually changed our stance from being less vocal to being more vocal, even at the detriment, potentially, of some people saying, 'I don't want to go somewhere where they're talking about these things,'" lead Pastor Jeremy McGarity said about the church's political engagement.[22] In an interview with the author in October 2021, McGarity said Skyline membership has grown during the pandemic to over five thousand. "They're coming to their church looking for answers. And if we're not able to give them the answers, they're going to go and get their answers from CNN and other places that probably aren't telling them the truth. At least we're going to give them the facts. We're going to give them the truth, and let them decide."[23]

The coronavirus pandemic revealed much that was great about America: Stoic medical personnel who donned cumbersome personal protective equipment day after day, month after month to save lives; scientists who labored around the clock to concoct effective therapies and vaccines;

essential workers who put themselves at risk to ensure others had necessary supplies; and regular people who distributed food for the needy and donated homemade masks. The crisis has also highlighted enduring fault lines: Unequal access to health care; the fragility of the social safety net; and racial disparities related to infection levels and economic impact.

The national characteristics that underpin those fractures—individualism, mistrust of government, and faith in capitalism—are also deeply ingrained in evangelicalism. Private religious beliefs have consequences in the public arena. The pastors who held in-person services indoors and cast doubt on vaccines did not listen to science or public health experts. They sued governors and mounted protests when they didn't get their way. They didn't believe the rules applied to them. In normal times, the word of evangelical leaders is unchallenged. They believe they answer only to a higher authority.

What makes someone an evangelical? The term is derived from the classical Greek word *euangelion*, translated as "gospel" or "good news" in reference to the Gospels of the New Testament and the evangelists Matthew, Mark, Luke, and John. Scholars generally agree that evangelicals are Protestants who believe in "the literal or near-literal truth of the Bible," feel the missionary spirit to spread the word of God, and believe that a conversion or "born-again" experience is necessary for salvation.[24] Evangelicals often speak of having a personal relationship with Jesus that influences every aspect of their daily lives.[25]

Evangelicals encompass a wide range of Protestants—fundamentalists, dozens of Baptist groups, Pentecostal churches, and charismatics. Some are independent or nondenominational or are loosely tied to an association of churches. Predominately Black Protestant churches, such as the African Methodist Episcopal Church, evolved separately from the broader, largely white evangelical tradition that is the subject of this book. Many evangelical congregations in cities are a blend of races, ages, and income levels.

Evangelicals are more conservative theologically than mainline Protestants, who interpret the Bible through the lenses of modern science and scholarship. Their political liberalism can be traced to the Social Gospel movement of more than a century ago that believed it was the duty of Christians to correct social injustices. In recent years, many denominations have splintered over whether to sanction same-sex marriage or to ordain openly gay clergy. Mainline denominations include the Episcopal Church, the Presbyterian Church (U.S.A.), the United Methodist Church, and many Lutheran groups. The churches adhere to traditional standards of liturgical worship and their ministers report to ecclesiastical authorities. In contrast, evangelical entrepreneurs design their own services and create their own structures, whether it is a church, Bible institute, media-based empire, or a full-fledged university.

Surveys on religious affiliation rely on the self-identification of respondents, so gauging the true sizes of groups is challenging. The Public Religion Research Institute's 2020 Census of American Religion interviewed more than four hundred fifty thousand adults from 2013 to 2019. It found that white evangelical Protestants represented 14.5 percent of the U.S. population in 2020, down from a high of 23 percent in 2006. White mainline Protestants dipped from 17.8 percent in 2006 to 16.4 percent in 2020.[26] A Religious Landscape Study taken years earlier by the Pew Research Center looked at the groups in their totality. Pew reported that mainline Protestants dropped from 41 million in 2007 to 36 million in 2014, its most recent survey. Meanwhile, evangelical Protestants increased from 60 million to 62 million.[27] (The PRRI and Pew surveys did not measure depth of belief or intensity of activity among the respondents. Both polls agreed that the country's largest religious group was the religiously unaffiliated, often called the "nones.")

Evangelicals have flourished in America's religious marketplace by blending business principles and media savvy. As the first country in modern history constituted without an established religion, America provided the perfect climate for innovators. Persuasion, not coercion, would be the key ingredient to succeed in their mission to win souls for Christ. Early evangelists such as George Whitefield transcended sectarianism and took their message where the people were. Successors such as Charles G. Finney and ballplayer-turned-fundamentalist-preacher Billy Sunday understood how to create a sensation, and Dwight L. Moody united big business and revivalism.

Evangelical entrepreneurs learned that they had to excel at mass communication to thrive. Radio and television could spread the Gospel faster than even the most tireless traveling preacher. The flamboyant preacher Aimee Semple McPherson knew that radio's intimacy was ideal for listeners seeking a personal relationship with Jesus. Billy Graham and Oral Roberts built multimedia empires that packaged evangelicalism for a mainstream audience. Though not typically categorized as evangelicals, Norman Vincent Peale and Robert Schuller perfected an upbeat style of preaching, a mastery of media, and a consumer-focused approach to ministry that influenced evangelical megachurches.

For more than a century, corporate titans have funded evangelical enterprises that echoed their pro-business, anti-union beliefs. Such a worldview values individualism over collective action, private charity over government activity. When these ideals are preached from the pulpit and interwoven with politics, they land with a compounded force. Liberal programs are portrayed as socialist threats to personal freedoms. They are even considered to be anti-Christian and un-American. Jerry Falwell Sr. pushed evangelicals into political activism while engaging in the business of winning souls through his megachurch and media ministry. White evangelicals have remade the modern Republican Party in their own image.

Two of the nation's largest evangelical churches were created through market research and management principles, inspiring countless imitators. Bill Hybels left a career in business to found Willow Creek Community Church in the Chicago suburbs. He canvassed neighborhoods to find out what people liked and didn't like about church and organized Willow Creek around meeting those needs. A few years later, Rick Warren did much the same in Southern California when he started Saddleback Community Church. Warren, the bestselling author of *The Purpose Driven Life*, who has cited management guru Peter Drucker as a key influence, created a consultancy for pastors as Hybels did. "Seeker-sensitive" churches like these target the unchurched and present a full menu of activities to keep them engaged all week.

"Prosperity gospel" megachurches such as Joel Osteen's Lakewood Church in Houston are more explicit about linking belief to material wealth. Other like-minded preachers, such as World Changers Church International's Creflo Dollar (who asked his congregation for $65 million to buy a Gulfstream G650 jet) and Relentless Church's John Gray (who purchased a $200,000 Lamborghini as an anniversary gift for his wife), exude material signs of success that amplify their message that faith will be rewarded in this world as well as in the kingdom to come. If people are struggling spiritually, emotionally, or financially, perhaps they can achieve a better life through faith—a powerful idea that has profoundly shaped American life.

1

AWAKENINGS

Early Evangelists and the
American Creed of Religious Liberty

I am persuaded the generality of preachers talk of an unknown
and unfelt Christ. The reason why congregations have been
so dead is because they have dead men preaching to them. . . .
How can dead men beget living children?

—George Whitefield[1]

At first glance, they seem like the oddest of couples, one a nonsectarian
polymath in Pennsylvania and the other an itinerant Anglican cleric
from England. And yet Benjamin Franklin and George Whitefield struck
up an unlikely friendship that reveals much about the origins of evangelicalism and religious freedom in America.

Whitefield was at the forefront of the First Great Awakening, a period
of religious intensity in colonial America in the 1730s and 1740s. The evangelist studied acting and theater in London, which added a dramatic flair to
his sermons. Audiences were held spellbound by his vivid reenactments of
biblical stories. Franklin estimated that about thirty thousand people heard
Whitefield's voice during an appearance in Philadelphia. "Every accent,
every emphasis, every modulation of voice, was so perfectly well turned
and well placed, that, without being interested in the subject, one could
not help being pleased with the discourse; a pleasure of much the same
kind with that received from an excellent piece of music," Franklin wrote.[2]

But many ministers believed Whitefield's popular appeal posed a challenge to the established order. Whitefield, though an Anglican, needled the
church's hierarchy as out of step with the passions of revivalism—a fervor
that emphasized a conversion, or a "new birth," through the workings of
the Holy Spirit. William Vesey, the Church of England's commissary in
New York, summoned Whitefield and requested he hand over his license

to preach in a pulpit. When Whitefield declined, Vesey blocked him from speaking in Anglican churches. "As he had denied me the church without my asking the use of it, I would preach in the fields for all places were alike to me," Whitefield wrote.[3] (He tartly pointed out that Vesey was a frequent visitor to the city's taverns.)

Churches were too small to hold his throngs of admirers. Franklin helped arrange the construction of a large hall in Philadelphia when churches spurned Whitefield during his visit in 1740.[4] The building was designed to be nonsectarian, a perfect setting for traveling preachers like Whitefield who attracted crowds of all denominations and even curious nonbelievers. Whitefield's years on the road taught him how to stage his appearances for maximum effectiveness.

Whitefield biographer Harry S. Stout wrote that the preacher "introduced religion to a dawning consumer age" and marketed his product wherever he found a thriving population.[5] Franklin, who ran a printing business and founded a constellation of civic organizations, recognized a kindred entrepreneurial spirit in Whitefield. Franklin's newspaper promoted Whitefield's revivals and his press printed the sermons, showing the preacher the power of taking his message directly to the people.

The two exchanged warm letters for many years. Franklin even expressed a starry-eyed wish that the king would send him and Whitefield to settle a colony in the Ohio territory consisting of "a large strong body of religious and industrious people." If they did so, "I firmly believe God would bless us with success," he wrote in 1756.[6] There is no record of a reply from Whitefield.

Franklin's relationship with Whitefield is intriguing because he had little use for religious dogma. Franklin confessed a belief in God and thought deeply about moral questions, but never found a denomination that could contain his questing mind. Near the end of his life, Franklin wrote favorably of Jesus of Nazareth's system of morals but admitted "some doubts as to his divinity."[7] Ever the practical man, Franklin rewrote the Lord's Prayer to make it more accessible. He altered "Our Father which art in Heaven" to "Heavenly Father" because it is "more concise, equally expressive, and better modern English."[8]

Whitefield tried without success to convert him. After praising Franklin for his scientific experiments, Whitefield wrote, "As you have made a pretty considerable progress in the mysteries of electricity, I would now humbly recommend to your diligent unprejudiced pursuit and study the mystery of the new birth."[9] Whitefield and Franklin agreed to disagree on the subject.

They did share a belief that virtue could be harnessed for the common good. When Whitefield made the hard journey to preach in the new settlement of Georgia, he proposed building an orphan house, a project Franklin admired. However, Whitefield believed slave plantations were necessary for Georgia to prosper and advocated legalizing slavery in the colony in 1751.[10] (Franklin owned enslaved people and spoke out against slavery much later in life.)

Franklin marveled at Whitefield's skill at extracting money to execute his plans. He recalled attending a Whitefield revival and resolved not to contribute to the collection plate. After hearing his sermon, Franklin felt a sense of shame and handed over his copper money, then his silver, and finally, "I emptied my pocket wholly into the collector's dish, gold and all."[11] Whitefield picked up more money in one Philadelphia engagement than many ministers received in a year.[12]

Despite their different perspectives, both disdained clerics who fixated more on hair-splitting theological debates than acts of public charity. Franklin wrote of visiting a Presbyterian service where the rambling minister's aim seemed "to be rather to make us Presbyterians than good citizens."[13] Whitefield's spirit of civic-minded engagement was unusual for a religious figure of the era, and it helps explain his appeal to a religious skeptic like Franklin.

Whitefield transcended sectarian boundaries, a recurring theme of the evangelical movement in America. So too is the emphasis on the individual conversion experience as the guiding star of faith. Whitefield and other revivalists were willing to make their case directly to the people. The question for colonial leaders like Franklin was how free the religious marketplace would be.

Many modern-day evangelicals believe that America needs to be saved by restoring it to an idealized past of Christian piety. This is incorrect. Religious fervor dimmed after the First Great Awakening dissipated around 1750. Scholars estimate that roughly 10 to 20 percent of colonists were formal church members—much lower than any era that followed in American history.[14]

Another myth is that the nation's founders were devout Christians. (Nor, as some liberals maintain, were they atheists.) They were undoubtedly steeped in Christian writings and practice, but they were also children of the Enlightenment. Most of them read deeply of philosophy and science, and were knowledgeable about non-Christian faiths. They were men of reason who also observed the presence of the Creator—or the Almighty or

Providence. They respected the value of religion as a basis for morality and social harmony, but most were wary of personally committing to a denomination. Some could be described as Deists, who through rational thought accepted a Creator that did not intervene in human affairs. Above all, the founders valued individual conscience in religious matters.

Like Franklin, Thomas Jefferson did not submit to conventional Christianity. He revised scripture to suit his rational approach to faith, wielding a razor to slice out the supernatural aspects of Jesus to assemble his own New Testament. He appreciated the teachings of Jesus—"the most sublime and benevolent code of morals which has ever been offered to man"—but did not believe Jesus to be the son of God and did not accept the Trinity.[15] Clerics and church dogmas distorted Christianity's "primitive simplicity of its founder," in Jefferson's words.[16]

The founders understood religious faith to be a voluntary activity that should not be coerced or directed by government authorities. Jefferson noted that New York and Pennsylvania did not have an established church—a denomination recognized by law as the official church—yet religion flourished and social peace was preserved even with dissenters. "They have made the happy discovery, that the way to silence religious disputes, is to take no notice of them," he wrote.[17] The church and state separation in Roger Williams's Rhode Island inspired greater experiments.

Jefferson's *Virginia Statute for Religious Freedom*, introduced into the Virginia General Assembly in 1779 to disestablish the Anglican Church but not passed until 1786, crystallized his thinking on religion and the state. Jefferson wrote that God gave man free will and thus "fallible and uninspired" civil and ecclesiastical leaders have no right to impose their religious opinions on others.[18] The statute barred religious tests for public office, not only because they infringe on individual liberty, but they also corrupt civil government and religion itself.

Meanwhile, Virginia legislator James Madison fought a proposal by Patrick Henry for a tax to support Protestant ministers. Madison's *Memorial and Remonstrance against Religious Assessments* in 1785 argued that religion is a God-given natural right—not something bestowed by government. It reasoned that religion existed before any earthly institution, so civil society has no standing and certainly no competence to interfere with a person's relationship with his or her Creator. Like his ally Jefferson, Madison believed that state support of religion corrupts all involved. The tax assessment bill was defeated.

Madison observed that the variety of religious practices in the colonies was an advantage because no one denomination could claim to be the one national religion. "This freedom arises from that multiplicity of sects, which pervades America, and which is the best and only security for religious liberty in any society. For where there is such a variety of sects, there cannot be a majority of any one sect to oppress and persecute the rest," he wrote.[19]

The idea of religious liberty was enshrined in the First Amendment to the United States Constitution: "Congress shall make no law respecting an establishment of religion, or prohibiting the free exercise thereof."[20] Historian Garry Wills believes disestablishment to be "the only original part of the Constitution."[21] No nation had ever been founded without an official church or religion. (The Constitution also barred religious tests for public office.) Churches were left to succeed or fail on their own.

Some evangelicals today complain about the "godless Constitution" because it does not cite "God" or "Christianity." After all, they argue, the Declaration of Independence contains the ringing words "We hold these truths to be self-evident, that all men are created equal, that they are endowed by their Creator with certain unalienable Rights." The Declaration also makes mention of "Nature's God," "the Supreme Judge of the world," and "divine Providence" (but notably not "Jesus" or "Christianity").

The two founding documents were written in entirely different contexts. The Declaration was a righteous call to arms by a people under siege; the Constitution was a blueprint for setting up the machinery of government. The Constitution represents the spirit of religious freedom of the men who debated and wrote it. Scholar John M. Murrin considers the Constitution "the eighteenth-century equivalent of a secular humanist text." Murrin estimates that the only born-again Christian at the Constitutional Convention in 1787 was Delaware's Richard Bassett, a devout Methodist who was not a factor in the debates.[22]

That the Constitution failed to make an explicit appeal to the divine did not mean the banishment of God or religion from public life. The reverse side of the Great Seal of the United States adopted in 1782 includes the motto "*Annuit cœptis*"—Latin for "God (or Providence) has favored our undertakings"—which is taken from Virgil's *Aeneid*, not sacred scripture.[23] The eye atop the pyramid is an allusion to the watchfulness of Providence. George Washington, though not a man of formal religious faith, placed his hand on a Bible at his first inaugural in 1789 and supposedly added the words "so help me God" after taking the oath.

The ceremonial displays of religion that are commonplace today made some early presidents uneasy. As president, Jefferson declined requests from religious groups to designate days of fasting or thanksgiving proclamations as infringements of religious freedom. In his famous reply to the leaders of the Danbury Baptist Association in Connecticut, Jefferson wrote in 1802 that "religion is a matter which lies solely between man and his God, that he owes account to none other for his faith or his worship, that the legislative powers of government reach actions only, and not opinions."[24] He then quoted the First Amendment and interpreted its meaning as "building a wall of separation between Church and State." Civil authorities had no business prescribing religious exercises, in Jefferson's view.

Madison resisted making religious proclamations as president for the same reasons, though he reluctantly made an exception during the passions evoked by the War of 1812. Madison was also unhappy with congressional chaplains opening sessions with prayers. Strictly speaking, the practice violated the First Amendment, but he knew that it was unlikely to be rescinded. Such prayers were symbolic in nature and thus Madison opted to apply the legal maxim *de minimis non curat*, Latin for "the law does not concern itself with trifles."[25]

As a young man in Virginia, Madison had successfully opposed the idea that government and the church needed to prop up each other to survive. In retirement, Madison looked with favor on the American experiment with church and state. As he had foreseen, no one denomination dominated the others. He noted that some old-style churches had fallen into ruin because their flocks shifted to other styles of worship and built new churches. America's dynamic religious marketplace allowed for improved religious training for preachers and the expression of religious zeal among their followers. "The number, the industry, and the morality of the Priesthood, and the devotion of the people have been manifestly increased by the total separation of the Church from the State," he wrote.[26]

As the first country in modern history constituted without an established religion, America was ideally suited for religious innovators. Success would come to preachers with a compelling message packaged for mass consumption. Evangelicals would be the ideal messengers.

They came on wagons and carriages over rutted country roads to a "communion" in Cane Ridge outside Lexington, Kentucky. Word had spread about outbreaks of religious fervor seen at revivals on the frontier, but this one in the summer of 1801 would exceed all expectations. As many as twenty thousand people journeyed to Cane Ridge in a state where the largest city had a population of less than two thousand.[27] When the visitors arrived, they crammed into cabins, found lodging out of town, or camped out in the fields. Presbyterian minister Barton W. Stone had witnessed other "camp meetings" and felt moved to organize a similar event in his log cabin church in rural Bourbon County. Stone invited fellow Presbyterian ministers as well as Methodist, Baptist, and local preachers to conduct services in a modest meetinghouse and nearby tent erected for the occasion.

What happened at Cane Ridge was a religious convulsion on a scale never seen before in America. Visitors were led in spiritual exercises that produced physical responses such as shouting, barking, and dancing. Wails of distress and shouts of ecstasy broke out among the assembly. Falling spells of believers "slain in the spirit" made the grounds look like a battlefield. One witness reported people acting as if they were having seizures. "Their heads would jerk back suddenly, frequently causing them to yelp, or make some other involuntary noise," the witness reported. "Sometimes the head would fly every way so quickly that their features could not be recognized."[28]

Ordinary people rose to testify about the Lord's presence in their lives while skeptics looked askance at the emotional outbursts. The Cane Ridge meeting lasted nearly a week that August, highlighted by the mass distribution of Communion on Sunday. Conversions were estimated to be in the thousands. It would be called "America's Pentecost," a reference to the Christian belief that the Holy Spirit descended on the apostles after Jesus ascended to heaven.

The widely reported revival at Cane Ridge is considered a landmark of the Second Great Awakening from 1795 to 1835. Cane Ridge showed how revivals could transcend sectarian boundaries. Worshippers only needed to bring a willingness to be transformed. Preachers were judged on their popular appeal, not by the depth of their formal religious education. The Bible's truths required no special learning to unlock. Disestablishment allowed upstart revivalists to organize their own camp meetings and offer up the prayer, "Lord, make it like Cane Ridge."

The biggest beneficiaries of this grass-roots movement were the Methodists. At the beginning of the 1800s, the breakaway Anglican group barely registered in American religious life. By the 1840s, Methodists were comfortably the nation's biggest denomination, vaulting over the more traditionalist Episcopal and Congregational churches.[29] Methodists "constructed almost as many churches as there were post offices and employed almost as many ministers as there were postal workers," wrote Mark A. Noll, a leading scholar of evangelicals.[30]

Camp meetings were so much a part of Methodist experience that a *Camp Meeting Manual* by B. W. Gorham in 1854 outlined favorable revival locations, recruitment strategies, a suggested hour-by-hour schedule, and practical instructions on constructing platforms and erecting tents. ("The seats should be of plank, and sixteen feet long, if possible.")[31] Most important, of course, was the quality of preaching, "not dry, dogmatic theorizing; not metaphysical hair splitting; not pulpit bombast; but plain, clear, evangelical, Bible truth, uttered with faithful, solemn, earnestness, and with the Holy Ghost sent down from heaven."[32]

The Methodists were in tune with the times and their audience. They held that the individual had the power to decide to follow Christ, and that salvation was possible through a conversion experience alone. Settlers on the frontier paid no mind to the dictates of distant bishops and scholars. The church dispatched hundreds of preachers to far-flung communities to find the "common people," serve their needs, and convert them. Their targets were generally unchurched and lacked formal education, so the preachers—also largely unlettered laymen—had to convey simple messages in an entertaining way to win converts.

One of the most colorful Methodist "circuit riders" was Lorenzo Dow, a gaunt figure widely known as "Crazy Dow." His unkempt appearance belied a steely work ethic. Dow's touring schedule took him through much of America and across the Atlantic to England and Ireland. Dow supposedly preached to more people than anyone else of his era, but he also took time for one-on-one meetings. "Thus round the circuit I went, visiting from house to house, getting into as many new neighborhoods as I could, and sparing no character in my public declarations," he wrote in his bestselling autobiography in 1859.[33]

The most influential revivalist of the time was not a Methodist circuit rider but an ordained Presbyterian minister named Charles Grandison Finney. Born in Connecticut in 1792 and raised in western New York, Finney had launched a promising law career when he felt a sudden terror about the state of his soul. The faithful churchgoer prayed on his knees for hours in the woods and returned to a darkened law office seeking spiritual guidance. Suddenly, the room filled with light and Finney felt the presence of the Lord. "My heart seemed to be liquid fire within me. All my feelings seemed to rise and flow out," he recounted in his memoirs.[34] A humbled Finney delivered his confession of faith and reported receiving a "mighty baptism of the Holy Ghost." After undergoing his conversion experience, Finney pledged to use his lawyerly skills of persuasion as an advocate for God.

Finney ignored urgings that he should attend Princeton's theological school and instead trained with his pastor for two years. His outlook seemed more Methodist than Presbyterian. Finney did not adopt a strict interpretation of the Westminster Confession of Faith, the creedal foundation for Presbyterian and Congregational churches. Multiple readings and revisions of it over the years resulted in subtleties that were lost on average churchgoers. Finney sensed that parsing the legalisms of a document drafted by theologians in the 1600s was not the way to reach the masses.

Finney joined a group of traveling preachers called the Oneida Evangelical Association. At a slim six feet two inches with deep-set, piercing eyes, Finney cut an imposing figure. His fame grew as newspapers reported on his dramatic preaching style. "After he came the Spirit of God was shed down with such power that nothing seemed able to resist it," read an account of his appearance in Rome, New York, in 1826. "The revival was remarkable for its solemnity and deep heart-searching."[35]

Finney carefully prepared the ground to ensure big turnouts. Church members fanned out into communities and went door to door with printed invitations. Finney lined up the cooperation of local ministers for his week-long meetings and used their churches when possible. His sermons stressed "the fundamental truths" that leaned on the divine authority of the Bible. Finney told his large crowds that a change of heart was enough for a person to be counted as a believer. People had the power to decide the course of their spiritual lives.

Among Finney's innovations was the "anxious bench," a front pew reserved for people considering conversion. Finney could then focus on them and encourage the assembly to lend prayerful support. Trained staffers looked for people who seemed to be undergoing a spiritual awakening and herded them into "special inquiry rooms." Finney would close with a call for sinners to convert. "Another moment's delay and it may be too late forever," he urged.[36]

Critics such as fellow Presbyterian minister Lyman Beecher complained that these conversions were too hasty to be lasting. Those who felt a religious experience should retreat in isolation to study their Bibles and embark on a long conversion process. Finney retorted that following such advice would only make it more likely that a sinner will delay accepting Christ or, worse, backslide into old habits and never make a decision at all.

The zeal unleashed at Finney's meetings fell short of the excesses at Cane Ridge, but it was enough to trigger concerns of some clergymen. They didn't care for his "new measures" that stirred up crowds at the expense of their more ritualistic churches. To Finney, creating a sensation was essential. He compared it to politicians who circulate pamphlets and run flag-festooned wagons through towns to promote their candidacies. "All these are their 'measures' and for their *end* they are wisely calculated. The object is to get up an excitement, and bring the people out. They know that unless there can be an excitement it is in vain to push their end," Finney wrote in his *Lectures on Revivals of Religion*, a guidebook for ministers. "The object of our measures is to gain attention, and you *must have* something new."[37]

Finney was suspicious of seminaries that churned out ministers proficient in dead languages but unable to speak in the common tongue. Ministers needed to find a balance between doctrinal and practical preaching because one without the other was useless. Finney urged ministers to tell stories from everyday life. After all, Jesus used parables simple enough for children to understand. Higher religious education had its place, he thought, but not if it diverted attention from the paramount goal of winning souls to Christ. To Finney, the formula was simple: "Ministers should be educated to know what the Bible is, and what the human mind is, and know how to bring one to bear on the other."[38]

Finney practiced this when he preached. He believed that ministers had no excuse for not knowing the religious opinions of every member of their congregations. If a preacher does not understand his audience, how can he possibly minister to them? The best way for ministers to connect with people was for them to cast aside their notes and speak from the heart. "Gestures are of more importance than is generally supposed. Mere words will never express the full meaning of the gospel. The *manner* of saying it is almost every thing [*sic*]," Finney wrote.[39] He recalled a missionary who was engaging everywhere except for in the pulpit, where he turned into a "perfect automaton." Finney related the story of a London bishop asking the celebrated English actor David Garrick why he moved people to tears with his performances and why ministers lulled people to sleep. "It is because we represent fiction as a reality, and you represent reality as a fiction," Garrick replied.[40]

Presbyterian and Congregational churches objected to such theatrics as unworthy of the dignity of the pulpit. But the lawyer in Finney saw little difference between making extemporaneous arguments to sway a judge and jury in a courtroom and off-the-cuff sermons to convert people at a revival. "It was remarked by a lawyer, that the cause of Jesus Christ has the fewest able advocates of any cause in the world. And I partly believe it," Finney wrote.[41] He praised Methodist preachers for their warm, commonsense preaching style. Their growing assemblies were proof that their approach was working and put to shame rule-oriented Presbyterian ministers.

Religious innovators like Finney have always been in conflict with traditional churches. Finney pointed out that many years ago ministers were expected to wear a cocked hat and a wig, but the formal vestments fell away and the churches did not suffer. In Finney's time, the introduction of choirs and instrumental music provoked bitter splits in congregations. Even organs were controversial—one Presbyterian synod considered disciplining a church for having one. Finney's meetings included choir singing and encouraged contemporary hymns. "The church is yet filled with a kind of superstitious reverence for such things. This is a great stumbling block to many minds," Finney wrote.[42] Such customs were human creations, not divinely inspired. The Bible is indeed silent on appropriate ministerial dress and musical worship stylings.

The free exercise of religion promised in the Constitution seemed to have been realized in practice. Near the end of the Second Great Awakening, Alexis de Tocqueville visited America to study the maturing democratic republic. The Frenchman was immediately struck by the vitality of religious life compared to Europe. Tocqueville befriended a variety of clergymen and laymen to understand why and "to a man, they assigned primary credit for the peaceful ascendancy of religion in their country to the complete separation of church and state," he wrote in his landmark work *Democracy in America* in 1835.[43]

Since churches in America were forced to stand solely on their own power, they were much more durable than state-supported churches. "In Europe, Christianity allowed itself to become the close ally of temporal powers. Today those powers are collapsing, and Christianity finds itself buried, as it were, beneath their debris," Tocqueville wrote.[44] In contrast, he found American–style Christianity to be refreshingly free of dogma. "I know of no country in which Christianity is less cloaked in forms, rituals, and symbols than in the United States, or in which it lays clearer, simpler, or more general ideas before the mind of man," he wrote.[45]

Tocqueville's upbeat view of religion in America contained a warning about the political consequences of intertwining religious zeal with patriotism. The powerful hold of Christianity on the American people could dominate nonreligious institutions. Tocqueville related an account of a New York judge who refused to swear in an atheist witness on the grounds that his testimony would lack credibility. "Americans so completely confound Christianity with liberty that it is almost impossible to induce them to think of one without the other. For them, moreover, this is by no means a sterile belief, a legacy of the past that lies moldering in the depths of the soul, but a vital article of faith," he wrote.[46]

American preachers also emphasized earthly rewards more than their counterparts abroad, another potential hazard. Ministers who encouraged people to gratify their selfish desires could take the focus off uplifting souls to achieve heaven. "Seeking to touch their listeners all the more effectively, they are forever pointing out how religious beliefs foster liberty and public order, and in listening to them it is often difficult to tell whether the chief object of religion is to procure eternal happiness in the other world or well-being in this one," he wrote.[47] For evangelicals, that would be an ongoing struggle.

2

TABERNACLE EVANGELISM

Moody and the Big Business of Mass Revivals

I don't see how a man can follow Christ and not be successful.

—Dwight L. Moody[1]

The organizers of what became known as Philadelphia's Grand Depot Revival left nothing to chance. After a triumphant two-year run in the British Isles, evangelist Dwight L. Moody had just sailed back to the United States. The spiritual connections he had made were extraordinary, as was the accompanying increase in his fame. By the time his steamship pulled into New York Harbor in August 1875, Moody was the best-known preacher since Charles G. Finney. (Finney died two days after Moody's return.) Moody's plainspoken style and Ira David Sankey's sprightly musical direction were a formidable combination overseas, and reporters were eager to know Moody's next move in America.

Moody, who had run the Young Men's Christian Association and founded a church in Chicago, knew that cities were ripe territory for evangelists. On his tour, he had received rapturous responses in Edinburgh, Manchester, Liverpool, and London. Post–Civil War America was transitioning into a more urban, industrialized society. "Water runs down hill and the highest hills in America are the great cities," Moody said. "If we can stir them we shall stir the whole country."[2] Moody accepted invitations to preach in Brooklyn and Philadelphia.

The city where George Whitefield created a sensation more than a century earlier went out of its way for Moody. Large crowds were expected, so holding the meetings in an existing church would not do. Business leader John Wanamaker, who was deeply moved by one of Moody's earlier appearances in Philadelphia, offered his Pennsylvania Railroad depot rent-free to Moody. (Wanamaker later built one of the nation's first department stores on the site, at Thirteenth and Market streets near City Hall.) The abandoned freight warehouse underwent significant renovations. Hundreds of workmen pulled up railroad tracks and laid down slightly sloped wooden flooring to allow all a view of the tiered platform. A thousand gas burners would provide illumination for the expected capacity crowds of ten thousand people.[3]

Organizers launched a promotional blitz. Committee secretary and Philadelphia YMCA leader Thomas Cree received $30,000 to spend on publicity efforts that included advertising in newspapers and creating posters to lure interdenominational audiences.[4] Armies of volunteers circulated one hundred sixty-two thousand leaflets at the depot-turned-tabernacle and at local congregations.[5] Hundreds of church singers were recruited to serve in the choir. Wanamaker pressed three hundred of his employees into service as ushers.

Moody's campaign began with a Sunday morning service on November 21, 1875. A banner behind the platform read "Behold I bring you good tidings of great joy which shall be to all people." Five hundred choristers and an array of prominent ministers assembled as the audience of about eight thousand settled in their seats.[6] Moody declared that the tabernacle's doors would always be closed on time and latecomers would not be admitted, in keeping with his blunt reputation. The stocky, bearded preacher had an appealing everyman quality. Witnesses noted his earnest, conversational style of preaching, "which clothes the most trite saying with the thrilling beauty of fervid eloquence."[7]

Moody's message resonated and his team's promotional efforts paid off: An estimated 1 million people attended about 250 meetings over nine weeks. Many couldn't make it inside the tabernacle; one disappointed Philadelphian lamented, "It's harder to get into the depot than heaven."[8] President Ulysses S. Grant attended a meeting in December and business titans such as Jay Cooke and Anthony J. Drexel were frequent guests. Attendees jammed the tabernacle's three specially designed "inquiry rooms" to meet with Moody and his aides for further counseling. About four thousand people converted. Philadelphia-area Presbyterian churches reported sharp increases in membership after the meetings.

Moody's revival also did well by earth-bound metrics. Costs were low due to the free rent and volunteer labor, and private donations defrayed remaining expenses. Moody and Sankey's popular hymnbook made $35,000 in royalties during their years overseas, and a new edition printed in time for the Philadelphia meetings was a financial bonanza. A committee of executives ensured the book's overall earnings of about $300,000 were channeled to religious and philanthropic causes—not into Moody's pocket. (Organizers were not above auctioning off Moody's towels after he left Philadelphia.)[9]

Moody's businesslike approach to the Grand Depot Revival influenced generations of evangelical entrepreneurs. Moody courted wealthy benefactors, instilled organizational discipline, and used press coverage and advertising methods to great effect. Moody's coordinating committee was "as systematic as an astronomer," wrote the journalist and politician John Forney. Moody's style of large-scale worship was not "content alone to trust some higher power."[10]

There was little in Moody's childhood to indicate he would become an important religious figure. Born in 1837, in Northfield, Massachusetts, Dwight Lyman Moody was the sixth of seven children in a family left destitute by the sudden death of his whiskey-loving stonemason father in 1841. Twins came soon after, leaving Moody's mother a widow with nine children, a heavily mortgaged homestead, and creditors to satisfy. Financial support from family members helped her keep the farm.

The children enrolled in a Unitarian Sunday school and were baptized in the church of their parents. They would walk barefoot, carrying their shoes and stockings and putting them on when they approached the church.[11] Moody was a reluctant attendee as a child, recalling that a preacher rousted him when he fell asleep during a service.[12]

Moody loved pranks. As the ringleader of the town's boys, he stampeded a neighbor's cattle, whooping and yelling all the while. To break up the tedium of rural life, he wrote a false announcement for an out-of-town speaker coming to town to address a temperance meeting and posted it on the schoolhouse door. A confused crowd gathered on the appointed day and Moody joined the others in blaming the nonexistent lecturer on some unknown practical joker.[13] Moody received whippings at school and from his mother for such naughtiness.

For the Moody children, finding employment was a matter of survival, so formal schooling suffered. Moody did not make it past seventh grade. He went to work in the fields and looked for jobs in neighboring towns. His lack of education revealed itself in his early grammar-challenged sermons. Wanamaker, his friend and business ally, noted that Moody "murdered the King's English" when he first heard him speak.[14]

Moody learned to refine his public appearances, but he knew his unvarnished approach was part of what endeared him to the masses. "I am tired and sick of your 'silver-tongued' orators. I used to mourn because I couldn't be an orator. I thought, Oh, if I could only have the gift of speech like some men! I have heard men with a smooth flow of language take the audience captive; but they came and they went. Their voice was like the air—there wasn't any *power* back of it; they trusted in their eloquence and their fine speeches," Moody wrote.[15]

At seventeen, Moody left home for Boston where, after a period of feeling adrift and homesick, asked his uncle for a sales job in his shoe store. As a condition of employment, Moody's uncle required him to abstain from the temptations of city life and regularly attend his Congregational church. At the store, Moody grew impatient waiting for customers to come to him and pulled in people off the street. At church, Moody took a Bible study class and realized how little he knew about scripture and seemed hungry for more.

Moody's conversion experience was pedestrian compared to the wild emotionalism seen at revival meetings. Moody's Sunday school teacher made an unannounced visit to the store and approached Moody while he was wrapping up shoes. "I simply told him of Christ's love for him and the love Christ wanted in return. That was all there was. It seemed the young man was just ready for the light that then broke upon him, and there, in the back of that store in Boston, he gave himself and his life to Christ," said the teacher, Edward Kimball.[16] Moody abandoned Unitarianism and joined the Congregationalists.

Moody moved west to Chicago, a fast-growing city in the 1850s where he would leave a lasting mark. He stuck with sales work and landed successively higher-paying jobs at boot and shoe companies. He scoured hotels and train depots for prospective customers and rang up sales numbers that outpaced his fellow salesmen. "I can make more money here in a week than I could in Boston in a month," Moody wrote in a letter to his brother in Northfield.[17] The company rewarded Moody's ingenuity by sending him on the road as a sales representative and as a debt collector. The thrifty Moody set a goal of earning $100,000—an astonishing amount for the time.

The excitement of Chicago and Moody's business ambitions didn't eclipse his religious commitment. He became a member of Plymouth Congregational Church and applied his persuasiveness to Christian service. Moody pledged to rent a pew every Sunday and did so without fail, even if he had to trawl boardinghouses, saloons, and street corners for congregants. Soon, Moody's ragtag collections of worshippers were filling four pews for each service.[18] Being himself a child of poverty, he discovered a mission

Sunday school and volunteered to round up needy children for others to instruct because of his lack of biblical knowledge.

Moody's religious work connected him to other churches. He struck up a fruitful friendship with the wealthy dry-goods wholesaler John V. Farwell at the First Methodist Church, and at the First Baptist Church he met Fleming H. Revell, whose sister, Emma, Moody married.[19] Moody joined the Young Men's Christian Association, an interdenominational evangelical group that offered a haven from the dangers of urban life. There he performed janitorial duties and other tasks to keep the office running.

In 1858, Moody started a Sunday school in a Chicago slum known as "the Sands," a lakefront brothel district. The children met in an old saloon. Attendance boomed and Moody convinced the mayor to let him use the city's North Market Hall rent-free for his meetings.[20] When enrollment swelled to about a thousand pupils, Moody proposed to raise $10,000 to construct a building.

Even in its makeshift setting, the school attracted notice. Abraham Lincoln visited the school at North Market Hall weeks after winning the presidency in 1860. Addressing the hundreds of hardscrabble boys, Lincoln remarked, "I was once as poor as any boy in this school, but I am now president of the United States, and if you attend to what is taught you here, some of you may yet be president of the United States."[21]

Moody abandoned his sales career to turn his full attention to evangelistic work. He took his $7,000 in savings—well short of his target—and vowed to make it last, God willing. Moody opened Illinois Street Church in 1864 with seating for fifteen hundred people and plenty of space for his thriving Sunday school. Moody performed church rites even though he was not an ordained minister. The church developed its own faith system that floated above denominational strictures. A plaque on the building read, "Ever welcome to this house of God are strangers and the poor." The church hosted nightly gatherings for mothers and young women, Bible study, rallies, and children's prayer meetings.[22]

Moody threw himself into wider religious work, attending conventions nationwide and in Britain on behalf of the YMCA. At one such meeting, Moody met Sankey, the composer who became a keystone of Moody's revival campaigns. The YMCA offered a refuge from the dangers of life on the streets, where young people could study the Bible and enjoy recreational activities. Moody also helped kindle a nationwide Sunday school movement. He traveled to cities and states and encouraged them to base their programs on his system in Illinois.

At twenty-eight, Moody was named president of the Chicago YMCA, a position that put him into regular contact with the city's political and business elite. The former shoe salesman had not lost his talent for extracting money from wallets. "He begged for men's money as simply and directly as he begged for their conversion; he trusted implicitly that God would grant him both; and he was rarely disappointed in either. The poor offered him small sums; the rich gave with a magnificent liberality; he accepted both as his Master's due," William Revell Moody wrote of his father.[23]

Moody led the drive to erect a building and wisely received a state charter exempting the YMCA's real estate from taxation. Fellow YMCA leader Farwell, the wealthy merchant, donated the property. A stock company was formed to raise construction funds, and the first $10,000 cash subscription was secured from Cyrus McCormick, the industrialist and inventor of the mechanical reaper.[24] The building—Farwell Hall—was dedicated in 1867. When a fire destroyed it four months later, Moody commissioned a new building. When the Great Chicago Fire of 1871 destroyed the second Farwell Hall as well as his Illinois Street Church, Moody again solicited funds from his benefactors to rebuild.

Throughout those turbulent times, the YMCA hosted daily prayer meetings at noon that drew office workers and people off the street. The unchurched were encouraged to attend, even if just for a few minutes. During the service, Moody would put newcomers on the spot, asking if they loved the Lord. If someone wavered, Moody jumped into the crowd and asked the person directly, "Do you want to be saved, now?"[25] During the summer months, Moody stood on the steps of Courthouse Square every night and preached to all who showed up. Nearby prisoners pressed up against their iron grates to hear Moody speak.

The construction delays slowed his work in Chicago, so Moody accepted invitations to conduct revival meetings in the British Isles. In 1872, Moody met evangelical leaders who offered inspiration and counsel. He observed conversions on a scale he had never seen before. At his request, hundreds would rise up and profess they were Christians. Moody's "inquiry rooms" were jammed with people thirsty for deeper religious instruction. He believed the system to be the most effective means of securing lasting conversions.

Moody and Sankey returned to Britain in 1873 for an extensive tour that would bring Moody international acclaim. Upon their return to America, they conducted the Grand Depot Revival in Philadelphia and then a ten-week meeting attended by nearly 1 million people in New York

City at P. T. Barnum's Great Roman Hippodrome. J. Pierpont Morgan and Cornelius Vanderbilt II were among the tycoons who defrayed the cost of converting the circus arena into a venue suitable for a religious meeting.[26] "The Hippodrome work is a vast business enterprise, organized and conducted by business men, who have put money into it on business principles, for the purpose of saving men," one observer noted.[27] Moody made a triumphant visit to Chicago in 1876 to lead a revival campaign. As in New York, some captains of industry, such as George Armour, developer of the grain elevator system, were put on the organizing committee to rally the private donations and corporate support necessary to fund Moody's specially built tabernacle.

Moody's events received intensive coverage in the popular press. Some found his brusque manner to be off-putting. "He is simply a ranter of the most vulgar type," wrote the *London Saturday Review* in a review of Moody's work in England. "It is possible that his low fun and screechy ejaculations may be found stimulating by the ignorant and foolish; but it is difficult to conceive how any person of the slightest culture or refinement can fail to be pained and shocked."[28] The American biographer Gamaliel Bradford offered a more balanced appraisal after reading Moody's sermons: "The language gets there. It is amazingly simple, direct, and vivid. . . . The sharp, rude energetic vigor with which he makes this appeal must have been almost irresistible when accompanied by his commanding tone and personality."[29]

By then, Moody was in his forties and his hair was getting thinner, his beard thicker, and his suits broader. His stern appearance resembled the run of stocky, bewhiskered Republican presidents who dominated the Gilded Age. Moody himself was as much a chief executive as a preacher. Before Moody would agree to conduct a revival in a city, he demanded the full support of local evangelical ministers. Then a businessman–dominated executive committee appointed chairmen to oversee finance, publicity, tickets, volunteer training, and other tasks.[30]

Moody criticized denominations such as the Episcopal Church for distancing themselves from the revival spirit of his meetings. "The older a church is the more it needs to be revived, because the tendency is into formalism," Moody said.[31] He said he heard of a minister warning his congregation against attending a Moody revival meeting because of the "undue excitement" it was sure to provoke. To Moody, that was exactly the point. "Don't be afraid of a little excitement and a little 'sensationalism.' It seems to me that almost anything is preferable to deadness," Moody said.[32]

Moody critiqued churches that displayed too little of what he called "Holy Spirit power" derived from the Gospels. "They don't desire it; they want intellectual power; they want to get some man who will just draw; and a choir that will draw; not caring whether any one is saved," Moody wrote.[33] He condemned churchgoing people who were more interested in the quality of their choirs and organs than in discussing the "risen Christ and a personal Savior." Churches uninterested in soul winning were destined to wither and die, he believed.

Skeptics of his revivals charged that the thousands of conversions they supposedly inspired evaporated soon after the meetings left town. Moody acknowledged that backsliding was part of human nature, but said such failures did not mean it was not worth the effort. "The professed converts did not hold out in Christ's day," he said. "Suppose that the farmer should refuse to sow because all his seed doesn't take root and ripen. Suppose that we should cut down our apple trees because all the blossoms don't mature."[34] In large part, Moody was preaching to the converted. Many attendees were respectable people who were already churchgoers and attended multiple meetings.

In city after city, Moody perfected his mechanistic approach to mass religion. "It doesn't matter how you get a man to God provided you get him there," he remarked.[35] He rejected theological complexities and spoke of the "Christian fundamentals" in the "good old doctrines of our fathers: Man is fallen; Christ comes to seek, redeem, and save him."[36] Moody preached that conversion was simply a matter of changing one's heart: "Remember, salvation is a free gift, and it is a free gift for us. Can you buy it? It is a free gift, presented to 'whosoever' will accept it."[37] In return, Jesus would bear your burdens. "There is not a need that you feel in your heart today but that Christ can meet if you let Him. God sent Him here to meet man's need."[38]

It's an irony of history that Moody—a lay preacher hostile to dogmas—did so much to elevate the doctrine of premillennialism. The theology predates Moody and is critically important in understanding the way evangelicals see the world and how they respond to it.

Before the late 1800s, the vast majority of Protestants believed in postmillennialism, which holds that the Second Coming will occur only *after* Jesus's followers establish a "millennium" of ever-increasing peace and righteousness on Earth. (Depending on one's interpretation, "millennium" can mean "a very long time" or literally "a thousand years.") The practical effect of this optimistic worldview meant that Christians must work for greater social justice to usher in the return of Christ and the final judgment.

Premillennialism is a wholly different interpretation of the end times described in the book of Revelation and other parts of the Bible. It holds that the world is becoming more wicked and cannot be redeemed except by God's direct intervention through the return of Jesus. Thus, Christ would return *before* the "millennium." In this view, churches were not responsible for reforming society.

Anglo-Irish theologian John Nelson Darby devised a system he called "dispensationalism," which divides history into seven "dispensations," or eras. The seventh and current dispensation is that of the Christian church. His breakthrough was the idea that God had separate plans for the earthly people of Israel and the heavenly people of the church.[39] The Jews were bound by past prophecies while Christians existed on a timeline that was still unfolding. Darby's interpretation held that the return of the Jews to Palestine would be a sign of the "end times."[40] This belief has been a lodestar for apocalyptically focused evangelicals ever since.

What became known as dispensational premillennialism had a profound effect on evangelical thought. It taught that the end of the current church age could come at any time, thus adding urgency to preachers' appeals for conversion to avoid being "left behind." Only true Christians will be "raptured" up to the air to meet Christ and be saved from the cataclysmic tribulation and the appearance of the Antichrist. After achieving final victory in the battle of Armageddon, Christ will bring his saints back to Earth and establish his millennial reign.

The teaching gained favor in the 1870s and 1880s and appealed to believers because they would be spared the tribulation to come. But, at its heart, premillennialism offers a pessimistic view of the world. If disaster is always lurking just around the corner and the world is becoming more wicked, what's the point of trying to make it better? Everything will soon be swept away. What matters most is saving souls, not saving society. As Moody observed, "I look on this world as a wrecked vessel. God has given me a life-boat, and said to me, 'Moody, save all you can.' . . . This world is getting darker and darker; its ruin is coming nearer and nearer."[41]

This was a decisive break from postmillennialists like Finney, an abolitionist who pushed for social reform as president of the progressive Oberlin College in Ohio. Congregational minister Washington Gladden extended that work through the Social Gospel movement, a liberal theology that applied Christian values to solve the world's problems. "Christianity would create a perfect society, and to this end it must produce perfect men; it would bring forth perfect men, and to this end it must construct a perfect society," Gladden wrote.[42] He supported labor unions and opposed racial segregation—unusual stances for the era.

The Gilded Age also featured clergymen such as Phillips Brooks and Russell Conwell, who argued that it was un-American for government to remedy the plight of the poor. They equated wealth with God's favor, thus perhaps the poor were poor because they were sinful. William Lawrence, the bishop of the Episcopal Diocese of Massachusetts, preached "godliness is in league with riches." "In the long run," he said, "it is only to the man of morality that wealth comes."[43]

For all of his early work with the YMCA and in the slums, Moody showed little sympathy for people mired in poverty. It was their fault for drinking too much, smoking too much, gambling too much. The only way out was to accept Christ, not to hope for a handout. Asked at a YMCA convention what advice he had for the unemployed, Moody replied: "First of all, to seek the Kingdom of God and His righteousness, believing in His promise, which I never knew to fail, that all things will be added to them. Second, to pray to God for work."[44] His extended remarks did not mention a role for government or secular organizations. Moody's brand of personal religion meant that it was up to the individual to find a solution, with God's help. Not incidentally, these were attitudes shared by his business-owning friends.

Moody's premillennial thinking—inconsistent as it was—steered him toward a dim view of social reform. "The word of God nowhere tells me to watch and wait for the coming of the millennium, but for the coming of the Lord. I don't find any place where God says the world is to grow better and better. . . . I find that the earth is going to grow worse and worse," he wrote.[45] Such a mindset could lead to more conversions. "I don't know of anything that will take the men of the world out of their bonds and stocks quicker than [the thought] that our Lord is coming again."[46]

Moody's educational efforts proved to be his most lasting legacy. In his hometown of Northfield, Moody founded a seminary for girls in 1879 and a school for boys two years later in the hope that many would grow up to be ministers and Christian workers. He started a series of summer conferences for college students in Northfield, which built a network of foreign missionaries.

Moody founded a school to train people he called Christian "gap-men" who would perform routine tasks that professional clergy wouldn't need to do. Such an undertaking required aggressive fundraising, and Moody again collected pledges from Chicago's leading businessmen:

Farwell donated $100,000, Cyrus McCormick Jr. gave $25,000, and department store founder Marshall Field pitched in $10,000.[47] In 1889, the Reverend Reuben A. Torrey was installed as the first superintendent of the Chicago Evangelization Society's Bible institute. (It lives on today as the Moody Bible Institute.)

If Moody built the institute's frame, it was Torrey who painted the picture. Torrey, a graduate of Yale and its divinity school, possessed the intellectual firepower that Moody lacked. Torrey had been a Congregational minister before heading to Chicago to work for Moody, who gave Torrey the additional task of pastoring his Chicago Avenue Church. From these influential platforms, Torrey promoted dispensational premillennialism and the Holiness movement, which taught that a "second work of grace" or blessing can allow believers to live a holy, or even a sinless, life. The nondenominational Bible institute produced hundreds of graduates who absorbed these doctrines and spread them widely.

Moody died in 1899, but Torrey carried his flame for decades. Torrey conducted revival meetings around the world—Australia, India, China, Japan, and the British Isles—and in American cities. Torrey followed Moody's template by hiring a musical director, Charles Alexander, and befriending businessmen. In Chicago, Quaker Oats Company founder Henry P. Crowell organized a laymen's council to spearhead Torrey's revival there.[48] In Philadelphia, Wanamaker was again one of the business leaders who reactivated the machinery of revivals.

Torrey was a starchy presence in the pulpit—"I cannot say I fully advocate the old-time style of revival where emotion was the chief instrument," he said—and his rigid theology proved to be divisive.[49] He left the revival circuit and concentrated on writing books that attacked science and settled scores with liberal critics. Torrey left Chicago to accept a position as dean of the newly formed Bible Institute of Los Angeles where he waged his crusade against modernity. The battle would be joined by a scrappy former ballplayer providentially named Billy Sunday.

3

THE FUNDAMENTALS

Billy Sunday's Trail Hitters
and the Assault on Modernism

There are lots of preachers who don't know Jesus. They
know about him, but they don't know him. Experience will
do more than 40 million theories.

—Billy Sunday[1]

The fusion of Christianity and patriotism was a theme Dwight L.
Moody sounded in a sermon near the end of his life. "There is nothing I am more concerned about just now than that God should revive His
church in America. I believe it is the only hope for our republic, for I don't
believe that a republican form of government can last without righteousness. It seems to me that every patriot, every man who loves his country,
ought to be anxious that the church of God should be quickened and
revived," Moody said in an 1899 sermon in his hometown of Northfield,
Massachusetts.[2]

Billy Sunday followed Moody's business-friendly template for traveling preachers and added a fighting spirit to it. Sunday boldly linked evangelicalism and Americanism and became one of the best-known people in
the country. His message curdled into nativism in his later years, and his
feverish style fell out of fashion as the age of radio dawned. Yet his life story
is a guide to understanding the political attitudes and flamboyance that are
hallmarks of evangelicalism to this day.

William Ashley "Billy" Sunday was born in a log-cabin home near
Ames, Iowa, in 1862, about a month before his father died of pneumonia
while serving in the Union Army. Sunday's mother was left impoverished,
and after years of struggle, Billy and his older brother were shipped off to
a soldiers' orphanage. Billy later returned to work at his grandfather's farm

and then set out on his own for good at the age of fifteen.[3] He competed in regional running competitions and played for his town's baseball team.

Sunday's speed caught the attention of Adrian "Cap" Anson, an Iowa native and player-manager of the Chicago White Stockings, a charter member of the National League later known as the Cubs. (The city's American League team, confusingly, is the White Sox.) Anson, one of the game's greatest players, signed Sunday as a backup outfielder in 1883. Sunday became known more for his ability to steal bases than for his prowess at the plate, posting a .248 career batting average. Baseball at that time was a game for roughnecks, and players were notorious for their exploits off the field. Sunday wasn't a carouser of the first rank, but he also didn't have much interest in religious morality.

His life started to change in 1886, when he heard gospel singers from Chicago's Pacific Garden Mission while out on the town with his teammates. Sunday felt moved to attend a service and kept going back until one day he publicly accepted Christ as his personal savior. Sunday started attending a Presbyterian church and met Helen "Nell" Thompson, a devout daughter of a businessman who blanched at the thought of her dating a ballplayer.

Sunday took classes in rhetoric, signed up for Bible study courses at the Chicago YMCA where he heard Moody speak, and married Thompson after demonstrating the requisite piousness. After being shuffled around to various National League teams, Sunday wrapped up his playing career after the 1890 season and accepted a full-time position with the Chicago YMCA as assistant secretary of the religious department. In that role, he recruited speakers for midday prayer meetings and handed out religious pamphlets on street corners.[4]

Evangelist J. Wilbur Chapman hired Sunday to be an assistant for his revivals, an apprenticeship that lasted for nearly three years. As an advance man, Sunday learned how to drum up publicity, select meeting halls, and train volunteers to be ushers and outreach workers. When Chapman accepted a pastorate at a Presbyterian church, Sunday stayed on the road and led revivals in the rural Midwest. His skills as a preacher were raw—much of the style and content of his sermons was cribbed from Chapman—but Sunday's enthusiasm made up for his lack of polish.[5]

Sunday was well into his ministry career when he applied to be a Presbyterian clergyman in 1903. With his unusual background and absence of theological training, Sunday was far from a typical candidate. He struggled under the board's questioning, but his track record as a soul winner was good enough for ordination. Sunday never served as a pastor, preferring the excitement of life on the road.

In his early days, Sunday preached in opera houses or under rickety canvas tents. When his crowds increased, Sunday constructed wooden tabernacles with sawdust floors and a barn-like appearance. He hired Homer Rodeheaver as musical director to lighten the proceedings just as Moody had done with Ira David Sankey. The preacher's wife, invariably called "Ma" Sunday in press reports, signed on as business manager. And like earlier revivalists, Sunday secured the support of local pastors before agreeing to come to town. Churches were expected to suspend services during Sunday's campaign to avoid competition.[6]

Rodeheaver, a trombonist, trained choir members to belt out hymns such as "Onward Christian Soldiers" and "The Old Rugged Cross." Prayer groups and Bible classes were organized in local churches and homes leading up to Sunday's appearances. There were special nights for businessmen, businesswomen, and children. Blocks of seats were reserved for civic groups, church societies, and veterans' organizations.[7]

He won over audiences with simple messages animated with an athleticism honed on the baseball diamond. In the pulpit, Sunday swung his arms like a whirligig and dashed across the platform like a runner heading for home. He smashed chairs to emphasize a point about damnation or the devil, and pounded away at the lectern. When his energy flagged, Sunday lay on his stomach and extended his arms as new converts approached the platform.[8]

His colorful language was as memorable as his antics. Sunday declared in a sermon that Pontius Pilate "was a stand-pat, free-lunch, pie-counter, pliable, plastic, lickspittle, rat-hole, tin-horn, weasel-eyed, ward-healing, grafting, whiskey-soaked politician of his day, pure and simple."[9] The preacher spooled out epigrams called "Sundayisms" such as "Your reputation is what people say about you. Your character is what God and your wife know about you" and "Some of the biggest lies ever told are to be found on gravestones."[10]

Traditional ministers played it safe, in his view. "Too much of preaching today is too nice; too pretty; too dainty; it does not kill," he complained. "Some people won't come to hear me because they are afraid to hear the truth. They want deodorized, disinfected sermons."[11] An early biographer referenced the accusations that Sunday stole material for his sermons without giving credit. "Sunday is not an original thinker. He has founded no school of Scriptural interpretation. He has not given any new exposition of Bible passages, nor has he developed any fresh lines of thought. Nobody learns anything new from him," wrote William T. Ellis in 1914.[12]

Sunday preached biblical inerrancy—the notion that the Bible is free of all error—thus, people only needed to read the Bible for themselves and obey it. "I want to say that I believe that the Bible is the Word of God from cover to cover. Not because I understand its philosophy, speculation, or theory. I cannot; wouldn't attempt it; and I would be a fool if I tried. I believe it because it is from the mouth of God; the mouth of God has spoken it," he said.[13] Sunday blasted "those ossified, petrified, mildewed, dyed-in-the-wool, stamped-in-the-cork, blown-in-the-bottle, horizontal, perpendicular Presbyterians" interpreting the Bible for their congregations.[14]

Sunday's belief system could fit on an index card: "With Christ you are saved, without him you are lost."[15] He put the consequences simply: "You are going to live forever in heaven or you are going to live forever in hell. There's no other place—just the two. It is for you to decide. It's up to you, and you must decide now."

John Wanamaker, the businessman in Philadelphia who backed Moody years earlier, approved of Sunday's stern message. "Billy takes his doctrine from the Bible and not from advanced schools of theology. Let those who deny the divine personality of Jesus make the most of it. If they can get into Heaven past these sayings of Christ, let them do it; it is not Billy Sunday's fault if he sticks to the text," he said.[16]

Letter writers attested to Sunday's down-home appeal. A millworker from Pittsburgh wrote in 1914 that he stopped going to school when he was nine years old, "so I must think with a child's words. . . . Big words are strangers to me." He complained about not being able to comprehend most preachers' messages. Not so with Sunday. "Billy I heard you twice, I know every word you said."[17] Others poured their hearts out to him. A woman named Mrs. Theodore W. Jones lamented that she was unable to make it to Sunday's crusade in Syracuse, New York, in 1915. "I am asking you if I am too late to give my soul to Jesus," she wrote. "Am a farmer's wife and have a hard life, always like to go to Church when I can, but am not a Christian."[18]

Others dismissed Sunday as a vulgar showman, even a charlatan. James F. Newton, a pastor in Dixon, Illinois, did not cooperate with Sunday's local meetings and attended them as a newspaper correspondent. Newton objected to the rallies as playing on people's basest fears of God's vengeance rather than inspiring true divine love.[19] Another writer noted that Lutheran and Episcopal churches did not endorse Sunday's Pittsburgh campaign but offered backhanded praise: "This buffoon of an evangelist made religion a subject of ordinary conversation. People talked about their souls as freely as about their breakfasts."[20]

Sunday's views offended Protestants steeped in the liberal theology that had dominated seminaries and colleges. The ministers that emerged from them did not accept biblical inerrancy and pressed for social reform. They formed the Federal Council of Churches in 1908 and adopted a "social creed" calling for an end to child labor, mandates ensuring workplace safety, and a living wage for all workers. The creed included a ringing statement of purpose: "To the toilers of America and to those who by organized effort are seeking to lift the crushing burdens of the poor, and to reduce the hardships and uphold the dignity of labor, this council sends the greeting of human brotherhood and the pledge of sympathy and of help in a cause which belongs to all who follow Christ."[21]

Such principles permeated many Methodist, Episcopal, and Presbyterian churches, but those denominations were losing ground.[22] From 1900 to 1910, the churches barely kept pace with population growth.[23] Sunday pointed to his sensational attendance numbers and noted that thousands more were turned away from his tabernacles that seated up to twenty thousand. He asserted that he knew how to reach people who had fallen away from traditional churches. A successful preacher "will put his cookies on the lower shelf. He will preach in a language that the commonest laborer can understand," Sunday said.[24]

Sunday, a premillennialist, attacked the Social Gospel movement in liberal Protestant churches for being too concerned with solving the world's ills at the expense of saving souls. The only true reform was for people to make a personal conversion to Christ—not to push for legislation or a new government program. Treating churches as just another charitable organization was "godless social service nonsense," he said.[25]

Sunday portrayed such efforts as threats to the American capitalist system. He teamed up with business barons such as Wanamaker, John D. Rockefeller Jr., and Henry Clay Frick to bankroll his campaigns. "Religion is good business. It has become a primary economic factor. Look at the big businesses that are backing religion. See the big men who are Christians. I tell you it is good business," Sunday said in 1917.[26]

Organized labor leaders complained that Sunday was a "strike-breaker, and that he gets the backing of great capitalists because his influence on working men turns their attention away from problems of hours and wages and the demand for more equitable conditions," wrote Horace J. Bridges in 1918. Sunday castigated people for sins of the flesh, Bridges pointed out, but the sins of "an individualistic and monopolistic industrialism—these he seldom casts an eye upon and never rebukes."[27]

Rockefeller's involvement in Sunday's 1917 New York campaign angered union leaders. They blamed the son of the oil tycoon for orchestrating the 1914 Ludlow Massacre in which a militia attacked a tent colony of striking coal miners in Colorado. Two labor union officials met with Sunday to discuss their concerns. After the discussion, the Labor Forum released a statement: "You have asked a representative of the most conspicuous House of Mammon in the world to sit on the platform with you, and have not accorded equal recognition to the plain people whom Christ conspicuously honored when he selected fishermen and humble workers to be His spokesmen and closest associates. That goes far to nullify all the good you do."[28]

Rockefeller stayed on as the keystone of a finance committee that raised $65,000 to cover the costs of building the New York tabernacle, which was 334 feet long and 247 feet wide.[29] The "glory barn" at 168th Street and Broadway accommodated up to eighteen thousand people. "Sunday and his helpers made it clear that they were going after souls as a successful commercial corporation would go after sales," according to an account of Sunday's ten-week campaign in New York in 1917.[30]

Sunday rang up impressive numbers of what he called "trail hitters," people who converted and promised to "hit the sawdust trail" for Jesus. They were counted and classified in the way a company reports revenues and dividends. In his New York campaign, there were 98,264 "trail hitters"; in Philadelphia in 1915, there were 41,724 signed cards.[31] Sunday reckoned that each conversion cost about two dollars when weighed against his campaign expenses.[32] He scrapped the "anxious benches" and "inquiry rooms" of earlier eras to streamline the conversion process.

Critics charged that many signatories were already church members or were people who joined one but didn't stay or never joined one at all. Retired Episcopal clergyman William A. Wasson dismissed Sunday's Philadelphia revival as a circus, adding "his converts believe they have found religion, but really they have lost their mental balance."[33]

Accusations of greed dogged Sunday as his fame grew. Sunday walked away from his 1916 campaign in Detroit with a "thanks offering" of $46,102.28 in cash, and less valuable items such as "fancy socks" and "many presents of flowers and fruits."[34] (The cash payout translates to well over $1 million today.) Henry M. Leland, founder and president of Cadillac, presented Sunday with an $8,000 limousine with special features such as a hidden pocket designed to hold a Bible.[35] Leland also mailed Sunday a check for $1,000 in appreciation for "the awakening of the moral, civic and religious consciousness of our city."[36] Leland had served on the Sunday campaign's executive committee.

Sunday regarded the offerings as fees for his personal use, and he spent them lavishly. He wore well-tailored suits when he preached, purchased a vacation home in Oregon, and built a handsome Arts and Crafts–style house in Winona Lake, Indiana. He also heavily donated to causes such as the YMCA and the Red Cross, especially after the United States entered World War I in 1917.

For Sunday and his successors, Christian service and financial success were intertwined. If people loaded collection buckets so full of coins, cash, and checks that Sunday's aides strained to lift them, it was a sign of God's blessing for the work being done in his name.[37] If Sunday could rise from a log-cabin childhood to a position of wealth and fame, maybe his admirers could, too. Sunday biographer Robert F. Martin wrote that the preacher appealed to the common man—that is, native-born white people—because he "embodied the myth of success in which they believed and because he had achieved that success by conducting his affairs in accord with the rule of the business world to which they belonged or to which they aspired."[38]

Other prominent Protestants subscribed to the ethos that religion could instill the virtues of discipline and thrift, leading to material success. "Material prosperity and godliness go hand in hand," said the Reverend A. B. Kendall of the United Society of Christian Endeavor in 1927. "The nation that sows morality and spirituality will reap peace and prosperity."[39] Advertising executive Bruce Barton cast Jesus as the founder of modern business in *The Man Nobody Knows: A Discovery of the Real Jesus*, a bestselling book published in 1925. Barton reduced Jesus' teachings into breezy homilies for the free-enterprise system. "He picked up twelve men from the bottom ranks of business and forged them into an organization that conquered the world," Barton wrote. "He thought of his life as *business*."[40]

Sunday's ebullience won him broad popular appeal. When his party pulled into town, thousands flocked to the train station in the hope of catching a glimpse of him. Photographers tracked Sunday's every move and reporters filled newspaper columns with his vivid remarks. *American Magazine* published a nationwide poll in 1914 asking people to name "the greatest man in the United States" and placed Sunday in eighth place, tied with Andrew Carnegie.[41] (Former president Theodore Roosevelt easily topped the list, with Thomas Edison finishing second.) In 1915, Sunday met with President Woodrow Wilson at the White House and lunched afterward with

Secretary of State William Jennings Bryan, a devout Presbyterian and later a notable opponent of Charles Darwin's theory of evolution.

Sunday and other conservatives who attacked the Social Gospel approved of government intervention in private matters of vice and morality. Sunday's most notable contribution to public policy was his fervent support for Prohibition. Protestants of all stripes had long backed "temperance" and advocates won restrictions on the sale of alcohol in some states. Sunday put the full force of his popularity and rhetoric behind it. "The saloonkeeper and the devil are both pulling on the same rope," he told a crowd of nine thousand at a revival in 1915. "Whisky is all right in its place and, take it from me, its place is in hell."[42]

His appeals "to get on the water wagon" were braided with nativism given that German immigrants dominated the brewery business. In a speech at the University of Michigan, he goaded students to campaign for a statewide ban on alcohol. "I will fight them till hell freezes over," he said about beer and liquor interests. "Then I'll buy a pair of skates and fight 'em on the ice."[43] On January 16, 1920, the day before the Eighteenth Amendment took effect, Sunday held a triumphant revival meeting in Norfolk, Virginia, telling the crowd of ten thousand packed inside his tabernacle, "The reign of tears is over. . . . Hell will be forever for rent."[44]

The anti-German hysteria that propelled Prohibition and America's entry into World War I supercharged Sunday's jingoism. "Christianity and patriotism are synonymous terms, and hell and traitors are synonymous," he thundered.[45] Sunday appointed himself "God's recruiting officer" in the fight to rout a "bunch of pretzel-chewing sauerkraut spawn of blood-thirsty Huns."[46] Sunday routinely waved an American flag from the platform to wild applause from the audience. The New York drama critic Heywood Broun measured Sunday against George M. Cohan, the composer of patriotic songs such as "The Yankee Doodle Boy," and wrote, "It is true that Cohan waved the flag first, but Billy Sunday has waved it harder."[47]

Sunday welcomed the postwar Palmer Raids that relied more on suspicion than legal warrants as justification to jail and deport thousands of communists and radical leftists. "If they don't like the way we do things, let them get out of here and leave. We don't propose to adjust the country to suit a lot of anarchists," he said as a "Red Scare" convulsed the country.[48] Sunday also backed the immigration laws of the 1920s that tightly restricted the entry of Southern and Eastern Europeans—many of them Catholics and Jews—and blocked the immigration of people from Asia. Sunday's views have reverberated through the generations in sentiments such as "America: Love it or leave it."

Sunday marshaled his premillennial beliefs—that Jesus could come again at any time—into a war against modernism in all of its forms. Once when he spotted a liberal theologian in an audience, Sunday shook his fist at him and shouted: "Stand up, you bastard evolutionist; stand up with the infidels and atheists, the whoremongers and adulterers."[49] Such an uncompromising attitude would become an evangelical hallmark.

Sunday was the most visible exponent of a rising movement that rebutted the ideals of liberal Christianity. Dispensationalist teachings were enshrined in the annotated *Scofield Reference Bible*, which has millions of copies in print since it was first published in 1909. Between 1910 and 1915, a series of essays by scholars and Bible teachers was published in twelve booklets called *The Fundamentals: A Testimony to the Truth*. Union Oil Company founder Lyman Stewart and his brother, Milton, conceived and paid for the expensive project. Lyman Stewart, a Presbyterian unhappy with his church's liberalization, ordered the free distribution of hundreds of thousands of the volumes to ministers, theological students, and YMCAs.

Among the editors of *The Fundamentals* was Reuben A. Torrey, leader of the Bible Institute of Los Angeles (now Biola University) that Lyman Stewart cofounded in 1908. Another project supervisor was A. C. Dixon, pastor of Moody Memorial Church and a fierce opponent of European scholars' "higher criticism," that raised questions about the Bible's veracity, authorship, and dating.[50] *The Fundamentals* contained attacks on Roman Catholicism, Mormonism, and Christian Science—religions the writers considered to be heretical—as well as broadsides against Darwin's theory of evolution. Other essayists defended tenets such as biblical inerrancy and the virgin birth of Jesus or described personal religious testimonies. The volumes formed the bedrock of Christian fundamentalism, a term first used in 1920.

One of its leaders was William Bell Riley, a Moody acolyte who transformed a Baptist church in Minneapolis into a bastion of fundamentalism. Riley opposed all forms of liberalism, and his answer to all social ills was individual conversion to Christ. "The whole impetus of Riley's social message seems to have been based on his own personal experience. Hardworking and poor, he had . . . made it to the very top of his profession. He could not understand why his pattern could not be universalized," wrote historian Ferenc M. Szasz.[51] Riley attacked divinity schools and seminaries that denied "every fundamental of our faith" and broadened his assault to all of higher education in his 1917 book, *The Menace of Modernism*.[52] In his view, intellectuals at colleges and universities promoted moral decay by pushing religion to the margins in the name of secularism. He founded a Bible school, a seminary, and a liberal arts college to correct that imbalance.

The fundamentalists believed the mass destruction and social upheaval wrought by World War I gave credence to their apocalyptic interpretation of biblical prophecy. Signs were piling up that Armageddon was near, so there was no time to waste. The Bolshevik-led Russian Revolution in 1917 and the rise of the Soviet Union seemed to represent the power from the North, referred to as Magog in the Hebrew Bible, preparing for the battle of Armageddon.[53] Premillennialists also believed that the redrawing of the map in the Middle East increased the chances of a new Jewish homeland in Palestine—another prophetic sign.[54]

The first meeting of the World's Christian Fundamentals Association in 1919 brought together six thousand ministers and heads of Bible schools to coordinate their doctrinal beliefs. Riley, who was chosen to lead the association, persuaded pastors to join the movement, and organized hundreds of conferences.[55] The association's work kindled fundamentalist groups across the country that sought to fracture Presbyterian and Baptist churches.

The opposition to modernism found its fullest expression in the battle over teaching evolution in public schools. William Jennings Bryan, the three-time Democratic presidential nominee and renowned orator, emerged as the most visible defender of the fundamentalist position. Bryan argued that the theory of evolution was incompatible with scripture—there was nothing in Genesis about man being descended from apes—and that no school should be forced to teach it. Bryan also worried about the political consequences of the survival-of-the-fittest, "natural selection" ethos of Social Darwinism. Bryan, a Presbyterian elder but not a fundamentalist, unsuccessfully ran for moderator of the Presbyterian General Assembly in 1923, falling short against a minister who endorsed the teaching of evolution at his college.

The next front in the war over evolution shifted to a small town in the South. A young science teacher named John T. Scopes was arrested in Dayton, Tennessee, for violating a state law barring the teaching of evolution in public schools. The American Civil Liberties Union used it as a test case to challenge the law as a violation of free speech. The ensuing 1925 trial turned into a tragicomic carnival with a cast of characters that included the celebrated lawyer Clarence Darrow defending Scopes, an ailing Bryan assisting the prosecution and testifying as an expert witness on the Bible, and the acerbic newspaper columnist H. L. Mencken skewering the whole spectacle. It was presented as a battle of modernism against fundamentalism, of science against faith, local yokels against intellectual elites, freedom of speech against freedom of religion.

Given the exhaustive coverage of the "Scopes Monkey Trial," its concrete legal result was absurdly minute—Scopes was found guilty and fined $100. (His conviction was overturned on appeal. The law at issue in Tennessee remained on the books for forty-two years.) The spectacle ridiculed fundamentalism in front of a national audience. In a dramatic confrontation on the courthouse lawn thronged with spectators and newsmen, Darrow poked holes in Bryan's knowledge of the Bible and geology and forced him into logical contortions. Darrow got Bryan to agree that biblical scholars had dated Noah's Ark to 4004 BC and sprang his trap:

DARROW: "What do you think?"

BRYAN: "I do not think about things I don't think about."

DARROW: "Do you think about things you do think about?"

BRYAN: "Well, sometimes."

(Laughter in the courtyard.)[56]

The faceoff in the summer heat continued with an examination of the claim in Genesis that God created the Earth in six days. "You think those were not literal days?" he asked Bryan, who replied, "I do not think they were twenty-four-hour days." That created an easy opening for Darrow. "The creation might have been going on for a very long time?" he asked. "It might have continued for millions of years," Bryan said to a stunned crowd.[57] The statesman's last gasp on the stand was a feeble one: "I want the world to know that this man, who does not believe in a God, is trying to use a court in Tennessee to slur at it." Darrow responded, "I am examining you on your fool ideas that no intelligent Christian on earth believes."[58] (Actually, millions of Christians—not just fundamentalists—rejected evolution and it remains a contentious issue today.)[59]

To the popular press, Bryan's testimony—which was not heard by the jury or entered into the official record—exposed biblical literalism as ridiculous and fundamentalists as ignorant. Darrow was hailed as the winner of the showdown against Bryan, who was denied the chance to question Darrow and deliver his carefully crafted speech to the court. Bryan died in his sleep five days after the duel in Dayton, dramatized in the play and movie *Inherit the Wind*. In response to a suggestion that Bryan died of a broken heart, Darrow snapped, "Busted heart nothing; he died of an overstuffed belly."[60]

At Bryan's burial service at Arlington National Cemetery, the Reverend George R. Stuart reflected on Bryan's life and said, "We thank Thee for this great hero of the common people."[61] The death of the "Commoner" inspired a tribute in Ohio where robed Ku Klux Klan members held a service and cross burning. The inscription on the cross read, "He stood at Armageddon and battled for the Lord."[62]

Fundamentalists lashed back in wounded defensiveness. Riley blasted "the blood-sucking journalists" and another minister attacked Darrow's questioning as "repulsive, abusive, ignorant, tiresome twaddle."[63] Riley and others scored scattered victories against the teaching of evolution, but they were portrayed as backward thinkers in a modern age. The *Christian Century*, a journal geared to liberal Protestants, said that fundamentalism was "wholly lacking in the qualities of constructive achievement or survival" and would be "a disappearing quantity in American religious life."[64] Fundamentalists retreated from the public square but they did not vanish. In exile, they nursed their grievances and created their own subculture to keep their ideas alive.

As the curtain fell on the morality play that was the Scopes trial, Billy Sunday was entering the sad twilight of his preaching career. Sunday's influence declined in the 1920s and his revival meetings retreated to smaller towns. A respectful but candid letter sent to Sunday from Homer Rodeheaver, his longtime musical director, outlined some of the problems. "It never comes to you, but in every city we know splendid men and women who are alienated from you and your work because of the drastic, disagreeable things you say about the money from the platform," Rodeheaver wrote in 1929.[65]

Rodeheaver observed that Sunday stopped meeting with local ministers and brushed off other important people who wanted to meet him. Even members of his own party were treated like strangers. Sunday lengthened his sermons to over an hour, lacing them with bizarre warnings about occultism, vegetarianism, and demons. This sliced into the time allotted for music. "Your crowds get tired and that is one of the reasons that you have not been getting great results in these latter years," Rodeheaver wrote.[66]

Sunday's nativism attracted an appreciative letter from the Kanton Klan of Canton, Ohio. "May we take this opportunity to congratulate you upon excellent service rendered our community in the furtherance of God's Kingdom and the perpetuation of our American heritage," the Ku Klux Klan affiliate wrote in 1931. "We pray your efforts in all future campaigns will be as richly blessed as they have in the past."[67]

Sunday's political clout had eroded. Skirmishes between the "wets" and the "drys" raged throughout the 1920s as the failures of enforcing Prohibition became obvious. In 1928, Sunday worked hard to elect Republican Herbert Hoover over Democrat Al Smith, whom Sunday believed to be unacceptable because he was "wet" and Catholic. Hoover declined an invitation to make a campaign stop at Sunday's tabernacle in Winona Lake, Indiana. Hoover won, but his hapless response to the Great Depression doomed his term in office. Sunday tried to buck up Hoover as the 1932 election neared. "Your fight against the elements that would wreck our nation if their socialistic revolutionary views become law is analogous to the fight Lincoln waged in the dark days of slavery," wrote Sunday, with the signoff, "Your friend to the last ditch."[68] Hoover lost to Franklin D. Roosevelt in a landslide, and the misbegotten experiment of Prohibition was repealed in 1933.

Sunday grasped the immense potential that the new technology of radio broadcasting held for evangelism, and he appeared on some programs, but he was too old and too much of a creature of the road to adapt. Radio preachers were reaching exponentially more people than Sunday ever could in his wooden tabernacles, which were not equipped with microphones or loudspeakers. His final years were deeply unhappy ones. He buried his only daughter and endured the suicide of his oldest son. Slowed by heart trouble, Sunday died in 1935, at seventy-two.

His death was front-page news in the *New York Times* and more than three thousand mourners filled Moody Memorial Church in Chicago for his funeral. A hymn was sung with the wistful refrain "we'll say 'good night' here, but 'good morning' up there." Presbyterian minister John Timothy Stone delivered the eulogy and said simply about the man who had preached to millions, "There has been no greater soul winner among men."[69]

4

SISTER AIMEE

The Birth of Pentecostalism
and the Dawn of Radio Preachers

I'm after souls and where the services are held matters little. . . .
My pulpit is the whole world.

—Aimee Semple McPherson[1]

For Aimee Semple McPherson, the opening of her majestic church
across from Echo Park Lake in Los Angeles on January 1, 1923, was
the fruit of two years of visionary planning. "Sister Aimee" had relentlessly
traveled across the country, honing her "Foursquare Gospel" message in
front of electrified crowds at tent meetings and auditoriums. Her unlikely
rise to fame and her tumultuous personal life made her an object of admiration and ridicule. Among the first religious figures to become a radio
celebrity, she attracted controversy with her claims of using the Holy Spirit
to heal the sick, provoking some newspapers and clergymen to declare her
a fraud. McPherson fittingly settled just up the road from Hollywood, the
fledgling dream factory of overnight stars and lurid scandals.[2]

But much of that lay in front of her. The dawn of the new year began
in classic Southern California style with the Tournament of Roses parade
of marching bands and floral floats coursing through Pasadena's streets.
McPherson entered the parade to promote her church, Angelus Temple,
which would open later that day. She directed volunteers to painstak-
ingly arrange thousands of pink roses and white carnations to resemble the
imposing church, and placed it atop the largest truck she could find.[3] An
organist performed gospel tunes from inside the fragrant structure, singers
walked alongside it to stir the early morning crowd, and workers handed
out leaflets about the church's official dedication ceremony later that

afternoon.[4] The enchanting float won a prize in its division, and, most important for McPherson, created a buzz of expectation.

The concrete façade of the semicircular church on Glendale Boulevard looked like one of the era's unfussy neighborhood ballparks, but the inside was something else. The largest unsupported dome in the nation at that time crowned the sanctuary that sat more than five thousand.[5] An artist designed and constructed eight stained-glass windows at a cost of $15,000. Visitors waited for hours to witness the architectural marvel for themselves.

Most of all, they were there for McPherson, the evangelist referred to in newspaper headlines as a "female Billy Sunday," "faith healer," and "miracle woman." She appeared on a temporary platform outside the church, knelt as she read the prayer of Solomon, and laid the church's dedicatory plaques.[6] One of them read, "Dedicated unto the cause of interdenominational and worldwide evangelism." The ceremony doubled as the founding of McPherson's International Church of the Foursquare Gospel.

The temple's doors then flung open and congregants streamed in, filling every seat. A section of the floor was reserved for "gypsies," who were among McPherson's most ardent supporters. "Each gypsy brought to the temple an offering of flowers as a token of gratitude to Mrs. McPherson for the new faith that she has brought to them, and as a token of worship to a new God—her God," the *Los Angeles Times* wrote.[7] A choir opened the service and a musician from Australia performed several solos on a golden harp. Ministers from an array of denominations took part in the program, and McPherson preached a triumphant sermon. Hundreds pushed up to the front when she made her altar call.

McPherson reflected on the momentous occasion in an interview after the service. "Today is the happiest day of my entire life. I can hardly believe yet that his great temple has been built for me—that so much of my work has been accomplished," she said. Her call to do God's work, her years of hosting evangelistic services across the country, her heartbreaks—all of these struggles must have been part of God's plan and thus worthwhile. "I have never been so happy," she concluded.[8]

Just three miles from Angelus Temple, a revival had taken place sixteen years earlier that ignited Pentecostalism as a worldwide force, deeply influencing McPherson. In 1906, a Black preacher named William J. Seymour had relocated from Texas and pastored an unusual mission in Los Angeles. Seymour, who went blind in his left eye after contracting smallpox, was the son of enslaved people and had been steeped in the Holiness movement and premillennial theology.

Seymour was the student of the preacher Charles Fox Parham, who ran a Bible school in Topeka, Kansas, where a woman "spoke in tongues" on January 1, 1901. The phenomenon, also known as glossolalia, was described in the biblical account of Pentecost, when the Holy Spirit descended upon the apostles and other followers of Jesus in Jerusalem fifty days after Easter Sunday. According to the second chapter of Acts, a mighty wind came down from heaven and filled them with the Holy Spirit—a spirit baptism—as Jesus had promised. Then they began to speak in languages they did not know, testifying to the works of God.

Parham and other believers interpreted these "tongues of fire" as a gift from the Holy Spirit that could mark the recipient as capable of healing the sick and issuing prophecies. Paul's first letter to the Corinthians, chapters 12–14, identifies the speaking and interpretation of tongues as among the spiritual gifts, or "charismata." But the notion of people suddenly worshipping in unlearned languages—whether human or supernatural in origin—was controversial, and Seymour was locked out of the Holiness church within days of his arrival in Los Angeles.

When no other church would have him, Seymour led Bible study sessions at a house on North Bonnie Brae Street where a Black couple lived. On April 9, 1906, some in Seymour's group started speaking in tongues. When word spread of what had happened, so many worshippers showed up at the tiny house that the front porch collapsed.[9] Seymour and his followers moved to an abandoned box-like building on 312 Azusa Street, which became known as the Apostolic Faith Gospel Mission or, less formally, the Azusa Street Mission.

Many in the city did not welcome the congregation's unusual worship style. A front-page report in the *Los Angeles Daily Times* on April 18, 1906, was heralded by stacked headlines:

WEIRD BABEL
OF TONGUES.
New Sect of Fanatics Is
Breaking Loose.
Wild Scene Last Night on
Azusa Street.
Gurgle of Wordless Talk by
a Sister.

The report described worshippers "breathing strange utterances and mouthing a creed which it would seem no sane mortal could understand." The reporter noted "colored people and a sprinkling of whites" in the assembly who howled in prayer and swayed for hours in supplication. Seymour was not mentioned by name but was insultingly portrayed as "an old colored exhorter" who clasped a miniature Bible and directed worshippers to "let tongues come forth." As midnight approached, a Black woman came forward and fell to the floor and "began a wild gesticulation, which ended in a gurgle of wordless prayers which were nothing less than shocking." Seymour whispered in awe, "She's speakin' in unknown tongues," then added, "Keep on, sister."

The exuberant outbursts at the Azusa Street Mission spurred a flurry of noise complaints from neighbors. The worshippers—variously called "holy kickers," "holy jumpers," and "holy rollers"—carried on well into the night, and police broke up the spiritual exercises when they got too rowdy. The rambunctious services attracted the curious who stood on benches to witness the proceedings. The worshippers seemed electrified. They did not need to be told what to do. "No choir led this gathering in song. Someone happened to want to sing a song and started it. Every one followed," a witness marveled. "No one in particular led in prayer. They all prayed."[10]

Racism tinged the distaste for what was happening on Azusa Street. An article in the *Los Angeles Times* about an Azusa Street service mentioned a white woman who testified that she had left her husband and children in order to follow the Black preacher. "At least a dozen young white women declared their intention of casting their lot with the negro ranters," said the article, which noted that Black women "threw themselves on the floor and cackled and gabbled."[11] Blacks and whites, men and women held hands during the service, and slung their arms around each other's shoulders in solidarity. "The surprise is that any respectable white person would attend such meetings as are being conducted on Azusa street," the article concluded.[12]

Other churches worried about what it would mean for them. The Reverend E. P. Ryland, president of the Los Angeles Church Federation, worried that the excitement of these "new creeds" was drawing people from traditional churches. Ryland thought they had lessons to teach about being more effective missionaries, but their rituals were too alien for his taste. Ryland witnessed a woman speaking in tongues at an Azusa Street service and saw it as a sign of fanaticism. "I had no doubt the woman was sincere, but she had worked herself into an excitement that made her irresponsible," he said.[13]

Even a rumor that such teachings had permeated religious institutions provoked outrage. "I would be very sorry indeed to have the impression get abroad that we sanctioned the Azusa Street church doctrine here," said L. Maria Deane, superintendent of the nearby Training School for Christian Workers. She recalled a woman she knew to be modest and quiet who turned into "a person under great nervous tension" after acquiring the gift of tongues.[14]

The Azusa Street Revival dissipated within a few years, but it had set fire to a movement. Pentecostal evangelists spread their message across the country and won masses of converts, although the Pentecostal denominations to come would not reflect its interracial origins. The believers were widely mocked and some ministers denounced their doctrines, but as in Cane Ridge a century earlier, their faith showed that common people could receive the gifts of the Holy Spirit. In their view, divinity degrees and refined education were obstacles to achieving religious ecstasy in anticipation of the imminent return of Christ. Few would do more to popularize Pentecostalism than Aimee Semple McPherson.

She came from a place a world apart from the bustle of Los Angeles. Aimee Elizabeth Kennedy, born on October 9, 1890, was raised on a small farm near Ingersoll, Ontario, Canada. She was an only child whose father, James, was a Methodist and her mother, Minnie, was active in the Salvation Army, an evangelistic ministry geared to the destitute. Aimee said she began doubting her religious upbringing in high school when her class studied evolution. If the Bible was wrong about the origins of life, it was probably mistaken about many other things, she reasoned. "The more I read and observed the lives of Christians, the more skeptical of the reality of God I became," she wrote in an early memoir, *This Is That*.[15]

Aimee's mother was alarmed and directed her to join a church immediately. Aimee stumbled upon a small Pentecostal mission in her town and was transfixed by a handsome Irish preacher named Robert Semple. His messages of repentance "pierced my heart with conviction" and lifted her spiritual crisis.[16] Aimee soon spoke in tongues and received the baptism of the Holy Spirit. She married Semple and they participated in revival campaigns in England and Ireland and performed missionary work in China. Robert Semple died in Hong Kong after contracting malaria and dysentery in 1910, leaving Aimee eight months pregnant and a nineteen-year-old widow.

Aimee and her infant daughter, Roberta, joined Aimee's mother in New York City to regroup and work for the Salvation Army. There Aimee met accountant Harold McPherson, and they quickly married and had a son, Rolf, and seemed ready to settle into domestic life in Providence, Rhode Island. A nervous breakdown and a string of health setbacks followed, however, including a serious bout with appendicitis. It was then that she heard the call to resume her evangelistic efforts. She took her children and returned to her family farm in Canada to launch her solo preaching career. Harold McPherson reluctantly assisted his wife at her tent revivals, but their marriage had frayed beyond repair. They divorced in 1921.

Aimee then spent several years crisscrossing the continent, sometimes with her mother in a "Gospel Car" with the words "JESUS IS COMING SOON—GET READY" printed along the side. Female preachers were a rare sight when women were just securing the right to vote in the United States, but McPherson was undaunted in the face of sexist attitudes. "Churches today will permit a woman to stand in the pulpit and recite for entertainment, but when she suggests preaching, religious folk hold up their hands in horror," she said. "A woman is able as a man to speak the truth."[17]

Reports spread of miraculous instances of "faith healing" at her meetings. About thirty people in Philadelphia in 1920 claimed they had been cured of their physical ailments after McPherson prayed for them. Robert Locke, who suffered from infantile paralysis and had to be carried into a McPherson revival, removed his brace and walked away unsupported.[18] Another man who was nearly blind declared that his sight had been restored. Unneeded canes, crutches, and braces were tossed into piles.

She conveyed a message of hope rather than damnation. Her personal appeal pulled in crowds that extended beyond strict Pentecostals. McPherson was not interested in parsing denominational differences because they interfered with her mission of trying to appeal to as many people as possible. Sister Aimee herself contained multitudes: Assemblies of God credentials as minister, a Methodist exhorter's license, and a Baptist preaching license.[19] She accepted basic evangelical doctrines like premillennialism but did not get bogged down in Pentecostal discussions such as whether speaking in tongues was a requirement to be baptized in the Holy Spirit.[20]

McPherson launched a West Coast tour in early 1921 to popular acclaim and intensive press attention. A reporter in San Diego noted that McPherson was far gentler with her listeners than Billy Sunday. "She has a sweet voice and pleads with her audience to accept of her religion," the article reported.[21] The message may have been delivered with a smile, but the content was similar. McPherson warned of the imminent return of Jesus Christ and urged all to reform and accept him, dividing all people into Christians or sinners. She railed against signs of moral laxity such as carousing in Tijuana, poolrooms, gambling, cigarette smoking, profanity, and dance halls. McPherson also complained about jazz when the noise from a nearby band disrupted her service.

Her meetings in San Diego culminated at Balboa Park's Organ Pavilion where more than eight thousand people watched her treat three hundred people with a range of ailments. They came up one by one in a process that took five hours. McPherson, wearing her trademark white, long-sleeved servant's uniform adorned with a black cape, stretched up her arms in prayer, laid her hands on the afflicted, and anointed them with oil. "Praise the Lord—I pray Jesus that this patient be healed here and now," she exclaimed, and told the ailing they would be healed if they had faith.[22] She declared three thousand conversions in her five-week revival and thanked the city's pastors for their assistance in her nondenominational work.

McPherson's series of meetings in San Jose later in the year came to a close with a service that attracted more than ten thousand people, many from out of town who sought to be healed. A girl from Montana came forward on crutches with one leg encased in a steel brace. McPherson unfastened the brace and the girl walked on her own power as the audience cheered and her mother wept. A child whose legs were paralyzed was able to stand and walk after professions of faith and the assembly's prayers. McPherson connected with children and adults alike because her message was simple: Jesus is as present now as he was yesterday and will be tomorrow. "If we understand it rightly and have faith, the Bible will show us how we can be delivered from sorrow, sickness, from uncertainty and struggle, from all ignorance and limitation," she preached. "The Bible only says the same thing over and over again, by parable, allegories and other ways. But it is always the same."[23]

Many took these stories of healing at face value, but one newspaper did not. A series of critical articles published in the *Sacramento Bee* in February 1922 scrutinized McPherson's claims. The reporter, Darwin J. Smith, followed up with people who said they had been healed at McPherson's revivals in Lodi and Fresno. A deaf woman identified as Mrs. H. F. Wheaton came forward at the Lodi event, and McPherson prayed for her and anointed her with oil. McPherson then questioned her in front of an auditorium, and Wheaton replied that she could hear. McPherson praised the Lord for the miracle. Two days after the meeting, Wheaton told a reporter that she could hear no better than before.[24]

The reporter searched McPherson's monthly magazine, *The Bridal Call*, for more claims of miracle cures and also found them to be false. An issue contained a statement attributed to a woman who said she was cured of her deafness after being anointed at a San Jose meeting. In a statement to the newspaper, she said that was incorrect: "I have never claimed that

I was healed of the deafness with which I have been troubled for eleven years. I was not cured and am still being treated by an osteopath."[25] The writer concluded that he could find no cures or miracles. "What relief, if any, came to these people was purely of a religious or mental nature, not physical healings."

McPherson responded to the controversy while at her tabernacle in Lodi. "It is easy to be a muckraker. Every man can find something wrong if he wishes to close his eyes to the good," she said. "All who come to us cannot be healed, as the healing is a matter of their faith alone."[26] Wheaton backtracked from her earlier statement about McPherson's effect on her hearing, saying it was her fault for not being ready to be healed. "My soul is being helped all the time, and I know that when the time comes I will be healed. I don't blame anything but the condition of my faith for the fact that I am not healed, but I know I am getting better," she said.[27]

Others believed McPherson's "divine healing" activities were causing physical harm. A deputy sheriff in Fresno said the county jail handled about ten people "afflicted with mental derangement on the subject of religion and the subjects of the McPherson meetings."[28] The physician of Mrs. Alta Roberts, who was in good physical and mental health, said she apparently suffered a breakdown related to McPherson's sermons and was sent to a private sanitarium in Stockton.[29] Roberts died at forty-two, leaving behind a husband and three sons. In a letter to the *Sacramento Bee*, the Reverend J. A. Craig of the Church of Christ in Madera wrote that he had spent a day at McPherson's meetings and "was thoroughly convinced that a greater fraud has never been perpetrated in the name of religion. . . . I have yet to find one who received any real lasting benefit from her work but can trace many who have been deceived and are really worse off."[30]

Another *Bee* exposé alleged that McPherson's mother and business manager, Minnie Kennedy, screened the people who were to come forward for healing at the revivals.[31] They first had to demonstrate a high level of faith and sincerity of conversion. (A Catholic who sought healing but wanted to remain a Catholic would not be selected, for example.) People on crutches and in wheelchairs attended meeting after meeting in the hope of getting a coveted card qualifying them for anointing by McPherson. Kennedy placed them in a reserved section and summoned them when it was their turn.

McPherson denied that she possessed divine power to heal the sick. "I do not claim that all that are prayed for are healed at these meetings. It is a matter of the strength of their faith. Those who have absolute faith in the power of Jesus certainly are helped," she said. "They must have even more than faith, they must have a real and goodly motive for being cured. They must be ready to give their life to the Lord in the future."[32] To the audience, it appeared that these were randomly selected people who were cured by divine visitation. To critics, it was a cheap magic trick or an example of mass psychology.

With mounting furor over her methods, McPherson canceled her revival meetings in Sacramento. "The ministers up there need waking up. The people need waking up everywhere in the matter of religion, but at Sacramento the ministers need somebody to wake them up," she said.[33] It was just as well because only two of the twenty-seven members of the city's Protestant ministerial union supported her visit. "I am joyful Mrs. McPherson is not coming to Sacramento, because I believe her so-called miracles are fakes," said union president E. H. Mowre, a Methodist pastor. "I feel it's a terrible thing to prey upon the sick and afflicted."[34] Another pastor blamed a revival in San Jose for hastening the death of a member of his congregation who he thought would have been better off healing at home.

Accusations of money-grubbing added to McPherson's troubles. A pastor produced an article about McPherson's lengthy revival in Denver—where she had been permitted to use a city auditorium for free—that reported she left town with $21,000 for her personal use, with much of it earmarked to build her temple in Los Angeles.[35] She brazenly asked for temple donations in her magazine, *The Bridal Call*, with this appeal: "We have faith to believe that for every dollar given, a precious soul will be won for Christ. . . . Oh! What eternal interest!"[36]

She also faced charges that she inflated the numbers of people converted and cured. A neurologist who observed the McPherson meetings in Denver found claims of cures to be baseless. Dr. C. S. Blumel told *The Rocky Mountain News* that a young man suffering from tuberculosis left his hospital bed, attended the service, publicly pronounced himself cured, then died thirteen days later. Another man with paralysis on his left side went up to be healed and in his zeal mistakenly waved his right hand to the audience. "The remaining 'cures' which form almost the total of a faith healer's achievements, are based on the patient's affirmation, and this is an expression of his credulity and enthusiasm rather than his judgment. With sufficient enthusiasm, he may certainly convince himself," the doctor said.[37]

McPherson pushed ahead with her revival meetings with an eye to opening her own tabernacle in Los Angeles, a fast-growing market primed for an innovative church to exploit. "We can't get along with a weak-kneed trembling church, but must have one that is strong, fearless, clear thinking and has a clean Gospel," she said in Oakland, where she was drawing tens of thousands each day to her tabernacle. She sharpened her critique of ministers who fell short of that goal. "I'd rather hear a man who had just let go the handle of a plow, who was filled with the Holy Spirit, than some well read, highly educated professor who did not have it," she said.[38]

McPherson's "Foursquare Gospel" stemmed from her sermon on the prophet Ezekiel's vision of God as four creatures with the face of a man, an ox, a lion, and an eagle on each side. McPherson interpreted it as the elements of Jesus's ministry: Man was Christ as savior; ox was Christ as healer; lion was Christ as baptizer with the Holy Spirit; and eagle was Christ the coming king.[39] Some of these ideas had surfaced in evangelical circles, but McPherson popularized them. She cannily incorporated and copyrighted the term and used it in the name of her International Church of the Foursquare Gospel.[40] The message was conveyed by a square logo with the words "Health," "Holiness," "Heaven," "Happiness" framing an open Bible with a "4" on it.

McPherson displayed a savvy business sense in getting Angelus Temple built. She found a contractor willing to accept her objection to debt on conscientious grounds and start construction on faith that she would pay.[41] Much of the labor and material was donated. She collected contributions at revivals as far away as Australia, sold temple chairs for $25 each as a fundraiser, and wrangled donors for the temple's stained-glass windows.[42] The temple cost about $250,000 in total and was debt-free when it opened.[43]

The "interdenominational" temple hosted healing services, prayer meetings, children's services, musical performance hours, Sunday school, and multiple worship services on Sundays. Volunteers staffed the temple's "prayer tower" around the clock. McPherson staged pageants and "illustrated sermons" featuring actors in elaborate costumes and sets worthy of nearby Hollywood. (The church continued to enter floats in the Tournament of Roses parade.) Visits from prominent figures such as William Jennings Bryan and Billy Sunday added credibility to McPherson's mission.

McPherson organized a Bible institute—later known as the Lighthouse of International Foursquare Evangelism, or L.I.F.E.—to instruct students on practical ways of saving souls, something she believed most theological students never learned how to do. "A minister who does not save souls is as much a failure as the real estate salesman who shows lots, but never gets to the point where he says, 'Sign here,'" she said.[44] They learned how to open meetings, deal with potential converts, and hold street revivals from a decorated truck.

But even the loudest megaphone could reach just so many people compared to the emerging medium of radio. McPherson delivered sermons on a Los Angeles station that donated time to Protestant preachers on Sundays.[45] She decided to open her own station and was the first American woman to hold a radio broadcasting license.[46]

The 500-watt station dubbed KFSG—Kall Four Square Gospel—was installed in the temple at a cost of $25,000, which was paid for through her followers' contributions. ("Help convert the world by radio!" exclaimed the donation drive in McPherson's magazine.)[47] Two radio towers on the temple's roof and an antenna suspended between them transmitted the powerful signal. The temple was filled to capacity when the station—then only the third operating in Los Angeles—made its debut on February 6, 1924. Among the speakers at the dedication was Harry Chandler, *Los Angeles Times* publisher and city powerbroker. He praised McPherson and reflected on the larger meaning of radio in American life. "It annihilates distance. It goes where the newspaper cannot follow, where there are few books, where there is loneliness, and where isolated thousands are longing for human contact and companionship," he said. "It brings the voice from the pulpit into the home."[48]

Radio allowed preachers the chance to make their case to audiences at a scale that would be unfathomable to a Whitefield or a Moody. The medium favors colorful, persuasive communicators, and evangelicalism has never suffered from a shortage of big personalities with compelling stories to tell. They are populists capable of filling arenas who also know how to connect with people one-on-one in their living rooms. The intimacy of radio is ideal for preachers who urge listeners to seek a personal relationship with Jesus.

The first licensed commercial radio station in the United States, KDKA in Pittsburgh, was also the first to broadcast a church worship service on January 2, 1921.[49] The exciting medium thrilled Americans; by the end of 1922, there were a million people listening to nearly six hundred commercial stations. Pastors who were early adopters enjoyed fruitful growth.[50] In 1923, R. R. Brown, founder of the Omaha Gospel Tabernacle, aired the first nondenominational services. By the early 1930s, Brown's *Radio Chapel Service* reached a half of a million listeners a week and admirers called him "the Billy Sunday of the air."[51]

Among the radio revivalists was Paul Rader, who had been a cowboy, a boxer, and a football coach before his conversion. Rader pastored Moody Memorial Church before starting the Chicago Gospel Tabernacle in 1922, a steel-framed structure popular with fundamentalists. The mayor of Chicago, William H. Thompson, owned a radio station and offered airtime to Rader. The preacher jumped at the chance. In 1925, Rader broadcast an all-day program on Sundays, *The National Radio Chapel*, on Thompson's station.[52] He warned of a collapse of morality. "I believe America is in the greatest crisis hour of her career. . . . We are not only filled with lust and luxury, but crime, which is the outcome of lust and luxury," Rader wrote in 1925, the heart of the libertine Jazz Age.[53]

Rader upgraded to a higher-wattage transmitter that his ministry called "The Cathedral of the Air." His broadcasts reached "sick rooms, hospitals, sanitariums, asylums, county homes, old peoples' homes, jails, churches, restaurants, army and navy barracks, lighthouses, homes of the poor and rich."[54] The program touched people who were homebound or lived deep in the backcountry where there were no churches to attend. His broadcasts inspired up to three thousand letters a week from listeners. "Mother and I are all alone. Mother is 81 years old and I am 61 years old," wrote one grateful listener from Bland, Missouri. "We live out in the country, but we don't get lonesome on Sunday nights—that wonderful band and music we get from your station!"[55] A fan from Tennessee wrote, "I'm an old woman and can't get out to church, but I thank God for the Radio, which enables me to hear the Gospel preached."[56] Tabernacle staffers sent thousands of mailers and experimented with musical formats and programs for children.

Meanwhile, the Bible Institute of Los Angeles founded its own station in 1923, as did the Moody Bible Institute in 1926. The Chicago school's station, WMBI, used its programming to build its enrollment and connect other evangelicals. The station invited guest speakers and musicians on its broadcasts and publicized events. Radio staffers broadcast meetings in nearly three hundred churches in the region as well as conferences and guest speakers.[57] Other programs like the foreign-language *Bohemian Hour* and *Teen-Age Bible Study Class* targeted niche audiences.

Fundamentalists and other evangelicals found traction on local stations but were effectively boxed out of national commercial networks. The Federal Council of Churches, a group representing mainline Protestantism, successfully lobbied the National Broadcasting Corporation (or NBC, founded in 1926) and the Columbia Broadcasting System (or CBS, founded in 1927) not to sell time slots to religious groups and instead give free time to council members.[58] That satisfied public-service requirements, but it upset fundamentalists and others who were not included.

A newer network, the Mutual Broadcasting System, founded in 1934, accepted payments for religious programs, including sermons by the Moody

Bible Institute's president. Fundamentalist preacher Charles E. Fuller was kicked off CBS when it halted paid religious programming in 1931. He continued to preach on the Los Angeles station KNX, but he had to find a new outlet when CBS purchased it in 1936. Fuller moved to Mutual a year later and began his *The Old-Fashioned Revival Hour*. Paying the network fees was a burden, so he conducted "radio rallies" and asked listeners for financial support. The program's formula of traditional sermons, gospel hymns, and the reading of listener letters proved to be a winner. *The Old Fashioned Revival Hour* boasted the largest audience in network radio—more than 10 million listeners tuned in to hundreds of stations each Sunday night.[59]

Fuller's success was also good for business; by the 1940s, religious programming represented about a quarter of Mutual's revenue.[60] Preachers from theologically conservative churches like the Lutheran Church-Missouri Synod and Seventh-day Adventists dominated the lineup. In frustration, the liberal Federal Council of Churches pressured Mutual in 1944 to adopt rules that limited paid religious programming to Sunday mornings, cut the programs to no more than thirty minutes, and barred the use of air time to solicit funds. In response, evangelicals bought time on independent and local stations—an early form of syndication—and organized the affiliated National Religious Broadcasters group as a counterweight to the council.[61]

Evangelicals overcame establishment opposition, fought for airtime, and showed that they could attract large audiences. In 1932, fundamentalists accounted for 246 of 290 weekly quarter-hours of religious broadcasting in Chicago.[62] A report ten years later found that 61 percent of Protestant programs on Chicago radio were fundamentalist.[63] Radio amplified their teachings and shifted them into the mainstream of American religious life.

Aimee Semple McPherson's foresight to control her own station meant that she didn't need to scramble for time slots. KFSG carried midnight organ recitals, children's programming, and her sermons. She frequently intertwined her compelling life story with the lessons of the Bible. The approach irritated fellow Los Angeles preacher "Fighting" Bob Shuler, who said McPherson built her following around her personality and that her congregation was there to worship her. "Her answer to all opposition is the story of herself," he fumed.[64]

Her personal travails were the stuff of a Hollywood melodrama. On May 18, 1926, McPherson went for a swim at a Los Angeles beach and disappeared. Thousands of church members and followers combed the beach by day, and searchlights beamed across the waters at night. Many believed she had drowned. More than a month later, McPherson emerged at a Mexican border town near Arizona after escaping from a couple that she said had kidnapped her at the beach in California. McPherson said they put a blanket over her head while driving to a shack in the Mexican desert. She said she was tied up and that her fingers were burned with a lighted cigar.

McPherson's followers were thrilled by her return, but others doubted her story. The Los Angeles County District Attorney's Office filed a complaint against McPherson and others, charging conspiracy to obstruct justice, fabricating evidence, and lying to a grand jury. It alleged that McPherson pretended that she had been kidnapped to cover up an affair with Kenneth Ormiston, former radio operator at the temple, at a cottage in Carmel. The parties denied the charges and they were dismissed due to lack of evidence. That didn't stop salacious coverage in the press.

The episode damaged her reputation and took a personal toll. She suffered a nervous breakdown in 1931, and her followers kept a constant vigil in the temple's prayer tower. McPherson recovered and eloped later in the year with David L. Hutton, a member of her choir. While traveling to Central America, she contracted a tropical disease and suffered a concussion. Their marriage ended in divorce in 1934. McPherson split with her mother and grew estranged from her daughter.

On September 27, 1944, McPherson died suddenly at the age of fifty-three while in Oakland for a church dedication, one of hundreds of Foursquare churches in the United States. Her death, ruled as an accidental overdose of barbiturates, evoked an outpouring of grief. Mourners remembered how the Angelus Temple provided meals, jobs, and clothing for the poor during the Great Depression. Some bewildered temple members didn't believe it to be true. Maybe she might rise again like Lazarus, a few hoped.

At McPherson's funeral in Angelus Temple, five hundred floral tributes estimated to cost $50,000 surrounded her open casket. The packed temple and crowds at overflow sites heard the 150-member choir and band perform some of McPherson's compositions, "Rest, O Weary Pilgrim, Rest" and "Songs of Paradise." Her son and designated successor, Rolf, delivered an impromptu eulogy and urged the congregation to carry on her work. "Mother today is not sorrowing, she is rejoicing with Our Savior," he said.[65] Thousands lined the streets to watch the procession to Forest Lawn Memorial Park. Boxes were spaced out along the long route where weary pallbearers could rest the twelve-hundred-pound bronze casket.[66]

The ministry continued with much less drama. Rolf McPherson proved to be a steady administrator and led his mother's church for forty-four years before retiring in 1988. During his tenure, it became a truly global church. When he died in 2009 at ninety-six, the International Church of the Foursquare Gospel claimed 8.4 million members in 144 countries.[67]

The Angelus Temple is a National Historic Landmark and looks much like it did in Sister Aimee's day—minus the twin radio spires because the radio station went off the air in 2003. The congregation today reflects the neighborhood's strong Latino character. Attendance may have tapered off, but as one of the first megachurches, its influence on evangelicalism is profound. Aimee Semple McPherson and the church she built blended celebrity, entertainment, business acumen, and mass communication into a much-copied formula.

5

EMPIRE BUILDERS

Evangelicals Organize, Billy Graham
and Oral Roberts Thrive

I did not choose to be a businessman. It was forced upon me
by the growth of the ministry. I had to learn the principles of
operating a business.

—Oral Roberts[1]

After the Scopes trial in 1925, Christian fundamentalists felt mocked by
the wider culture and turned inward. They kept busy during their wil-
derness years creating their own subculture of "congregations, denominations, mission societies, publishing houses, Bible camps, institutes, colleges,
and seminaries," wrote scholar Randall Balmer.[2] That infrastructure gave
shape to the broader "new evangelical" movement that took flight during
World War II.

Frustration had been building in fundamentalist circles with the liberal
Federal Council of Churches, which since 1908 had asserted itself as the
authoritative voice of Protestantism. Preachers going back to Billy Sunday
decried its emphasis on fixing social problems as a distraction from the work
of soul saving. The council also maneuvered to keep evangelicals off radio
networks, but the popularity of fundamentalist programs on independent
stations showed the appetite for their views.

Few despised the council more than Carl McIntire, a hard-line minister from New Jersey who broke from the Presbyterian Church USA to
found the fundamentalist Bible Presbyterian Church in 1937. Four years
later, he organized the American Council of Christian Churches, which,
despite its name, was a small band of dissatisfied fundamentalists. McIntire
labeled himself as "militantly pro-Gospel and anti-modernist."[3] He was also
militantly pro–private enterprise. His council declared "the presuppositions

of capitalism are in the Bible."[4] However, McIntire's views were too strident to act as an effective counter to the Federal Council of Churches.

The more moderate layman J. Elwin Wright assembled evangelicals at summer conferences and seminars in the 1930s as leader of the New England Fellowship. Wright, raised by a father who started a Pentecostal ministry, became a Congregationalist and joined Boston's historic Park Street Church. Wright bonded with the church's pastor, Harold John Ockenga. Through their travels and conversations, both men perceived the need for a national organization.

Wright chaired a committee that invited evangelical leaders to a National Conference for United Action among Evangelicals at the Hotel Coronado in St. Louis in 1942. Among the 147 attendees were Pentecostals and representatives from a spectrum of denominations. Ockenga delivered a speech titled "The Unvoiced Multitudes" that urged evangelicals to unite and engage with the wider world.

The founders were attempting to find a middle ground between liberal mainline churches and separatist fundamentalists like McIntire. They concluded that since millions of evangelicals had "no corporate means of making their wishes known in matters common to all," their new association was necessary.[5] The group's constitution took a veiled shot at the Federal Council of Churches: "We realize that in many areas of Christian endeavor that organizations which now purport to be representatives of Protestant Christianity have departed from the faith of Jesus Christ." Members were required to affirm that "the Bible is the inspired, the only infallible, authoritative word of God," among other doctrinal points.[6]

The group, which became known as the National Association of Evangelicals, incorporated in Chicago in 1943 and represented parts of fifty denominations. (The group purposely avoided the fraught label "fundamentalist" in favor of the less divisive "evangelical.")[7] Three years later, it attracted twenty-two full denominations with a membership of a million people, small in comparison to the Federal Council of Churches.[8] The NAE could never claim to speak for all evangelicals, but it did prove that it could organize effectively on a national scale. With Ockenga as president, the NAE formed the National Religious Broadcasters group to lobby for airtime on radio networks, created a wide-reaching missionary organization, and established a war relief commission for humanitarian assistance.[9]

The NAE's free-enterprise ethos won the backing of conservative business interests. "Confidentially, we have aroused the interest of some of the executives of the National Association of Manufacturers, who see in the N.A.E. an ally in their fight against collectivism and the spread of these anti-American doctrines through the Federal Council and other modernist agencies," Wright wrote in a 1944 letter to NAE board members. All board members were asked to invite "Christian industrialists in your own circle of interest" to an NAE conference so they could be hit up for large donations.[10]

Liberals had long dominated divinity schools at Harvard, Yale, and the University of Chicago, much to the chagrin of conservatives. Ockenga and Charles E. Fuller, the popular host of *The Old Fashioned Revival Hour*, founded the Fuller Theological Seminary in Pasadena in 1947. The institution was intended to be the "Cal Tech of modern evangelicalism."[11] The interdenominational school affirmed that "neo-evangelicals" welcomed education as the key to advancement rather than retreating to the usual evangelical stance of anti-intellectualism.

Among Fuller's faculty members was Carl F. H. Henry, a theologian who in his influential 1947 book *The Uneasy Conscience of Modern Fundamentalism* suggested that evangelicals must resist self-defeating isolation. "To say that evangelicalism should not voice its convictions in a non-evangelical environment is simply to rob evangelicalism of its missionary vision," he wrote.[12] But he recognized the limits of what could be achieved in the secular realm: "The evangelical task primarily is the preaching of the Gospel, in the interest of individual regeneration by the supernatural grace of God, in such a way that divine redemption can be recognized as the best solution of our problems, individual and social."[13]

Such evangelical "parachurch" organizations sprouted everywhere during the 1940s: InterVarsity Christian Fellowship/USA, founded in 1941 as a campus ministry to college students and faculty; and Youth for Christ International, founded in 1944 to reach teenagers with clean-cut entertainment and rallies featuring sports stars and even a horse that kneeled at a cross.[14] The groups kept churches stocked with young converts and trained a rising generation of evangelical leaders. Among them was Youth for Christ's first full-time evangelist, a lanky firebrand from the South named Billy Graham.

The story of evangelicalism in the twentieth century is in many ways the story of William Franklin Graham Jr. He was born November 7, 1918, near Charlotte, North Carolina, and spent his early years on the family's prosperous dairy farm. "Billy Frank" was raised in the Associate Reformed Presbyterian Church but credited his true religious awakening to revival meetings conducted by evangelist Mordecai Ham in Charlotte in 1934. Ham preached in a tabernacle on the edge of town, and Graham went with a friend to see what the fuss was about. Graham found a seat near the back and was transfixed by Ham's sermon. "In some indefinable way, he was getting through to me. I was hearing another voice, as was often said of Dwight L. Moody when he preached: the voice of the Holy Spirit," Graham wrote in his autobiography.[15] Ham was also an unrepentant anti-Semite. "Publicity, commerce, money are all in the hands of the Jew," he said in one of his Charlotte sermons.[16] Graham attended many more of Ham's meetings and ultimately came forward to publicly commit to Christ.

Upon graduating from high school in 1936, Graham took a job with the Fuller Brush Company to earn money for college. Graham and a few friends headed to South Carolina to sell brushes, staying in boardinghouses and cheap motels. Graham carried his case of sample brushes door to door from sunrise to sunset, refining his sales pitch along the way. He'd start by telling the housewife that he didn't come to sell anything, but instead wanted to give her a brush absolutely free. Once he had his foot in the door and opened his case to display his brushes, a sale was in the offing. "I was convinced that Fuller brushes were the best product money could buy, and I was dedicated to the proposition that every family ought to have Fuller brushes as a matter of principle," he said.[17] At the end of the summer, Graham ranked as the top Fuller salesman in the Carolinas.[18]

With his earnings, Graham registered at Bob Jones College in Cleveland, Tennessee, a fundamentalist school founded by Bob Jones Sr. Graham was put off by the college's authoritarian teaching style and severe social rules such as requiring chaperones on dates.[19] He transferred to the unaccredited Florida Bible Institute near Tampa. Graham found it to be a nurturing environment with an unusually broad-minded curriculum for a fundamentalist institution. Visiting lecturers from a variety of denominations were invited to campus and students were encouraged to think through problems for themselves.[20] During a lonely walk on a golf course one night in 1938, he heard the call to devote his life to ministry—a call he had resisted for years. This time, he accepted.

Graham received baptism by immersion and was ordained a Southern Baptist minister before graduating from the Florida Bible Institute in 1940. He was accepted at Wheaton College near Chicago, one of the leading evangelical schools in the country. The gregarious southerner acclimated to life in the Midwest, regularly preached at a nearby tabernacle, and broadened his intellectual life by studying anthropology. But by far the most significant event at Wheaton for Graham was meeting fellow student Ruth McCue Bell. She was born and raised in China and her father was Dr. L. Nelson Bell, a medical missionary at a Presbyterian hospital. Graham aggressively courted her and they married after graduating in 1943. Graham accepted the pastorate of a small Baptist church not far from Wheaton, and they organized prayer meetings, youth activities, and classes for children.

Torrey Johnson, pastor of a Baptist church in Chicago, heard about Graham's forceful preaching and invited him to take over his Sunday night radio program, *Songs in the Night*, on WCFL in Chicago. Graham won church approval for the $150 a week to buy the airtime and wrangled soloist George Beverly Shea to appear on the program. *Songs in the Night*, a mix of preaching and gospel singing, was a hit with audiences, drawing letters from listeners across the Midwest as well as financial contributions. With his profile on the rise, Graham spoke at out-of-town evangelistic meetings and backed away from spending his life as a small-town pastor. "I wanted to be moving, traveling, preaching, anywhere and everywhere. Ruth soon began to realize, as she later told me, that her life was going to be one of good-byes," he wrote.[21]

Johnson dangled another opportunity in front of Graham, this time to speak at an event geared to servicemen and young people in Chicago in May 1944. Graham preached to an auditorium crowd of about three thousand and was gratified when about forty people rose to accept Christ.[22] Graham spoke at similar rallies in other cities also coordinated by Youth for Christ committees. Seeing the strong response, Johnson wanted to unite the independent groups under a single national organization and asked Graham to be its first full-time field representative. Graham took the job, forcing him to resign as pastor—the only time he would ever lead a church.

The prospect of going on the road exclusively to preach for Youth for Christ thrilled Graham: "I was a traveling salesman again—not displaying a case of brushes this time, just brandishing my Bible."[23] He went by bus, train, and airplane across the country to promote the new movement. Johnson brought Graham and several others to Europe, which lay in ruins after World War II. Graham preached at rallies and youth conferences in the United States and Canada and returned to Great Britain for a campaign at his own expense. Graham brought choir leader Cliff Barrows and his wife, Billie, to play the piano. They packed their schedule with rallies and were joined later by Ruth for sightseeing in Europe.

Ruth flew back to her parents' home in Montreat, North Carolina, to care for their first child, Virginia, nicknamed "Gigi," and Billy stayed in Europe, worried he would soon run out of money. Graham wrote to industrialist R. G. LeTourneau, an inventor and manufacturer of earth-moving equipment. LeTourneau, known as "God's businessman," bankrolled causes such as the Christian Business Men's Connection and published an in-house Christian journal. Graham asked for $7,000, and LeTourneau mailed a cashier's check in that amount.[24] It would be first of many occasions Graham would rely on wealthy businessmen to further his ministry.

William Bell Riley, the fundamentalist standard-bearer, remembered Graham from a Youth for Christ rally in Minneapolis, and reached out to the traveling preacher. Riley wanted Graham to replace him as president of three institutions known as the Northwestern Schools in Minneapolis in 1947, the first of which he had founded in 1902. At eighty-six, Riley was ailing but still possessed the presence of an Old Testament prophet. He summoned Graham to his office and said, "Beloved, as Samuel appointed David King of Israel, so I appoint you head of these schools. I'll meet you at the judgment seat of Christ with them."[25] Despite this patriarchal blessing, Graham did not want to leave Youth for Christ and agreed to an honorary vice presidential position. But Riley died at the end of the year, and Graham, with a bachelor's degree in anthropology, became the nation's youngest college president at twenty-nine.

Graham, by his own admission, was an absentee president for much of the next three years while expanding his evangelistic efforts. He continued to appear at Youth for Christ rallies and conferences, but started to conduct his own campaigns geared to the entire community. Like previous evangelical preachers, Graham secured the broad support of churches before agreeing to citywide events. Months before his arrival, prayer meetings in churches heightened anticipation and advertising in newspapers raised awareness.

Graham assembled a close-knit ministry team: musicians George Beverly Shea and Cliff Barrows, and childhood friend and associate Grady B. Wilson. In 1948, they resolved to dispel the Elmer Gantry–style stereotypes of religious hypocrisy that clung to traveling preachers. Graham relied on prosperous sponsors and fundraising through local committees to avoid having to make public appeals for donations. They adopted the "Billy Graham rule" of not traveling, meeting, or eating alone with someone of the opposite sex, except for a spouse, to avoid even the appearance of sexual impropriety.[26] They also pledged to avoid criticizing other churches or exaggerating attendance numbers.

Graham recounts an intriguing interlude in his autobiography about a spiritual crisis he faced just before an important time in his life and ministry. He attended a conference where lectures by a string of distinguished religious scholars reinforced for Graham his lack of theological knowledge. Alone in his room one night, Graham immersed himself in the Bible. Was it completely true? Could he trust it fully? Graham became consumed with doubts about whether he could continue preaching. He went for a walk into the woods, dropped to his knees, opened his Bible, and prayed. "I was trying to be on the level with God, but something remained unspoken. At last the Holy Spirit freed me to say it, 'Father, I am going to accept this as Thy Word—by *faith*! I'm going to allow faith to go beyond my intellectual questions and doubts, and I will believe this to be Your inspired Word," he wrote.[27] Graham plowed ahead preaching biblical literalisms, even to the extent of outlining the precise dimensions of heaven—sixteen hundred miles in each direction—as spelled out in the book of Revelation.[28]

With his doubts resolved, Graham felt refreshed for his most ambitious campaign to date. The Christ for Greater Los Angeles committee asked Graham to hold a revival. He examined the offer and requested three changes: extensive cooperation of churches and denominations, triple the budget to allow more spending on promotion, and a much bigger tent for his meetings.[29] The committee, run by Christian businessmen, agreed to his terms, and the revival was scheduled to run for three weeks starting in September 1949. Evangelicals believed the home of Hollywood to be rife with crime and immorality, and they were unsure how receptive it would be to Graham.

Under a capacious tent at Washington Boulevard and Hill Street, Graham preached every evening and twice on Sunday—at 3 p.m. and 8:45 p.m. to avoid competing with morning church services. Newspaper ads heralded the campaign as "L.A.'s Greatest Revival Since Billy Sunday" and boasted its "Canvas Cathedral" could accommodate up to six thousand people. The organizing committee's fact sheet called him "tall, slender, handsome, with a curly shock of blond hair, Graham looks like a collar ad, talks like a North Carolinian and preaches like a combination of Billy Sunday and Dwight L. Moody."[30]

The campaign's touches—the gospel music, the tent, and the sawdust floors—did feel like a throwback to Moody and Sunday. Graham, who favored the loud ties then in fashion and flashy suits that hung loose on his wiry frame, echoed his forebears by focusing on finding salvation through Christ.

He wove in events ripped from the headlines—the Soviet Union had just successfully tested its first atomic bomb, ending the American nuclear monopoly—to illustrate the premillennial belief that the end of days was imminent and that Americans must not delay in committing to Christ. "Communism has decided against God, against Christ, against the Bible, and against all religion. Communism is not only an economic interpretation of life—communism is a religion that is inspired, directed, and motivated by the Devil himself who has declared war against Almighty God," he said.[31]

Graham's campaign attracted little press coverage, so he was stunned one day to see throngs of reporters and photographers. A story about Graham had appeared in two Los Angeles newspapers owned by William Randolph Hearst, who supposedly ordered his editors to "Puff Graham" and run a story about Graham's campaign across his sprawling chain of newspapers. Graham never met or corresponded with Hearst, but the aging press baron was familiar with Youth for Christ and shared the preacher's anticommunist sensibilities. Graham rocketed to national fame with upbeat reports in *Time* and *Life* magazines. The ministry team extended the campaign, which ended in late November after eight weeks.

The statistics were startling for such a young preacher: three hundred fifty thousand people attended the seventy-two meetings and they yielded about three thousand conversions, an assortment that included an associate of gangster Mickey Cohen, celebrities such as the singing cowboy Stuart Hamblen, and Olympian and war hero Louis Zamperini. Still, there was a sense that he was preaching to the converted with many repeat visitors. Nearly all of the campaign's churches were affiliated with the National Association of Evangelicals; Graham did not seek the support of denominations aligned with the liberal Federal Council of Churches.[32] Graham himself would be at the center of the tensions between fundamentalism and mainline Protestantism in the postwar era.

Billy Graham left Los Angeles a rising star in evangelicalism. His next campaign, in Boston, included sermons at Harold John Ockenga's Park Street Church followed by mass rallies in Boston Garden—and he filled out a management structure to sustain his momentum. He signed up Willis Haymaker, an organizer for Billy Sunday and others, to direct his rallies. One of Haymaker's first suggestions to Graham was to rebrand his events *crusades* instead of *campaigns*.[33] He carefully examined cities before committing to hold crusades, set up a local office to oversee every detail, and disbursed blocks of tickets to church groups.[34]

The momentous decisions made during Graham's crusade in Portland, Oregon, starting in July 1950 laid the foundation for his burgeoning empire. Three hundred churches there had requested Graham's presence, and volunteers constructed a wooden tabernacle following the template used in Sunday's campaigns.[35] Graham experimented with separate meetings for men and women to address problems of domestic life, and volunteers provided child care in special tents. Total attendance of the six-week crusade reached a half-million, and counselors collected about nine thousand signed decision cards for people committing to Christ. The revival closed with a triumphant "Crusade for Freedom" rally at a football stadium.

During the successful crusade, Graham and his associates were weighing how to amplify the upwelling of the Holy Spirit they were witnessing across America. One idea was to produce motion pictures. Graham hired filmmaker Dick Ross to shoot his Portland crusade in color and create a documentary. Pleased with the result, Graham merged the production company into Billy Graham Films (later World Wide Pictures) and opened an office in Burbank, California. The film company branched into feature films with the first, *Mr. Texas*, receiving a splashy premiere at the Hollywood Bowl. Graham's appealing personality and moral message were irresistible to rich men like J. Russell Maguire, an industrialist who wrote a $75,000 check to boost Graham's film business.[36] (Maguire was a rabid anti-Semite, a characteristic that Graham overlooked in others, which would haunt him later in life.)

Another wealthy ally was Texas oilman Sid Richardson, who Graham affectionately called "Mr. Sid." Richardson was hardly the prototype of a pious Christian—he enjoyed sipping bourbon and playing poker too much for that—but he and Graham struck up an unlikely friendship. Graham's 1954 feature film, *Oiltown, U.S.A.*, about a self-made Texas oil tycoon who found God, was something of a homage to Richardson. The film was advertised as "the story of the free-enterprise system of America, the story of the development and use of God-given natural resources by men who have built a great new empire."[37] It very well could have been describing Graham himself.

For years, Graham had dabbled in another medium—radio—and suddenly had the chance to claim a national platform. Walter A. Maier, longtime host of *The Lutheran Hour*, had just died and Philadelphia preacher Theodore Elsner, president of the evangelical National Religious Broadcasters, believed Graham could be a worthy successor. Elsner's son-in-law, Fred Dienert, worked at an ad agency in Chicago that handled religious broadcasts. Dienert and the agency's senior partner, Walter F. Bennett, approached Graham in Portland with a pitch for a weekly nationwide radio program. Graham joked that if he somehow raised $25,000 by midnight for that purpose, he would take that as a sign from God and do it. Graham told his capacity audience that night about the proposal, and was stunned to learn his team had collected $24,000 in donations. Short of his goal, Graham went out to dinner and returned to his hotel at 11:30. In Graham's telling, a clerk at the front desk informed him that he had two letters: each one contained a $500 check from businessmen who wrote notes encouraging

Graham to enter broadcasting. "Emotion so overcame me that I could not think straight. Clearly, the funds had come from God," Graham wrote later.[38]

Graham signed a thirteen-week deal with the American Broadcasting Company to put *Hour of Decision* on its coast-to-coast radio network, but the ministry team was flummoxed about what do with the $25,000 stuffed into a shoebox. Because the donations were earmarked to pay for radio airtime, they could not be deposited into the crusade bank account. Graham realized that he had no formal organization, no board of directors, and no corporate bank account. He phoned Northwestern Schools business manager George Wilson for advice, and Wilson suggested forming a nonprofit corporation. With Graham's approval, Wilson filed documents to formally incorporate the Billy Graham Evangelistic Association.[39] Wilson set up an office to process the influx of letters and donations after *Hour of Decision* first aired on November 5, 1950. The correspondence formed the core of the organization's all-important mailing list. A $50,000 gift from two Texas businessmen paid for a television version of the program in 1951.[40]

Much to his relief, Graham's resignation as president of the Northwestern Schools was accepted in 1952, allowing him to concentrate on realizing the Billy Graham Evangelistic Association's ambitious mission: "To spread and propagate the Gospel of the Lord Jesus Christ by any and all . . . means."[41] Graham received a fixed salary that allowed him to live comfortably but not lavishly, and enabled him to avoid having to take free-will offerings. The association supplied audited statements to satisfy any public concerns about graft.

By 1954, *Hour of Decision* had a weekly audience of 15 million across a thousand stations; his syndicated newspaper column, *My Answer*, reached another 15 million people; his book of reflections, *Peace with God*, was a bestseller; his crusades in Europe drew millions.[42] Oilman and philanthropist J. Howard Pew emerged as another generous patron. "God has given to me the ear of millions," Graham wrote to Pew. "He has given to you large sums of money. It seems to me that if we can put these two gifts of God together, we could reach the world with the message of Christ."[43]

Pew was a Presbyterian layman who severed ties with the liberal National Council of Churches, believing that their policies would "inevitably lead us into communism."[44] With Pew's financial support, Graham founded a magazine, *Christianity Today*, in 1956. Graham installed theologian Carl F. H. Henry as editor. (Graham's father-in-law, L. Nelson Bell, was listed as executive editor.) It was instantly an essential journal of evangelical thought.

Billy Graham was big business, and he in turn espoused free-market ideals. In 1954, he wrote an article in the U.S. Chamber of Commerce's magazine that explicitly linked Christianity with capitalism. "We have the suggestion from the Scripture itself that faith and business, properly blended, can be a happy, wholesome, and even profitable mixture. . . . Thousands of businessmen have discovered the satisfaction of having God as a working partner."[45] Businesses leaped at the chance to associate themselves with the attractive, all-American preacher. In 1951, Chicago and Southern Airlines invited Graham to dedicate its new aircraft, outfitted with a pulpit and organ. Graham gamely led the crew in a ceremony as the plane flew over Memphis, praying that "the great C&S Airline may be blessed as never before."[46]

Like Billy Sunday, Graham criticized organized labor and strikes, saying in 1952 that the Garden of Eden was a paradise with "no union dues, no labor leaders, no snakes, no disease."[47] He warned of the dangers of socialism and government interference in the free-enterprise system, urging instead "the rugged individualism that Christ brought."[48] "We must have a revolt against the tranquil attitude to communism, socialism, and dictatorship in this country," Graham told a crowd in front of the Texas Capitol in Austin in 1952.[49] Like his revivalist predecessors, Graham believed "personal salvation must come before social reformation."[50]

In another part of the country, far from the citadels of respectable Protestantism, another preacher from the tent revival circuit fused the verities of the Gospel with American-style capitalism to build an evangelical empire. Oral Roberts took divine healing out of the shadows and into the light of radio and television.

Born in the same year as Graham, Granville Oral Roberts traveled a much stonier path to notoriety. Roberts was raised in poverty in rural Oklahoma by a father, Ellis, who was a Pentecostal Holiness preacher, and a mother, Claudius, who had Native American roots. Oral stuttered from an early age, a stigma that followed him into adolescence. He showed signs of leadership and athleticism, but chafed under parental pressure to attend church and Sunday school. Oral left the suffocation of home life to follow his coach to another high school to play basketball. At seventeen, he contracted tuberculosis in both lungs and wasted away while confined to bed. Months passed, and doctors were doubtful he would recover.

The family believed in "the fact of healing through faith in God" and took the emaciated Roberts to a tent meeting run by divine healer George W. Moncey in July 1935. Roberts, sitting in a rocking chair cushioned by pillows, listened to Moncey preach and watched people come forward to accept Jesus as their savior. Then the evangelist asked people to line up if they needed healing. Moncey approached Roberts in his chair and asked him to stand up and prayed for him. "I felt the healing power of the Lord. It was like your hand striking me, like electricity going through me. It went into my lungs, went into my tongue, and all at once I could breathe. I could breathe all the way down," Roberts recalled.[51] Roberts climbed up on the platform and rejoiced that he had been healed. The stuttering stopped, too. "For the first time my tongue was free and the words came pouring out," he said.[52]

Roberts fully regained his strength after about a year, and tests revealed that he no longer had tuberculosis.[53] Roberts felt the call to serve God and apprenticed as a preacher under his father, spoke at young people's meetings, received the baptism of the Holy Spirit, and earned a license to preach in the Pentecostal Holiness church in 1936. He studied at Oklahoma Baptist University in Shawnee and wrote a church book on dispensational premillennialism, concluding that the rapture was near. Roberts improved as an evangelist on the revival circuit, energizing audiences and winning souls. Roberts married a preacher's daughter, Evelyn Lutman Fahnestock, and took on pastoral assignments.

Dissatisfied with the low pay of his church and lethargy of his congregation, Roberts launched an independent healing ministry in 1947. "I had allowed myself to become an echo of other men, and particularly of a denomination, instead of a voice for Jesus Christ with a total commitment to be like Him," Roberts wrote.[54] He preached divine healing at services and on his radio program. Reports of "miracle healing" spread throughout the Pentecostal community, and requests for his services poured in. Roberts returned to the life of an itinerant preacher with Tulsa, Oklahoma, as home base for his young family.

Sometimes his lack of experience showed. A woman on crutches approached Roberts in the healing line in Alton, Illinois, and he commanded her to toss them aside and walk. Roberts and the audience rejoiced when she threw up her hands, but then she wilted to the ground. Roberts helped her up, to much confusion in the crowd. "The Lord was trying to say something to me and He did," Roberts said later. "I became very, very careful from that point on."[55]

Roberts also realized he needed to be more cautious about money. Contributions failed to cover the rent on the auditorium he reserved in Chanute, Kansas, and he considered giving up the ministry. Evelyn pushed him back on the platform, seized the microphone, and appealed for help. "People, you don't know Oral like I do. He's not here for the money. He's here for the Gospel," she pleaded.[56] A new collection closed the gap.

In 1948, Roberts decided to stop holding services in local churches, preferring community-wide support for his events. He secured a bank loan to purchase a giant tent, bought a Hammond organ and a Steinway grand piano, and a truck and trailer to haul them from town to town.[57] In Durham, North Carolina, daily crowds numbered in the thousands and swelled as high as nine thousand for his closing service. One witness recounted an extraordinary wave of healing power: "As soon as the crippled were touched they threw their crutches away, deaf ears snapped open, people leaped off stretchers. Next morning crutches were lying all around the tent where they had been left."[58]

Roberts and his circus-size tent journeyed to bigger cities like Denver and Dallas, where he fielded requests from Pentecostal pastors to extend his stay to meet the rising demand. He started a monthly magazine, *Healing Waters* (renamed *Abundant Life* in 1956), and wrote guidebooks on divine healing. His earnest preaching style resulted in more than fifteen thousand conversions during his meetings in Florida in early 1949, and thousands came forward for healing at a single service. Roberts felt the power of God flowing like a current through his right hand and used it as his point of contact. He believed demons were the cause of most human suffering. "Demons recognize God's power in my life," he said.[59]

Roberts associate Bob DeWeese managed the healing lines by handing out cards and requiring seekers to sign a release that the service could not "guarantee healing."[60] A sponsoring pastor interviewed cardholders to ensure they had faith for God's healing, and then they were organized in the order they would approach Roberts for his touch. As with "miracle woman" Aimee Semple McPherson's revival meetings a generation earlier, skeptics viewed the system as a way to filter out the extremely ill. But Roberts prayed for them in an "invalid tent," emotionally exhausting encounters that would stay with him for years.

Roberts's tents expanded along with his campaigns. A tent seating 7,000 went into service in 1950; two years later, it was replaced by a $200,000 tent that could accommodate 12,500 people.[61] Roberts dispatched DeWeese to cities months in advance to sign up sponsoring pastors and nail down financial arrangements. Like Billy Graham, Roberts scheduled his meetings so they would not conflict with local church services. Unlike Graham, he took up contributions to help defray costs, though he did share them with sponsoring churches.

Roberts tapped into grassroots networks of Pentecostal businessmen to sponsor his crusades. One of the most important was Demos Shakarian, a dairyman who chaired the local committee for Roberts's crusade in Los

Angeles in 1951. Shakarian told Roberts he wanted to start a group that would encourage spirituality among businessmen. Roberts agreed and promised to help. Shakarian started out by hosting small breakfast meetings at Clifton's Cafeteria in Los Angeles and pitching the idea to Roberts's crusade audiences.[62] The organization, the Full Gospel Business Men's Fellowship International, broke across denominational lines and introduced Pentecostalism to the middle class. Shakarian entered the inner circle of Roberts's advisers.

Roberts revitalized his nonprofit organization founded in 1948—Healing Waters, Inc.—to keep up with his thriving ministry. He hired Holiness preacher O. E. Sproull as an associate evangelist to help with his healing crusades. Wealthy Holiness layman S. Lee Braxton pushed Roberts to construct a highly visible headquarters in Tulsa to house his magazine and the staff necessary to handle the volume of correspondence. Braxton negotiated a large construction loan for the building and encouraged Roberts to get involved in the city's business community. Roberts became an evangelist for the Chamber of Commerce and served on the board of directors of Tulsa's largest bank.[63]

Braxton set up a "partner system" of donors and conferences for businessmen to pay for broadcasting his radio program, *Healing Waters*, in new markets. In 1949, twenty-five stations carried the program; by 1953 the number ballooned to two hundred.[64] Roberts then worked out a deal to put his program on ABC's network, nearly doubling its number of stations. *Healing Waters* consisted of "deliverance sermons" and a healing prayer in which he would ask listeners to place their hands on their radio cabinets and intone, "I lay my hand over this microphone, and, lo, I am laying it upon you there in your home."[65] Roberts, who overcame childhood poverty and illness, had an uncanny ability to bond with regular people. They eagerly supplied the program with testimonials of being healed.

One of Roberts's signature touches was to send free "anointed cloths" to those who requested his prayers. Recipients were assured that Roberts "prays over each cloth separately and individually."[66] They were a tangible way of making believers feel connected. The Roberts organization reported mailing 96,173 prayer cloths in 1950, and hundreds of thousands more in the years to come.[67]

Roberts bristled at being described in the press as a "faith-healer"—he said it was God that healed, not him—and insisted "my main business, by far, is to win souls."[68] The Roberts organization released statistics on conversions as a bank would release earnings reports: 52,211 "souls saved" at rallies in 1950; 268,113 total conversions in 1954; 1,025,206 souls won in twelve months, according to a March 1959 report.[69] The accounting was dubious—the vast majority of converts were claimed via the radio and television ministries—but it showed the boldness of Roberts's goals.

Early on, Roberts perceived the power of television. His no-nonsense style and darkly handsome visage came across well on TV. In 1954, Roberts experimented with filming segments in a Hollywood studio, but the results were underwhelming. Fellow evangelist Rex Humbard told Roberts to film a crusade for television, which presented a host of technical challenges. Crews strained to capture the energy of the altar calls and the drama of the healing lines, and attendees were told to act as if the cameras weren't there. For the first program in 1955, Braxton bought time on sixty-one stations costing more than $8,000 a week.[70] After the initial broadcast, Braxton reported that the Tulsa headquarters received thousands of letters "telling how God blessed the people through the television program."[71]

The newly minted television star took his crusades overseas in the 1950s, speaking to large crowds in South Africa, filling London's Wembley Stadium, and touring the Holy Land. Such costly efforts put financial pressure on his organization, which he renamed the Oral Roberts Evangelistic Association, Inc., in 1957. It excelled at direct-mail fundraising—by the end of the decade, the ministry was the largest receiver and sender of first-class mail in Tulsa.[72] Nearly all of the letters sent to Roberts contained appeals for healing. The Roberts organization trained hundreds of typists to draft personalized responses—no form letters, Roberts insisted—and later used an IBM 1400 series computer to speed up the process.[73]

Roberts proposed a "Blessing Pact" in which partners were asked for a donation and "Brother Roberts" would pray that it would be returned to them from an unexpected source by the end of the year. If it didn't, Roberts would refund the original donation. Few asked for their money back. Donors were assured "that God will especially prosper you in your job, or your business, or your profession."[74]

This was an early form of what became known as the "prosperity gospel." In his 1954 book, Roberts cited 3 John 2—"Beloved, I wish above all things that thou mayest prosper and be in health, even as thy soul prospereth."[75] Roberts concluded: "God wants to save us, heal us, prosper us, bless us. This is His nature, His desire, His practice, His will." Thus, it was biblically correct for Christians and preachers to pray for success, an attractive message for his working-class base. Roberts would later call this teaching "seed-faith." "It gives people hope and expectation that seed sown to God will be multiplied in every area of life. It is a powerful principle," Roberts wrote in his autobiography.[76]

Perhaps out of jealousy, Pentecostal denominational leaders were growing uncomfortable with his independent success. The Pentecostal Holiness church considered revoking Roberts's ministerial credentials in 1953 because some leaders felt his healing revivals were incompatible with church teaching. The Churches of Christ called Roberts a fraud for his faith-healing claims. One critic accused Roberts of paying people on his TV program to falsely say they had been cured.[77]

Mainline Protestant clergymen also condemned the healing services as "offensive" and the "ultimate blasphemy."[78] Several reports could not verify that people had in fact been healed. Individual stories that leaked out reflected poorly on the revivals: A woman who believed she had been healed discarded her insulin and later died in a hospital; another elderly woman died en route to a revival, causing a physician to warn against "moving critically ill patients to a faith healer."[79]

Roberts did not publicly reply to specific criticisms, but they stung. "I do what I believe is right. If a person is healed, the evidence satisfied me and it satisfied them," he said. "I'm not quarreling with anybody. . . . I just promote my product."[80] He was indeed a skilled self-promoter and businessman. Roberts reportedly took an annual salary of $100,000—many times Graham's fixed salary and the equivalent of about $1 million today—and did not apologize for the lifestyle it bought him.[81] Being a Christian did not mean one had to be poor; in fact, the opposite was true, in his view.

Many of these conflicts were aggravated by Roberts's blustery personality. In contrast to Graham, who maintained relationships with press barons like Henry Luce of *Time* and *Life* magazines, Roberts was less at ease operating in such rarefied circles. When Roberts tried to explain his belief system to reporters, he would lash out when they mischaracterized it. Roberts had difficulty overcoming the lingering cultural bias of Pentecostal believers as "snake handlers" and "holy rollers."

Some newspaper columnists said Roberts's TV program was not in the public interest and should be pulled off the air. "To allow the enormously influential medium of television to be used week after week to show undocumented 'miracles,' with all their implied aspersions on the competency of medicine, seems contrary to the spirit, if not the letter, of the industry's code governing mature and responsible broadcasting," wrote *New York Times* TV critic Jack Gould in 1956.[82] Roberts asked his legions of supporters to write protest letters to the *New York Times*, and he had to spend time in Washington to lobby for his ministry's right to buy airtime.

Roberts and Graham were often lumped together in stories about evangelism in the 1950s despite their differences in style and doctrine. Although they were the same age and rose to prominence on parallel tracks, Roberts hungered for Graham's approval. Roberts first met Graham at his 1950 crusade in Portland, where Graham unexpectedly asked Roberts to offer the evening prayer. "His appearance on Graham's platform was unprecedented recognition for a Pentecostal to receive from an evangelical minister—especially from Billy Graham," wrote Roberts biographer David Edwin Harrell Jr. The gesture "placed Oral momentarily in a larger, more respectable, world than he had ever imagined he could be a part of."[83]

Their only other recorded in-person contact in the 1950s occurred in 1957 just after Graham had returned to the United States from his crusade in Australia. The year before, Roberts endured disastrous revival meetings in Melbourne marked by hecklers and attacks in the press. Both men happened to be in New York City and Graham went to Roberts's hotel, embraced him, and told a story about being trailed in India by a blind man who thought he was Oral Roberts and how he had felt bad that he couldn't help heal him.[84] The visit lifted Roberts's spirits immensely.

Roberts tried to improve his ministry's image by setting up a $1.5 million account with a New York public relations agency in the late 1950s. In interviews with key journalists, he deemphasized physical healing—"many 'cures' have been claimed by psychosomatic cases," he admitted—and focused on soul winning.[85] "I'm preaching that God is a good God—in a world of violence, distrust, fear, and hatred. . . . The second thing I am preaching is divine intervention. That God divinely intervenes in human affairs," he said.[86] The outreach seemed to work. "You might not personally care for his brand of teaching, but you cannot deny that the Oral Roberts organization fills a human need," wrote the *Tulsa Tribune* in 1959.[87] That is the mission of any entrepreneur, and explains the success of his ministry.

What Graham did for fundamentalism—smoothing out its rough edges and repackaging it as a more moderate "evangelicalism"—Roberts did for Pentecostalism. Both leveraged new forms of media and they partnered with businessmen to pay for it. Their organizations were maturing in an era of religious consensus in America, when evangelicalism graduated from canvas cathedrals to the pinnacle of political power.

6

THE AMERICAN WAY OF LIFE

Business, Politics, and Religion
Align under Eisenhower

Without God, there could be no American form of gov-
ernment, nor an American way of life. Recognition of the
Supreme Being is the first—the most basic—expression of
Americanism.

—President Dwight Eisenhower[1]

On a summer's day in Washington, D.C., in 1950, thirty-one-year-old
evangelist Billy Graham and his closest aides prepared for a private
meeting with President Harry Truman. Graham's campaign in Los Angeles
had catapulted him into national fame. Graham, whose courtly demeanor
masked a steely ambition, had begun collecting allies at the highest precincts of business and politics. The White House initially put off Graham's
request for a meeting and finally agreed to receive him on July 14, thanks
to the intercession of John McCormack, a Massachusetts congressman and
future House speaker.

Graham and his associates—Grady Wilson, Cliff Barrows, and Jerry
Beavan—wore summery light-colored suits, hand-painted ties, and white
buck shoes in tribute to the always dapper Truman. The quartet bounded
into the Oval Office at noon sharp. Graham discussed his campaigns and
praised Truman's handling of the war in Korea. With their time together
winding down, Graham quizzed Truman about his faith. The president,
a buttoned-up Baptist, replied, "Well, I try to live by the Sermon on the
Mount and the Golden Rule." Graham responded, "It takes more than
that, Mr. President. It's faith in Christ and His death on the Cross that you
need."[2] Truman stood up, signaling the meeting was over, and Graham
asked if they could pray together. "Well, I guess it can't do any harm,"
Truman said.[3] Graham put his arm around the startled president and prayed.

After leaving the Oval Office, Graham and his crew ran into the White House press corps. Reporters asked Graham about the meeting and he recounted their exchanges in detail, adding that they all had prayed together. A photographer asked if he could reenact the scene, and Graham, Wilson, Barrows, and Beavan all knelt on the White House lawn in solemn prayer before the cameras.

The photos and stories made national news and the coverage of the spectacle disgusted Truman, who refused to invite Graham to the White House again or endorse his crusades in Washington.[4] A mortified Graham realized he had made a rookie mistake in blurting out the content of a private conversation with an important person. "It began to dawn on me a few days later how we had abused the privilege of seeing the President," Graham wrote.[5] He did not make that blunder with Truman's successor.

It was Truman's predecessor who infuriated politically conservative Christians. In 1933, Franklin D. Roosevelt fulfilled his campaign promise to repeal Prohibition, dismantling one of their greatest achievements.[6] Rightwing ministers viewed Roosevelt's New Deal programs as dangerously collectivist, secular answers to problems that were essentially individual and spiritual in nature. They attacked initiatives such as the National Recovery Administration and the Social Security Act of 1935. Such government spending would create a "new class of citizens, the class of 'dole-loafers,'" declared Methodist minister Arno C. Gaebelien.[7] Fundamentalist John R. Rice founded the newspaper The Sword of the Lord and swung it against Roosevelt's expanding welfare state. Rice urged his readers to "free America from the hateful, immoral, unchristian New Deal which threatens to throttle private enterprise."[8]

James W. Fifield Jr., pastor of the First Congregational Church in Los Angeles, enlisted the business elite in 1935 to back his group, Spiritual Mobilization. Fifield said Protestant ministers had the duty to defend individual liberty and free enterprise against government power tilting the country toward socialism during the Great Depression. Oilman J. Howard Pew donated generously to the group and encouraged his corporate friends to contribute. Spiritual Mobilization published a monthly journal, distributed a magazine free to ministers, produced a radio program, and conducted conferences to spread its Christian pro-business message.[9]

Norman Vincent Peale, newly installed as pastor of Manhattan's Marble Collegiate Church, blasted liberal-minded ministers as underminers of capitalism. "A rugged individualism is decidedly superior to a shabby collectivism," Peale said from the pulpit in 1934.[10] Peale's broadsides against social activism drew a retort from the Reverend John Paul Jones, president of the Ministers Union of America, a group sympathetic to the plight of working-class people. Jones, also the pastor of a Brooklyn church, warned against "the common and fatal tendency to identify the Kingdom of God with the social scheme beneficial in the main to the class in power."[11]

Peale and other political conservatives indeed favored the free-enterprise ideals of the management class over the demands of union members. In 1937, the minister denounced the Congress of Industrial Organizations as leading a "wild and undisciplined predatory mob."[12] Business leaders and conservatives had long connected organized labor to the international communist movement. "I believe that labor, before it wrecks itself and this country, should be warned that it is being exploited by subversive elements, by fascist and communist influence," Peale said in a sermon that drew a rare burst of applause.[13] The way to repair the division was to get religion in the hearts of the working people and employers, he said.

One of the most effective conservative responses to Roosevelt and the New Deal was the National Committee to Uphold Constitutional Government, also known as the Committee for Constitutional Government. The group sprang to life in 1937, when Roosevelt proposed increasing the number of justices on the Supreme Court, which had scuttled some of his New Deal programs.

Peale's friend Frank Gannett, a right-wing newspaper publisher in Rochester, New York, and a committee cofounder, knew about the minister's strong anti–New Deal views and asked him to serve as chairman. Peale took on the job despite the presence of ultra-conservative members that pushed the group into taking extreme positions. The committee assailed the president's "court-packing scheme" as an unconstitutional power grab. It spurred a vigorous letter-writing campaign against the bill, which failed in Congress.

"A minister is a man before he is a minister, and a man or a minister who sees dangerous issues should raise his voice against them," he said in 1940.[14] That year, Peale denounced Roosevelt for breaking precedent to seek a third term: "The only way to restore this guarantee of democracy is to defeat not merely Mr. Roosevelt as a man and candidate but to rebuke by an overwhelming voice this affront against the American people."[15]

Roosevelt won the election against the backdrop of a world at war. The need for national unity after the Japanese attack on Pearl Harbor on December 7, 1941, muffled much of the criticism from conservative quarters. Roosevelt did not live to see the United States emerge from World

War II as the world's strongest economy, the lone nuclear power, and the architect of the postwar global order.

The nation boomed after the privations of wartime. Government programs such as the G.I. Bill opened the doors to college and vocational programs for millions of returning veterans who otherwise would have been shut out of higher education. A rising middle class thrived in a thrumming economy of rising wages, plentiful jobs, and modest inflation. New housing developments in the suburbs put homeownership within reach for working-class families, and many had enough left over to afford a car and a television set. Americans—that is, white Americans—enjoyed the world's highest standard of living.

Postwar America did seem to be a uniquely blessed country, a truly exceptional nation. Americans took comfort that God, or "the man upstairs" in the folksy parlance of the time, was always in their corner. With this prosperity came a surge of outward religious feeling. In 1940, only 37 percent of Americans were weekly attendees at a church or synagogue; by 1955 the figure jumped to 49 percent, according to Gallup polling.[16] Other metrics such as mainline Protestant church membership, Sunday school enrollment, and construction spending on religious buildings also increased throughout the 1950s.

Parachurch organizations—Christian groups that evangelize outside denominational lines—seeded this growth. They tailored their messages to popular tastes and have been described as "religion gone free enterprise."[17] One of the most vital was Campus Crusade for Christ, founded by Bill Bright. The Oklahoma native moved to Los Angeles after college and started a candy company and Bright's Purchasing Service in which he connected customers with wholesalers.[18] Bright, a Presbyterian, felt a call to reach out to university students and organized teams to visit sororities and fraternities. Billy Graham's crusade in Los Angeles in 1949 inspired Bright and his friends to step up their evangelism.

In 1951, Bright founded the first chapter of Campus Crusade for Christ at the University of California, Los Angeles. He and his wife, Vonette, targeted student leaders and prominent athletes. Bill Bright instructed his recruiters to read salesman and self-help author Frank Bettger's *How I Raised Myself from Failure to Success in Selling*. Bright demanded that his staffers must be immaculate in appearance and unfailingly cheery in disposition. He directed them in how to craft a sales pitch to potential clients, concluding with the question, "Are you ready to say 'Yes' to Christ tonight?"[19]

Confronting the threat of communist infiltration of college campuses was a main thrust of Campus Crusade for Christ's mission. Bright warned of professors under communism's sway who were "advocating the violent overthrow of the American government."[20] If they successfully indoctrinated young people, it would mean the downfall of the country. Bright believed his vision of Christian evangelism supplied an essential antidote, especially on secular, state-operated campuses. "God has been booted out of the very system of higher education which was established to bring light to the world," Bright said.[21]

Bright boiled down the mission into his *Four Spiritual Laws*: God loves you, sin separates man from God, Jesus Christ is the only way to God, and man must individually receive Christ as his savior. The booklet was one of the organization's most effective recruitment tools. Campus Crusade for Christ, now styled as "Cru" to avoid the negative connotations of "crusade," expanded into a national and then a global movement.

With Pew's financial backing, Peale founded another organization, the Christian Freedom Foundation, in 1950 to sell their views of "economic freedom" to Protestant clergymen. The foundation published a magazine, *Christian Economics*, that advocated "free enterprise—the economic system with the least amount of government and the greatest amount of Christianity."[22] The munificence of the Pew family propped up the magazine for years, allowing it to be distributed at little to no cost to nearly a hundred thousand clergymen.

These groups typified the business-focused, anticommunist thrust of evangelicalism in the 1950s when religious belief was nearly universal in the country. Surveys taken in 1953 and 1954 found each time that 98 percent of Americans believed in God, and nine out of ten believed in the divinity of Christ.[23] In 1952, Gallup reported that 75 percent of Americans said religion was "very important" in their lives, a record high.[24]

There was good reason, however, to question the depth of this supposed religious revival. For instance, Bible distribution jumped 140 percent from 1949 to 1953 to nearly 10 million volumes a year, but a Gallup poll found that 53 percent could not name even one of the four Gospels, suggesting that the volumes were admired more than they were read.[25] Another survey found that Americans' motivations for going to church were more social—"obedience to convention or duty" or "to set a good example"—than theological.[26]

Will Herberg, a Jewish sociologist and author of the influential 1955 book *Protestant-Catholic-Jew*, argued, "The American Way of Life is the operative faith of the American people."[27] He characterized it as a common belief in individualism, self-reliance, material achievements, and free enterprise—all bound by a general sense that religion is a supremely "good thing."[28] America's Cold War foe, the Soviet Union, opposed all of these ideals; thus, it was easy to "identify the American cause with the cause of God, and to convert our immense and undeniable moral superiority over communist tyranny into pretensions to unqualified wisdom and virtue," Herberg wrote.[29]

To likeminded thinkers like the liberal Protestant theologian Reinhold Niebuhr, such a triumphalist attitude smacked of arrogance. In his 1952 book *The Irony of American History*, Niebuhr cautioned against oversimplifying the Cold War as a clash between a "God-fearing and a godless civilization."[30] A righteous people "are never safe against the temptation of claiming God too simply as the sanctifier of whatever we most fervently desire," he wrote.[31]

Niebuhr cited an example of a president who possessed a more modest appraisal of religion's uses in public affairs. In 1865, as the Union Army neared victory, Abraham Lincoln reflected on the religiosity claimed by both sides of the Civil War. "Both read the same Bible, and pray to the same God; and each invokes His aid against the other. . . . The prayers of both could not be answered; that of neither has been answered fully. The Almighty has His own purposes," Lincoln said in his Second Inaugural Address.[32] Niebuhr said communist tyranny was as wrong as American slavery, but reminded readers that "the true God can be known only where there is some awareness of a contradiction between divine and human purposes, even on the highest level of human aspirations."[33]

Temperate religious intellectuals like Niebuhr were voices in the desert in an immodest time. Preachers like Billy Graham believed America would not survive unless it experienced a spiritual revival. "Either communism must die or Christianity must die, because it is actually a battle between Christ and anti-Christ," Graham said in 1954.[34] In the Atomic Age, the end of the world was no longer an abstraction, and so the righteous could wield God as the ultimate weapon. In this supercharged environment, political leaders rushed to endorse overt displays of religion.

Graham overcame his embarrassing encounter with Truman and held a crusade in Washington in early 1952. On the sidelines, he hosted luncheons and informal get-togethers with businessmen and politicians. (Truman refused to participate in any way, in spite of Graham's direct pleas and use of powerful intermediaries.) Graham boldly conducted a religious service on the steps of the Capitol—an unprecedented event. Tens of thousands attended, giving it the appearance of a presidential inauguration, and millions more listened in via radio. Graham asked Congress to dedicate a formal national day of prayer, saying, "There is a hunger for God today."[35]

The idea, which had been bandied about since the days of Lincoln, gained new force after Graham's direct appeal. Congress approved a joint resolution on April 17, 1952, that the president "shall set aside and proclaim a suitable day each year, other than a Sunday, as a National Day of Prayer, on which the people of the United States may turn to God in prayer and meditation at churches, in groups, and as individuals."[36] Truman approved the measure and issued a proclamation setting July 4, 1952, as a suitable day for the first National Day of Prayer. Every president since has followed suit.

Sid Richardson, an early Graham booster, introduced the preacher to fellow oilman Clint Murchison Sr., Senator Lyndon Johnson, and House Speaker Sam Rayburn, who waived the rules to allow Graham to preach at the Capitol. Another prominent friend was Dwight Eisenhower, who was in Europe serving as NATO's first supreme allied commander. Richardson wanted the famous general to run for president in 1952 and enlisted Graham to help persuade him. Graham wrote a flattering letter to Eisenhower assuring him of his prayers and saying "upon this decision could well rest the destiny of the Western World."[37] "That was the damnedest letter I ever got!" the general exclaimed to Richardson and asked to meet Graham.[38] Richardson paid for Graham to travel to France for their rendezvous. Despite their generational age gap, they established an easy rapport.

Eisenhower outlined to Graham his Kansas upbringing in the Brethren in Christ Church (River Brethren), a small Mennonite offshoot. Despite his Bible-centered childhood—he was said to have been named after Dwight L. Moody—Eisenhower fell out of the churchgoing habit as an adult.[39] Eisenhower mentioned to Graham that he and his wife, Mamie, rarely attended military chapel services. He inquired about Graham's crusades and what he preached to his followers. They agreed to keep in touch.

Four months later, after winning the Republican presidential nomination, Eisenhower called on Graham for both political and spiritual guidance. Eisenhower asked Graham to inject his speeches with a spiritual flavor, and Graham passed along some Bible verses. Eisenhower waited until after the election to join a church. After consulting with Graham on an appropriate denomination, he opted to become a Presbyterian like his wife. Graham recommended National Presbyterian Church in Washington and handed him an inscribed red leather Bible that Eisenhower kept at his bedside table for years.[40]

Eisenhower won easily. As president-elect, he spoke at a meeting of the Freedoms Foundation in New York and said the core of Americanism was embedded in the Declaration of Independence's promise that "all men are created equal, that they are endowed by their Creator with certain unalienable Rights, that among these are Life, Liberty and the pursuit of Happiness." Therefore, he said, it held that government's role was merely to secure such rights of divine origin. In contrast, the Soviets believed in the supremacy of the state and that religion was the opiate of the people.

To Eisenhower, the chasm between the two systems was unbridgeable. "Our form of government has no sense unless it is founded in a deeply felt religious faith, and I don't care what it is," he told the hotel audience. "It seems to me that if we are going to win this fight we have got to go back to the very fundamentals of all things. And one of them is that we are a religious people."[41] Eisenhower advocated a nondenominational form of religion—"a belief in belief"—that shaped his administration's outlook.

At a private meeting in a New York hotel room, Eisenhower looked at the teeming city below and said, "I think one of the reasons I was elected was to help lead this country spiritually. We *need* a spiritual revival."[42] Eisenhower requested Graham's assistance in selecting biblical passages for his inaugural address. To the surprised delight of Graham, Eisenhower read a personally composed prayer after taking the oath. One of the Bibles he used was opened to a passage of Graham's choosing—2 Chronicles 7:14: "If my people, who are called by my name, will humble themselves and pray and seek my face and turn from their wicked ways, then will I hear from heaven, and I will forgive their sin and will heal their land."[43]

Ten days after taking office, Eisenhower was baptized by the Reverend Edward L. R. Elson in a private ceremony at National Presbyterian Church. He is believed to be the only president baptized while in office. Eisenhower took up Elson's suggestion to open each Cabinet meeting with a prayer, and the minister offered to help coordinate them.[44] At times, Eisenhower's salty language from his military career would get the best of him. "Jesus Christ, we forgot the prayer!" he once exclaimed after emerging from the Cabinet Room.[45]

Four days after his baptism, Eisenhower spoke at the first Presidential Prayer Breakfast, held at the Mayflower Hotel in Washington, thanks to the backing of hotelier Conrad Hilton. The driving force behind the breakfast was a Methodist minister named Abraham Vereide, a Norwegian immigrant who had directed Seattle's Goodwill Industries in the 1920s and into the Depression.[46] Vereide had grown disillusioned with the effectiveness of social work and turned sharply to the right with the rise of the New Deal and labor strikes. In 1935, with the help of his contacts in the Seattle business community, Vereide organized prayer breakfasts for executives that fused Christ, conservatism, and capitalism. Vereide mobilized similar groups in other cities.

Vereide's attraction to power led him to Washington, D.C., where he gathered seventy-four men—mostly members of Congress—for a prayer meeting at the historic Willard Hotel in 1942.[47] With the help of a wealthy patron, Vereide bought a four-story mansion on Embassy Row that served as headquarters for his group, the National Council for Christian Leadership.[48] The capital's powerbrokers flocked to the prayer breakfasts. Vereide's stark message meshed with Cold War attitudes. "The choice boils down to this: 'Christ or Communism.' There is really no other. Those in between—playing neutral—are literally playing into the hands of the enemy," he wrote to members of the House breakfast group in 1949.[49]

Graham personally sounded out Eisenhower's interest in attending a national prayer breakfast. Eisenhower was reluctant to commit because he didn't want to feel obligated to come every year.[50] Vereide dispatched Senator Frank Carlson, a Kansas Republican and an Eisenhower confidant, to reach out directly to the White House. The courting wore down Eisenhower, though he requested no television or radio coverage of his appearance.[51]

At the Mayflower Hotel, the new president spoke to more than four hundred ministers, businessmen, and government leaders. Above the dais hung a painting of Uncle Sam on his knees in prayer, an image proudly designed and commissioned by Hilton himself.[52] Eisenhower told the ballroom gathering that "today I think that prayer is just simply a necessity" and that "all free government is firmly founded in a deeply-felt religious faith."[53] The event is an annual Washington ritual now known as the National Prayer Breakfast, evolved into an important nexus of religion, politics, and business.

Eisenhower's displays of piety spurred an appreciative letter from the National Association of Evangelicals and a request for him to take part in the organization's July 4 kickoff of its yearlong "March of Freedom" in 1953.[54] White House officials were unfamiliar with the NAE and asked the Library of Congress to look into the group before committing. Assured that "the organization is considered to be thoroughly reputable" and represented 10 million people, Eisenhower agreed to participate.[55] On July 2, he invited NAE officials and others to the White House for a signing of its declaration connecting a verse from Psalm 23 to a list of "seven divine freedoms."[56] The message was clear: America's foundational principles were divinely based.

Many of the totems of what has been called "civil religion" were enacted during the Eisenhower era: Congress inserted the phrase "under God" into the Pledge of Allegiance in 1954; the administration issued a postage stamp with the words "In God We Trust" above the Statue of Liberty's crown in 1954; and the government adopted "In God We Trust" as the nation's first official motto in 1956. The changes took effect with scant opposition or debate. The term "Judeo-Christian" also entered into popular use. It reflected a consensus around values such as a belief in the rule of law and the preeminence of the individual that were seen as synonymous with American ideals.[57]

Eisenhower kept in touch with Graham throughout his presidency for golf outings, reports on his foreign crusades, and advice on matters both spiritual and political. The question of race relations emerged as a primary subject. Although Graham was a son of segregation-era North Carolina, he refrained from the outright racism of many of his peers.[58] He found no support in the Bible for segregation and pressed for integrated crusades, although few Blacks attended.[59] Graham reluctantly accepted segregated seating in the South until the Supreme Court's *Brown v. Board of Education* decision in 1954, which declared racial segregation of public schools unconstitutional.[60] From then on, he refused enforced segregation at his crusades. However, Graham believed overcoming racism required changing hearts through Christ, not legislation and court decisions. Civil rights activists were getting tired of waiting.

In a letter to Eisenhower on March 27, 1956, Graham agreed to approach the leaders of denominations in the South to discuss ways to achieve racial progress. Graham urged a measured approach on an issue where his moral beliefs clashed with his understanding of practical politics. Raised as a Democrat in the one-party South, Graham even sounded like a political strategist to the Republican president in an era when religion was less partisan. "Immediately after the election you can take whatever steps you feel are wise and right. In the meantime, it might be well to let the Democratic Party bear the brunt of the debate," Graham wrote as Eisenhower's reelection campaign was gearing up. "I hope particularly before November you are able to stay out of this bitter racial situation that is developing."[61] Eisenhower quickly replied with a lamentation that the issue will be "dragged into the arena of partisan politics."[62]

Later that year, Graham reported to the president that he had held productive meetings with denominational leaders in the South and encouraged them to take a stronger stand on desegregation. He also spoke at Black universities and Protestant conferences where he urged patience. "If the

Supreme Court will go slowly and the extremists on both sides will quiet down, we can have a peaceful social readjustment over the next ten-year period," Graham wrote to the president.[63] In the same letter, Graham dispensed bare-knuckled campaign advice to Eisenhower: "I am somewhat disturbed by rumors that Republican strategy will be to go all out in winning the Negro vote in the North regardless of the South's feelings. Again I would like to caution you about getting involved in this particular problem."

The struggle over desegregation detonated a year later in Little Rock, Arkansas. Nine Black students were enrolled in the all-white Little Rock Central High School, but segregationist mobs backed up by the Arkansas National Guard blocked them from attending. The move by the governor, Orval Faubus, defied the Supreme Court's desegregation ruling. Television cameras captured the ugly scenes of white demonstrators yelling racist slurs at children and threatening them with violence.

Eisenhower, moderate to a fault on racial issues, faced rising criticism for letting this direct challenge to federal authority go unanswered. Eisenhower asked Graham for his thoughts—should he send in federal troops? Graham answered that he had no alternative but to do so.[64] The president dispatched soldiers from the Army's 101st Airborne Division to enforce the desegregation order and federalized the Arkansas National Guard. Troops escorted the nine Black students into the school and protected them from the white mobs, defusing the crisis. The troops' bayonets could not, however, prevent the torrent of abuse and harassment that white students directed at the Black students inside the school for the rest of the year.

When Eisenhower called Graham for his counsel on the Little Rock crisis, the preacher was in New York where he had just finished a crusade that drew about 2 million people. It confirmed Graham as the nation's leading religious figure, but it also tested his considerable political powers. Just as he had strained to find a middle ground on racial issues, he had tried to assemble a broad spectrum of Protestants under his roof. As with civil rights, it revealed the limits of consensus.

Graham's watershed crusade in New York began with a cable handed to him after playing at a golf club near Versailles where he had bumped into the Duke of Windsor, an indication of the lofty social circles he was moving in. The message was from George Champion, an executive at Chase Manhattan Bank and an official with the Protestant Council of the City of New York, informing Graham that the council voted to invite him to host a crusade.[65] The city's diverse population and perceived indifference to religion had long been seen as barriers to evangelism, and Graham had declined two earlier requests because few mainline Protestant ministers backed him.[66] Graham had since won over London and other cities in Europe, so he accepted the challenge of taking on New York in 1957.

The council claimed to represent seventeen hundred churches from thirty-one denominations and appointed an executive committee stacked with business leaders, city powerbrokers, and clergymen. Madison Square Garden was secured for Graham's use for six weeks starting May 15. The crusade's total cost was expected to be $900,000—his priciest to date. Graham did not want to charge for tickets, so businesses, individual donors, and church groups shouldered much of the expenses. Corporate chieftains and old-money New York backed Graham as they had Moody and Sunday.[67] Graham and his team would not receive any money from the crusade, though the New Yorker Hotel granted the Grahams the free use of a suite.[68]

Graham's crusade machinery sprang into action: special committees recruited choir volunteers, coordinated train and bus caravans for out-of-state churches, reached out to campuses, and organized prayer meetings.[69] Training sessions instructed counselors how to comport themselves when handling people who came forward during the altar calls. The advertising blitz included 650 billboards, 40,000 bumper stickers, and 500,000 leaflets.[70] "When you see an advertisement for a Cadillac, it just says Cadillac and shows you a picture. Billy is like a Cadillac. We don't have to explain," said Graham's public relations director, Jerry Beavan.[71]

The detailed preparation coupled with Graham's global fame left little doubt that he would fill the seats night after night. The golden-haired preacher always made good copy—a perpetual-motion machine commenting on news events, whirling through stadiums and arenas, consorting with presidents and prime ministers and even royalty. Plus, he was a one-man multimedia empire with his nationally syndicated newspaper column, best-selling book, *Christianity Today* magazine, feature films, weekly radio program *Hour of Decision*, and televised crusades. "In our crusades and work, we need every instrument of modern mass communications," Beavan said. "We've got the greatest product in the world to sell—salvation for men's souls through Christ. Why shouldn't we sell it as effectively as we promote a bar of soap?"[72]

The Billy Graham Evangelistic Association was the nerve center of his activities and promoted his brand of wholesome American-style Christianity. Its staff of nearly five hundred worked with brisk efficiency: One hundred million pieces of mail were sent out each year based on a master mailing list.[73] The ministry dispatched free books, pamphlets, and thank-you notes to donors large and small who sent in their cash and checks. Other letter-writers appealed for help and advice, and their requests were processed, too. George Wilson, who managed the organization in Minneapolis, said the association's job was "to dispense the world's greatest product with the greatest economy to the greatest number of people as fast as possible."[74] Graham's organization tailored that product to meet the needs of the masses.

For his New York crusade, Graham went out of his way to win broad support—even going so far as to meet with wary Catholic and Jewish leaders—but there were murmurings of discontent among some Protestants. Reinhold Niebuhr, a theologian at New York's Union Theological Seminary, thought Graham's message was too simple-minded to reckon with the world's complexities. Graham's evangelism "promises a new life, not through painful religious experience but merely by signing a decision card. Thus, a miracle of regeneration is promised at a painless price by an obviously sincere evangelist. It is a bargain."[75]

On the other end of the Protestant spectrum, such fundamentalists as John R. Rice, Carl McIntire, and Bob Jones Sr. (who Graham knew from his days as a student at his college in the 1930s) objected to the Protestant Council's sponsorship of the crusade. To them, teaming up with liberals was heresy. "Old-time Bible-believing fundamentalists insist that the Bible clearly forbids yoking up with unbelievers, even though one's motives may appear to be good," Rice wrote in his magazine, *The Sword of the Lord*.[76] The broadsides wounded Graham, who had been backing away from preaching fundamentalist biblical literalisms.[77] The New York crusade marked Graham's decisive break with fundamentalism, which retreated into a defiant separatism. Graham soldiered on under the banner of evangelicalism.

Graham doggedly promoted the crusade on secular outlets such as *The Steve Allen Show*, local radio programs, and a splashy spread in *Life* magazine. The crusade was expected to be the biggest in the city since Billy Sunday's revival in 1917. On opening night on May 15, Graham assured a nearly full Madison Square Garden that his meetings were not intended to be mere entertainment. "I believe we need a spiritual revolution in America. We need a revolt against materialism; a revolt against crime; a revolt against the emphasis on sex; a revolt against the sins and the wickedness in high places," he said.[78]

He frequently turned to his open Bible—and asked attendees to follow along—and read passages from the prophets Ezekiel and Isaiah while gesturing with a pointed finger for emphasis. "We've lost God. And we're restless, and that's the reason men and women tonight are searching frantically for peace and joy and happiness, and they can't find it."[79] Graham forcefully asked the audience to acknowledge their sins and receive Christ. More than seven hundred people walked down the arena's aisles to make their "decisions for Christ" in front of an interdenominational choir of fifteen hundred singers. Counselors led them to an inquiry room where the faint odor of a circus menagerie from several days earlier still hung in the air.[80] In a jab at his detractors a few days later, Graham accused some clergymen of acting so sophisticated about religion that "we can't bring it down to the common man."[81]

The common man was precisely Graham's target, and there was no better way of reaching him than television, which he called "the greatest method the church has ever known for getting over its message."[82] For the first time, Graham consented to coast-to-coast broadcasts of his crusades on four Saturday nights in June on ABC. The weekly cost of the airtime was $50,000, and he appealed for donations at weekday services, noting that the checks were tax deductible and an "investment in the kingdom of God."[83] Graham secured a commitment from Pew to underwrite half of the expense if necessary, clearing him to sign the contract.[84]

The experiment spurred a surge of donations and interest, forcing two extensions past the crusade's scheduled end date of June 30 through Labor Day weekend. (Graham also held his own in the ratings against variety shows hosted by Perry Como and Jackie Gleason.)[85] The city that in Graham's opinion worshipped money, fashion, and materialism couldn't get enough of him. Graham filled Madison Square Garden night after night and held special events throughout the summer: A sweltering service in Yankee Stadium where Vice President Richard Nixon sat on the platform set up on the baseball diamond; a noontime rally that blocked traffic on Wall Street; and a final event that packed Times Square over Labor Day weekend. In all, the Graham team said about fifty-five thousand people made "decisions for Christ" at the services plus many more souls won via the telecasts seen by millions.

The question that bedeviled revivalists for generations was raised again after Graham's crusade: Do sudden conversions stick? In January 1958, the *New York Times* surveyed 504 local Protestant clergymen asking them how many referrals they received, how many were new names, and how many attended their church regularly.[86] The newspaper received replies from 159 ministers who indicated the crusade had little lasting impact. The clergymen reported 3,997 referrals of which 2,552 were already members of their churches. Most of the others either didn't attend their church or could not be located.

Some pastors appreciated Graham's reinforcement of Christian principles, others viewed the crusade as a spectacle. As was the case with Dwight L. Moody and Billy Sunday, Graham preached mostly to the converted. "While a good many members of our church and congregation attended one or more sessions of the crusade, I am not aware of any positive impetus to the life and work of our church as a result, nor have I observed any stimulus from it to the work of the churches through the Protestant Council," wrote the Reverend Albert J. Penner, a Congregationalist minister.[87]

The results were paltry even by the sponsoring Protestant Council's measure, which estimated that as many as ten thousand people joined their seventeen hundred affiliated churches, an average of roughly six new members per church.[88] The church that benefited the most was Manhattan's Marble Collegiate Church, which received 373 referrals. Of those, 184 were new names.[89]

The church's longtime pastor was Norman Vincent Peale, whose 1952 book *The Power of Positive Thinking* unified psychology, practical business advice, and basic Protestant teachings and in turn made him rich and famous. In an admiring letter to Graham, Peale wrote: "My spiritual life is stronger and deeper as a result of your marvelous preaching. You have done me more good than I can possibly express. Our church has profited in a wonderful way from the crusade."[90]

Peale and Graham were rooted in very different theological traditions but both were restless entrepreneurs, constantly in the public eye with their books, TV and radio appearances, and newspaper columns. They shared an abiding faith in the goodness of American capitalism and a taste for the political arena. As author and historian William G. McLoughlin Jr. put it: "The pietistic fundamentalist and the mystical modernist meet in the realm of hope and miracles."[91] Peale was no physical "miracle worker" in the style of an Aimee Semple McPherson or Oral Roberts. The pudgy, bespectacled minister was from a mainline denomination, but his ideas helped form the framework of the large-scale evangelical churches that came to dominate the religious landscape.

7

MR. BRIGHTSIDE

Peale's Power of Positive Thinking and Schuller's Crystal Cathedral

Whatever your situation may be, you can improve it. . . . Hold
firmly in your mind a picture not of failure but of success.

—Norman Vincent Peale[1]

Norman Vincent Peale felt like a failure. In 1932, he had been chosen
as pastor of Marble Collegiate Church, a prestigious congregation
on Fifth Avenue in Manhattan. Marble Collegiate, affiliated with the Reformed Church in America, traced its history to 1628 and claimed to be
the continent's oldest continuous Protestant organization. But, like the
country, the church had fallen on hard times. A revolving door of temporary pastors had left it rudderless.[2] The inadequate facilities included a
dirt-floored basement, one meeting room, and a cramped kitchen.[3] The
sanctuary retained its austere beauty, but few were there to see it—only
two hundred people showed up for a typical Sunday service. The privations
of the Great Depression cast a pall of hopelessness over the empty pews.

When Peale ascended to the pulpit for his first sermon as pastor, he
acknowledged the fears weighing down his new flock. "Perhaps we think
so much in terms of failure that we have forgotten how to think in terms
of success. Perhaps we have fallen into the habit of minimizing our powers
and belittling ourselves," he said. "I tell you, if you fill your life with an
awareness of the presence of God, all fear and shrinking and sense of failure
will be cast out of you!"[4]

Peale prepared three different sermons a week—one on Wednesdays
and two on Sundays—and immersed himself in tedious administrative
work.[5] When he met with congregants individually, he discovered that
their struggles were more practical than spiritual in nature: Why do I have

trouble making friends? How do I overcome shyness in social settings? What can I do to make my marriage happier?

He traveled to England for a summer vacation with his wife, Ruth, and took stock of his efforts to revitalize Marble Collegiate. The assessment was bleak. He was exhausted, most of the pews remained empty, and he lacked the training to counsel people about their worries. At a peaceful hotel garden in Keswick, Norman wondered to his wife if he should accept that he had failed and step aside. Ruth replied that he should follow his own preaching of positivity and simply let Christ point the way forward.[6]

Upon his return to New York, Ruth suggested that Norman find a psychiatrist who could assist with church counseling. Norman got in touch with Dr. Smiley Blanton, an Episcopalian from Tennessee who had trained under Sigmund Freud. Blanton was pleased to finally meet a minister who saw psychiatry and religion as complements.[7] He agreed to review cases Peale brought to him. The connection boosted Peale's confidence because he felt equipped to address his congregation's needs. Church attendance jumped, and his partnership with Blanton deepened. Their insights into religion and the mind would help make Peale one of the most celebrated— and controversial—religious figures of the century.

The self-styled apostle of positivity suffered from waves of self-doubt early in his life. Born in 1898, in rural Ohio, Peale was the son of a Methodist minister and former physician, Clifford. Norman admired his father, but he wasn't sure he could follow his path even if he wanted to. "Perhaps the most difficult problem I ever faced as a youth was my consummate inferiority complex," Peale wrote in his autobiography in 1984. "I was shy and filled with self-doubt. In fact, I lived like a scared rabbit. I constantly told myself that I had no brains, no ability, that I didn't amount to anything and never would."[8]

Peale attended Ohio Wesleyan University where he was an indifferent student except for oratory class. After college, Peale worked as a newspaper reporter before heading to Boston University's School of Theology. Norman's father had risen to be a district superintendent in the Methodist Church and when a minister fell ill, he offered the pulpit to Norman. Peale followed his father's advice to use simple language and delivered his personal testimony. Norman never forgot the hush that fell over the congregation as he spoke and the warmth people showed him after the service.

Peale received his ordination as a Methodist minister and accepted pastoral assignments in Rhode Island and then in Brooklyn, New York, where he went door to door to meet people and invite them to services.

He assembled a mailing list and sent out weekly postcards that made claims such as "unchurched people of every Protestant denomination" were coming in increasing numbers.[9] Membership swelled to nine hundred and the Sunday school grew to be the largest in the borough.[10]

Church leaders noticed Peale's success in Brooklyn and, in 1927, called him to lead University Methodist Church in Syracuse, New York. A Syracuse University student named Ruth Stafford, the daughter of a clergyman from Detroit, attended the church and bonded with the young minister. After a two-year engagement, they got married in 1930 at the church with Peale's father as co-celebrant. When seeing the jammed pews, Norman regretted not taking up a collection.[11]

Through pastoral visits, Peale became convinced that the health of a person's spiritual life directly affected his or her mental and physical condition. He partnered with physicians on difficult cases—sometimes praying together in a patient's room—and observed striking results.

Out-of-town churches recruited Peale. In 1932, a group from New York asked him to speak at Marble Collegiate Church, and he accepted. A week later, he noticed officials from the church in attendance at his service in Syracuse. The church offered him the pastorate, but with a condition: He would have to change his denomination from Methodist to the Reformed Church in America. Peale had to weigh it against another invitation to fill a prosperous Methodist pulpit in Los Angeles. He concluded that New York was where God called him to be. Peale's intuition was correct: He led the church for fifty-two years.

Marble Collegiate's history dates almost to the founding of New Amsterdam as a Dutch colony; its earliest members included Peter Minuit and Peter Stuyvesant. The church's 215-foot steeple has loomed over Fifth Avenue and West Twenty-Ninth Street since 1854. The church's name was inspired by its white marble façade, which turns blindingly bright when the sun's rays strike it squarely. Radiant stained-glass windows—some created in the studios of Louis Comfort Tiffany—illuminate the narrow, high-vaulted interior.

Although he was a member of a mainline Protestant denomination, Peale would become a model for evangelical entrepreneurs. He was an innovator who eschewed sectarian dogmas and bureaucracies. He used simple language and mass communication tools to reach as many people as possible. He advanced political conservatism for decades. And he became an industry unto himself.

To Peale, Christianity was a power source that needed to be unlocked and harnessed. "Men everywhere should know that those who sincerely have faith in Christ according to the definite spiritual technique outlined in the New Testament can and do secure personal power," he told his congregation in 1936.[12] By reshaping their personalities, he believed that believers could cure themselves of the obstacles holding them back—not just spiritually, but in every aspect of life.

Peale applied it to his preaching style after hearing criticism about boring ministers. Peale stopped preaching from behind a lectern and learned to speak without notes. Despite his short stature and owlish appearance, Peale was a surprisingly dynamic speaker. He used a technique he called "picturizing" or "imaging" in which he would write the sermon and then visualize himself delivering it.[13] "You can be what you have pictured, and accomplish what you want your life to be," he said in a sermon. "The formula for good days ahead is to pray hard, work hard, believe hard—and picture hard."[14]

Peale's focus on "mind power" drew from an eclectic mix of religious and secular sources: Metaphysics, psychology, mysticism, medicine, and traditional evangelism.[15] One of his most intriguing inspirations was the New Thought movement. Its practitioners emphasized spiritual mind-healing and constructive thinking to promote well-being. They taught that God's spirit, which was a power only for good, dwelled in unity with nature and was made manifest in humanity.[16] Christian critics complained that it diminished the divinity of Jesus and deemphasized the centrality of sin.

In 1937, Peale put his theories into practice by teaming up with Dr. Smiley Blanton to found the Religio-Psychiatric Clinic. Blanton had undergone psychoanalysis from Freud and was a devout Christian. "If religion as it has usually been practiced is enough, why do we have unhappiness, anxiety and nervous breakdowns?" Blanton said. "Because barriers to personal development and a normal religious life have been built up in the subconscious mind, and a clergyman usually needs a psychotherapist's knowledge of behavior to help remove them."[17]

The free clinic attracted hospital patients as well as church attendees. The clinic's novelty helped boost the church's membership rolls by 203 in 1941—the highest annual growth in church history.[18] In 1951, Peale and Blanton founded the American Foundation of Religion and Psychiatry as an outgrowth of the clinic's work. Peale steered income from books and speaking engagements into the clinic, which by 1952 was receiving about three thousand patients annually.[19] Blanton supervised a staff of four ministers with clinical training, three paid and six volunteer psychiatrists, four psychologists, and a social worker.[20]

When the clinic needed more space, Peale asked his rich friends at the Kresge Foundation to pitch in for a new facility in 1955.[21] He also received research funding from General Motors executive Alfred P. Sloan. W. Clement Stone, a New Thought author who had become rich through his insurance business, contributed to the clinic and served on its board of directors. Stone believed a positive mental attitude was essential to his success and donated millions to groups that advocated his brand of self-help. By the 1960s, the clinic saw twenty-five thousand patients annually and established affiliates nationwide.[22]

Peale's activities stretched well beyond Marble Collegiate and the clinic. He had been on the radio as early as the 1920s during his ministry in Syracuse. In 1935, the Federal Council of Churches permitted Peale to host a weekly radio program, *The Art of Living*, on NBC affiliates. Peale's appearances inspired a flood of letters, assuring him that his message of practical Christianity was connecting with people. The program ran for a remarkable fifty-four years. Peale published his first book, *The Art of Living*, in 1937 and followed it with another slim volume, *You Can Win*, the year after.

The Peales founded a nonprofit organization called Guideposts in 1945 known for its namesake monthly magazine. It started as a modest pamphlet and evolved into a publishing powerhouse with circulation into the millions. The content consisted mostly of nondenominational testimonials about how religion has helped people. Peale revealed the periodical's true aim in a letter to businessman Edward F. Hutton, who paid for Committee for Constitutional Government ads warning against atheistic communism. "Our purpose is to put it in the hands of everybody in the country who might possibly be receptive to Communism," Peale wrote in 1947.[23] Peale persuaded corporate America to plump up the numbers for *Guideposts*: U.S. Steel alone purchased subscriptions for all of its one hundred twenty-five thousand workers.[24]

Peale's results-oriented ministry and his bullet-point approach to preaching appealed to the business class. He welcomed being billed as "a businessman's preacher." Peale understood that he had to present Christianity as something that worked. Peale went out of his way to meet businessmen where they were, both physically and spiritually. He relished speaking at trade conventions or to informal groups of salesmen, regaling them with well-practiced anecdotes and humorous stories.

Peale collected many of these lecture tips and anecdotes from his clinic's patients in the bestselling *A Guide to Confident Living*. His next book, *The Power of Positive Thinking*, would be a phenomenon. Published in 1952, the book presented simple problem-solving formulas. "By using the techniques outlined here you can modify or change the circumstances in which you now live, assuming control over them rather than continuing to be directed by them. Your relations with other people will improve. You will become a more popular, esteemed, and well-liked individual," Peale wrote in the introduction.[25] People could build up their self-confidence knowing that God is their companion and helper. "Affirm it, visualize it, believe it, and it will actualize itself. The release of power which this procedure stimulates will astonish you," he wrote.[26]

Peale urged readers to repeat peaceful words like "serenity" or lines from scripture as positive affirmations. He cited an unnamed businessman who developed a system of "prayer power" for overcoming problems. "It is a curious formula but I have practiced it and personally know that it works. . . . The formula is (1) PRAYERIZE, (2) PICTURIZE, (3) ACTUALIZE."[27] He described it as picturing a positive outcome, surrendering it to God's will, and watching the picture turn into reality.

Much of the book consists of handy lists such as ten rules for getting effective results from prayer, ten ways to stop worrying, ten rules for building self-confidence, and ten principles to win the esteem of others (topping the list: "Learn to remember names"). Peale summed it up as "applied Christianity; a simple yet scientific system of practical techniques of successful living that works."[28] Peale sprinkled his text with biblical quotations, but some of his chapter titles tilted toward the secular territory of Dale Carnegie: "Believe in Yourself," "How to Get People to Like You," and "How to Have Constant Energy."

The knives of his detractors sharpened as Peale's celebrity ballooned. Franklin Clark Fry, president of the United Lutheran Church of America, denounced Peale's "positive thinking," saying "there is nothing more sinister . . . than that instrumentalization of religion—the use of God to accomplish a specific aim."[29] Religious scholar William Lee Miller criticized Peale for claiming that positive thinking "can solve every problem just by denying it really exists and promise that every wish can be fulfilled just by 'thinking' it."[30] "He has the ability—and the nerve—to fit his message precisely to the exacting requirements of mass popularity," Miller wrote.[31]

For all of Peale's sermonizing about ignoring negative thoughts, he admitted privately that the attacks dredged up his old self-doubts. "It made me question whether I really belonged in a ministry where my motives could be so questioned," he wrote.[32] His church stood by him, and Peale concluded his critics were missing the point. "Many ministers said my book was oversimplified and wasn't couched in the correct ecclesiastical language," Peale told the *New York Times*. "This was true. It was written in simple language because I was trying to reach people who were not in church."[33]

By that standard, Peale was a smashing success. *The Power of Positive Thinking* resided on the *New York Times* bestseller list for 186 consecutive weeks, selling millions of copies. The genial pastor was on par with Billy Graham as a ubiquitous presence, with a weekly NBC radio program, a weekly television show, a nationally syndicated newspaper column, *Guideposts* magazine, regular contributions to *Reader's Digest*, and even a line of Hallmark greeting cards.[34] Peale's Foundation for Christian Living served as the clearinghouse for many of these ventures. Workers managed the center's direct-mail operation on his property in Pawling, New York. With all of these activities, it was almost an afterthought that Peale preached to thousands at his church twice every Sunday, with overflow crowds watching via closed-circuit television.

In 1955, Protestants commissioned a team to study how religious messages on mass media affected people in New Haven, Connecticut. A Congregationalist named John West was asked why he spread Peale's pamphlets to his employees. "There's so many things applicable to a businessman and his church in Dr. Peale's sermons—why we're both dealing in people," he said. It was good for business because it showed customers that his was a "good Christian firm and that our dealings are based on the Christian faith."[35] Asked what message stuck with him when he heard Peale preach in person, West couldn't recall anything he said.

Peale's self-help philosophy was perfectly tuned to the concerns of business and the individual. Peale taught that the answer to society's problems was for individuals to turn to God and pray for guidance. There was no place in his formula for government-run social welfare programs, which he had attacked since the New Deal. Peale toned down his political beliefs in public to avoid offending the unchurched people he so obsessively courted. Instead, he worked assiduously behind the scenes to advance them.

In his politics and his preaching. Peale reduced everything to the individual. Peale believed in the Horatio Alger myth of upward striving—pull yourself up by your bootstraps, pray hard, work hard, and good things will happen. "You want health? Pray for it. You want financial security? Pray for it. You want a life filled with abundant joy? Pray for it. You want to do something worthwhile in life? Pray for it. Pray big prayers and you will get big answers," Peale wrote.[36]

Peale's focus on the inner life blinded him to harsh social realities. Peale tells an anecdote in his 1957 book *Stay Alive All Your Life* in which "a Negro boy said to me glumly, 'I can never amount to much in this country.'" Peale pointed out to the boy that people like Jackie Robinson and Ralph Bunche overcame discrimination to become successes. Peale left the boy with these words: "If you will get self-doubt out of you mind, and rid yourself of the inferiority complex you are nursing, and believe that God will help you, and then you give everything you have to whatever you do, you will get along all right."[37]

Perhaps such advice would be well received if you were a comfortable member of Peale's Fifth Avenue church or a middle manager fretting about asking the boss for a raise or a promotion. But to a Black boy in the 1950s who lived in a country where racial discrimination was enforced by law and custom, such a blithe comment verged on being delusional. As another leading Protestant religious figure of the era—the Reverend Martin Luther King Jr.—would point out a decade later, "It's alright to tell a man to lift himself by his own bootstraps, but it is a cruel jest to say to a bootless man that he ought to lift himself by his own bootstraps."[38]

Peale's passions flared during presidential elections. In 1948, he urged the imperious right-wing General Douglas MacArthur to run for president and then backed Republican Thomas Dewey against Truman. In 1952, he supported the Eisenhower–Nixon ticket and condemned rival Adlai Stevenson for his divorce, prompting the erudite Democrat to quip, "I find the Apostle Paul appealing and the Apostle Peale appalling."[39] Peale admired Eisenhower for elevating the importance of religion in public life, and the respect was mutual. Eisenhower praised Peale at a 1957 ceremony attended by FBI director J. Edgar Hoover, a Peale acolyte who appreciated the minister's fervent anticommunism.

In 1960, Richard Nixon, the vice president and the Republican nominee, faced off against Democratic nominee John F. Kennedy, whose Catholicism had emerged as a flashpoint in the race. That summer, Peale sent a letter to Billy Graham asking if he would be willing to also go public with his support for their friend Nixon. Graham demurred but invited him to an evangelical strategy session. Peale was encouraged to attend a conference in Washington that would discuss the campaign and formulate a response. Graham urged Peale to go. (Graham, sensing a trap, wrote in his autobiography that he was "privately glad that I would still be in Europe and therefore unable to attend.")[40]

In September, Peale presided at a meeting of the group, the National Conference of Citizens for Religious Freedom, at the Mayflower Hotel in Washington. The 150 Protestant ministers and laymen unanimously agreed on a statement filled with warnings about the Catholic Church's baleful influence on politics. "It is inconceivable that a Roman Catholic President would not be under extreme pressure by the hierarchy of his church to accede to its policies with respect to foreign relations in matters, including representation to the Vatican," the statement said in part.[41]

The insinuation that Catholics could not truly be loyal to the United States touched off a furor. As the group's most famous member, Peale was saddled with the brunt of the criticism. "I find myself embarrassed and deeply troubled that Dr. Peale and his colleagues in Washington felt called upon to add fuel to a fire which has been fed well enough of late by hate-groups and extremists," said the Reverend Benjamin Minifie, rector of Grace Protestant Episcopal Church in New York. The group's statement amounted to "an incitement to bigotry," he said.[42]

Days later, Kennedy directly dealt with the "religious issue" in a high-stakes speech to the Greater Houston Ministerial Association. The Massachusetts senator told the skeptical Protestant clerics that he believed in an absolute separation of church and state in America, "where no public official either requests or accepts instructions on public policy from the pope, the National Council of Churches or any other ecclesiastical source." Kennedy deftly handled questions about his Catholicism, pointing out the Constitution's ban on religious tests as a qualification for office. "I am the Democratic Party's candidate for president, who happens also to be a Catholic. I do not speak for my church on public matters, and the church does not speak for me," Kennedy said.[43]

The backlash to the Protestant ministers' position grew. Peale announced that he had cut ties to the group, claiming that he attended as an invited guest and was not involved in preparing the statement. Peale followed up with a letter to his congregation in which he revealed that he offered to resign as pastor, which was not accepted by church elders.

The degree of Peale's participation with the group was undoubtedly exaggerated in the press, but he was hardly a political neophyte. By then, Peale was sixty-two and had worked for high-level conservative causes for decades. He seemed sorrier about getting caught up in the maelstrom than the substance of the meeting. "I felt a sense of concern about the matter of religious freedom and believe it is proper at any time for a Protestant to meet with fellow Protestants to discuss matters relating to our faith," he wrote. Kennedy eked out a victory over Nixon, prompting

Peale to write bitterly to friends, "Protestant America got its death blow on November 8th."[44]

Peale resumed his schedule of media obligations and out-of-town speaking engagements. He continued dispensing his positive-thinking homilies to a nationwide audience as well as from the pulpit of his Manhattan church. Among his regular congregants in the 1960s were two future presidents: Nixon, who worshipped there while living in New York; and a young Donald Trump, whose worldview would be influenced by Peale's teachings.[45]

His fusion of religious belief and mental health made him a "minister to millions" and an inspiration to other religious leaders. One of them was a fellow Reformed Church in America pastor who sought Peale's help in setting up his church on the other side of the country. The ambitious Robert H. Schuller restyled Peale's teachings as "possibility thinking" for his upwardly mobile Southern California audience and beyond.

Like Peale, Schuller was a son of the Midwest raised in a deeply religious setting. "I tell people I was born in a little house at the dead-end of a dirt road that had no name and no number, and you can go anywhere from nowhere," he often said.[46] Robert Harold Schuller was born September 16, 1926, near Alton, Iowa, the youngest of five children in a family of Dutch immigrants. The Schullers lived in a cloistered Dutch Reformed community. The Dutch minister, called the "dominee," was the town's unquestioned authority figure. Strict rules governed everyday life: No dancing, no alcohol, no movies, and no fishing on Sundays.[47]

Schuller's father, Anthony, assembled the farmhouse from a Sears-Roebuck kit, so it lacked electricity or running water. In the outhouse, toilet tissue consisted of pages torn out of the store's catalog.[48] The family milked cows and collected eggs to squeeze out a meager living. Schuller's mother, Jennie, baked bread that the family dipped into plates of hot melted fat and syrup as a rare treat.

One of Schuller's earliest memories was a visit from Henry Beltman, his mother's brother, an almost mythic figure in family lore. Beltman had served as a Christian missionary in China when leaving the county was a significant trip. Schuller was only four years old when his dashing uncle approached him, laid his hands on his head, and declared, "You will be a preacher when you grow up!"[49] The encounter was a defining event in Schuller's life, and he prayed every night for his uncle's proclamation to become true. He had a feeling God didn't want him to become a farmer.

He attended a one-room schoolhouse with two outhouses. In first grade, he felt the sting of being picked last for a team at recess, even being passed over for a girl. He was overweight, unpopular, and overly self-conscious. Schuller walked home alone, stewing over the taunts and holding to his dream of being a preacher. He delivered sermons to herds of grazing cattle, pretending he was standing in the pulpit of a grand church.

Schuller publicly committed to the church in high school and attended the Reformed Church–affiliated Hope College in Holland, Michigan, where his uncle went. After graduating in 1947, he advanced to nearby Western Theological Seminary and wrote his thesis on John Calvin. Schuller interpreted sin as a "condition" instead of an "action," and concluded preaching would be more effective if it focused on redemption rather than guilt.[50] On the occasion of preaching at his hometown church for the first time, Schuller was enchanted by a young organist who asked which hymns she should play. The student, Arvella DeHaan, would become Schuller's wife of sixty-three years.

Another important relationship in Robert Schuller's life began around then, but this time it wasn't love at first sight. He and some fellow seminary students packed into a car for Grand Rapids to hear Norman Vincent Peale speak at a city auditorium. Although Peale was a pastor of a church in their denomination, professors were skeptical of him and encouraged the students to critique his address. The capacity audience seemed delighted by Peale, but Schuller felt oddly unmoved. To him, Peale's style was undignified—too many wild gestures and simple-minded ideas. He and his classmates agreed on the ride back to campus that Peale was not someone to emulate.[51]

In 1950, Schuller earned his diploma from the seminary, received ordination in the Reformed Church in America, and accepted a call to be pastor at the thirty-five-member Ivanhoe Reformed Church in the Chicago suburbs. The newlywed Schullers faced the challenge of healing a bickering congregation and turning around the church's dire finances. Schuller went door to door to introduce himself to the community and invited his neighbors to attend a Sunday service. The church filled up week after week, but Schuller noticed that most of the newcomers didn't return.

At seminary, Schuller dwelled on theological arguments that were way over the heads of most people. They didn't teach him how "to win the respect of people who aren't at all religious." Schuller read Dale Carnegie's *How to Win Friends and Influence People* and Peale's *The Power of Positive Thinking*. Schuller got over his initial reservations about Peale and adopted a positive style of preaching. Attendance picked up, and Schuller could see that his sermons "should be designed not to 'teach' or 'convert' people, but rather to encourage them, to give them a lift."[52]

The expanding Schuller family—daughter Sheila was born in 1951 and son Robert Anthony in 1954—was struggling to make ends meet on a pastor's income. The church awarded him a raise of twenty dollars per month, a disappointment to Schuller.[53] After all, church membership had surged from thirty-five to nearly five hundred under his leadership, and he oversaw the construction of a new sanctuary, a new parsonage, and a Sunday school expansion.

Schuller was brooding about his future when he received a call from the Reformed Church in Los Angeles to found a church in Orange County. Upon arrival by train from Chicago, Schuller basked in the palm trees, orange groves, and colorful flowers that were such a contrast to the harsh Midwest winter he had left behind. The balmy climate and the opportunity for a fresh start were just too good to pass up. So, like millions of people in postwar America, the Schullers headed west.

World War II changed Southern California in incalculable ways. Its proximity to the war's Pacific theater, large swaths of undeveloped land, and pliant local governments made it an ideal setting for new military bases. In 1942, Camp Pendleton in north San Diego County and El Toro air station in Orange County were established as important Marine Corps installations; in 1943, the Navy opened a shipyard in Long Beach; and, in 1944, the Navy placed a weapons depot in Seal Beach. Aviation and defense industries flourished thanks to wartime production contracts: among them, the Lockheed assembly plant in Burbank, Consolidated Aircraft (later Convair) in San Diego, Douglas Aircraft in Santa Monica, and Northrop in Hawthorne.[54]

After the war, defense contractors and the military remained the engines that propelled the region's economy. Government spending on missile and aerospace technology poured into Southern California, and the plentiful job market attracted masses of workers from out of state. An estimated 3 million military personnel had passed through the West during the war years, and many returned to settle.[55] Orange County's population soared from 216,224 in 1950 to 703,925 in 1960—a 225.6 percent increase. Developers strained to keep pace, constructing twenty-five hundred housing tracts with one hundred forty-four thousand building lots in the county during that period.[56] The newly constructed Santa Ana Freeway connected these residents to their jobs and wholesome family attractions like Disneyland in Anaheim and Knott's Berry Farm in Buena Park. Sunny optimism prevailed in a land of seemingly endless possibilities and growth.

Churches rushed to minister to the influx of transplants that sought community. From 1950 to 1960, mainline Protestant denominations enjoyed solid gains: Methodists and Episcopalians each added seven churches in Orange County. But theologically conservative churches expanded even faster—the number of Baptist churches jumped from six to fifty-seven in the county's incorporated cities, and fundamentalist congregations mushroomed across the region.[57] Historian Lisa McGirr pointed out that their focus on personal salvation blended well with the region's individualistic, entrepreneurial culture. Southern California's defense-dominated economy also fueled political conservatism by reinforcing the "connection between capitalism, prosperity, and anticommunism," she wrote.[58]

Schuller embodied and extended such beliefs. He arrived in Orange County in 1955 with $500 from the church and a head full of ideas, but little else. Schuller was a pastor without a congregation, so he drew a $4,000 missionary's salary with half coming from the Reformed Church in America's missions board in California and the rest from the church's national missions board in New York, headed by Ruth Peale.[59] The Schullers had so little money that they had to take out a three-year loan to buy an electric organ they mounted on a trailer.

Schuller had the immediate challenge of finding a site for his Sunday morning services. During his honeymoon in 1950, he attended a service at a drive-in theater in Iowa where a Lutheran pastor mounted the roof of the snack bar and spoke to people sitting in their cars. On a much larger scale, the Methodist minister J. Wallace Hamilton ran a church in St. Petersburg, Florida, that allowed people to stay in their vehicles and listen to the service via a sophisticated amplifier system.[60] Schuller was fascinated by Hamilton's ingenuity.

With no other options, Schuller turned to a drive-in theater in the city of Orange, a few miles east of his church's future home of Garden Grove. The theater's manager agreed to rent it for ten dollars each Sunday to cover the cost of the sound technician.[61] What the Orange Drive-In Theatre lacked in amenities, it made up for with its convenient location and abundant parking. He placed a notice in the newspaper to promote his "drive-in church," and added the catchy tagline, "Come as you are in the family car!"[62]

His Southern California ministry began with an eleven o'clock service on March 27, 1955. Roughly fifty cars were sprinkled throughout the vast lot, with about a third belonging to choir members whom Schuller asked to arrive in separate cars to ensure at least the appearance of a crowd.[63] Arvella played the organ while Robert preached about "Power for Successful Living" from the tarpaper-covered roof of the snack bar. Worshippers in their cars followed along via speakers they mounted to their vehicles. The total offering amounted to less than a hundred dollars.

Schuller knew he would fail if he limited himself to attracting only members of his modest denomination. He criticized pastors of traditional Protestant churches for being satisfied with flat membership in their outdated buildings in decaying downtown areas. Schuller believed that if a church didn't grow, it would start to die. The only way for a congregation to grow was to reach unchurched people, who did not care about denominational labels. So Schuller chose the generic name Garden Grove Community Church instead of something more specific like the First Reformed Church of Garden Grove.[64]

On weekdays, Schuller knocked on doors asking people if they belonged to a church. If they said yes, he thanked them and moved along; if they said no, he asked what they would like to see in a church. He scribbled down their answers—programs for children, lively music, and practical preaching—and pledged that his church would someday grow big enough to address all of their needs. Ideally, he felt, churches should be like suburban shopping centers by offering ample parking, a convenient location, and something for everyone.

Schuller cut an impressive figure as a preacher, even from the roof of a refreshment stand. The taunts he endured in childhood for being fat were well in the past. He filled out into a strapping man who moved gracefully in his heavy clerical garments. His confidence shone through in his arresting preaching style in which his voice suddenly rose to a crescendo when emphasizing a point, and then just as quickly fell almost to a whisper, forcing listeners to lean forward in their seats to hear.

If Schuller's goal was to impress the unchurched, who better to make an impression than Norman Vincent Peale? In 1957, he asked Peale to speak "at the largest church in Orange County, with parking for 1,700 cars!"[65] Peale preached about hope and encouragement to a sea of cars at the Orange Drive-in Theatre. Schuller delighted in the publicity windfall and the legitimacy Peale's presence conferred on him.

Peale's insight that Jesus never condemned any person inspired Schuller to change his approach. If Jesus was more interested in people's strengths than their weaknesses, shouldn't preachers emphasize that? Schuller purged theological language from his sermons that might confuse newcomers. He selected seemingly secular topics such as "How to Make Marriage Succeed in Today's World" and wove in subtle biblical references.[66] He purged judgmental or negative messages and avoided political issues or controversial subjects. "People will rush to hear exciting good news!" he wrote.[67]

Schuller coined the term "possibility thinking," defined as using your God-given powers of imagination to dream up ways to achieve a desired objective.[68] Schuller had overseen the construction of a small chapel, but he thought it was time to think big. He sketched out his vision of an indoor-outdoor church of glass that would give worshippers the option of sitting in the sanctuary's pews or staying in their cars and listening via speakers. Making it into a reality would put "possibility thinking" to the test.

Schuller secured ten acres for $66,000 on Chapman Avenue at Lewis Street in Garden Grove, just west of the drive-in movie theater. He batted away "negative thinkers" on the church board who thought his building plans were ill-advised, insisting that his congregation—and God—would provide. Schuller hired the celebrated architect Richard Neutra to design the sanctuary and campus. "It was another attempt on our part to make a favorable impression on non-churched people. And it worked!" Schuller wrote.[69]

Garden Grove Community Church's new home opened in 1961, with the Peales present at the sanctuary's dedication. At the beginning of services, twenty-five-foot-high glass panels silently slid along an electric track, opening the modern sanctuary to the parking lot. Schuller dramatically appeared on a balcony positioned to allow him to preach to both sets of people. A network of 104 high-fidelity speakers amplified the music across row after row of automobiles.[70] The landscaped campus included four bell towers, decorative fountains, and floral gardens. Newspaper ads highlighted the church's enviable location—"a half-mile off the Santa Ana Freeway, 2 miles below Disneyland"—and noted that people could choose to worship "in the privacy of their cars."[71]

As Schuller's popularity soared in the 1960s—church attendance jumped to two thousand people each week—the minister stayed aloof from the tensions of the times.[72] His congregation and the surrounding suburban communities were almost exclusively white and thus felt detached from the civil rights movement. Racism may be wrong—even sinful—but demonstrations could easily spiral into violence and disorder, he thought. Schuller didn't speak out against civil rights marches, but he did not feel comfortable participating in them, either. Schuller believed mainline Protestant churches' preoccupation with social issues was a mistake because "the mental, emotional, and spiritual hurts of the average person were being totally ignored. As a result, millions of spiritually hungry souls were leaving their churches."[73]

However, Schuller was involved in Orange County's anticommunist groups and supported a school superintendent who sent mailers to families extolling Christianity and "American heritage."[74] Schuller's first book, *God's Way to the Good Life*, published in 1963, offers a window into his political thinking. He condemned the fervor for "statism" that "bombards us with the propaganda that the state must play the role of God, feeding the hungry, caring for the ill, providing for every need from the cradle to the grave."[75] Private, Christian charity should be sufficient to meet the needs of the truly needy. The price for depending on the state was always the loss of freedom, he wrote.

Like many conservatives, Schuller's point of reference was individual responsibility, not community action. For instance, he wondered why the government would provide free vaccinations for children. "Does that mean that the government will tax some corporation, private business, or some personal citizen's private wealth to give my child free vaccine? Well, I can afford to pay for my own child's vaccine. Let us get back to the great old idea of paying our own bills," he wrote.[76] Using that logic, he also questioned the wisdom of free public education.

Schuller interpreted the commandment "thou shalt not steal" as a guarantee that each individual has the right to own property. Thus, Christian beliefs and American capitalist ideals were threatened by communism and socialism. Government had no right to tax, take away, or "steal," those gains to create a welfare state. "Too, you have a God-ordained right to be wealthy," Schuller wrote. "Having riches is no sin. Wealth is no crime. Christ did not praise poverty. The profit motive is not necessarily unchristian!"[77] His message was a welcome balm to the consciences of the well-heeled. They could continue to accumulate wealth serene in the knowledge that it was the Christian thing to do. They were also being good Americans because capitalism and freedom went hand in hand.

Schuller needed the constant financial support of his congregation and the business community to realize his ever-unfolding dreams. In 1968, the Neutra-designed Tower of Hope, topped by a ninety-foot neon-lit cross, opened on the campus. The fourteen-story tower—then the tallest structure in Orange County—contained a twenty-four-hour telephone counseling service, classroom space, offices for the church's administrative and direct-mail operation, a chapel, and Schuller's office, which boasted panoramic views. In the following year, he founded the Robert Schuller Institute for Successful Church Leadership to teach other pastors his church-growth principles. Throughout the years, the seminars brought together thousands of pastors and laypeople, fostering the megachurch movement.

Schuller served on the planning committee for Billy Graham's crusade in Anaheim in 1969 and hosted the evangelist for a leadership seminar. The well-manicured campus impressed Graham and he suggested Schuller should televise his sermons. The cost would be steep: $400,000 a year to buy airtime and pay production expenses. Graham called his friend Gene Autry, owner of the powerful station KTLA, to ask if he could set aside an hour for Schuller on Sunday mornings.[78] Schuller floated the idea of a television ministry during a sermon, and his congregation pledged to donate more than half of the annual cost. To Schuller, the gamble was worth it. What better way to reach the masses of unchurched people than through television?

The program, *Hour of Power*, launched in 1970 and brought Schuller into living rooms throughout most of Southern California. Letters and donations flooded into Garden Grove Community Church, enabling *Hour of Power* to expand to other cities. Viewers were entranced by his upbeat message and the visuals of the attractive campus. By 1975, *Hour of Power* was carried on sixty stations across the country and viewed by 2.5 million people.[79]

Schuller peppered his sermons with upbeat catchphrases: "Inch by inch, anything's a cinch," "Turn your hurts into halos and your scars into stars," and "Tough times never last, but tough people do." Schuller pointed to his rise from poverty as proof that his teachings could work wonders. His books sold well and he was in demand on the lucrative speaking circuit. The Schullers owned a fashionable home in Orange, along with a beach cottage and a mountain cabin. Arvella believed the most important role of a pastor's wife was to support her husband. "He hates to decide what to wear in the mornings, so I find out what his schedule is and I hang out his suits and pick out his ties and shirts. He likes to look nice, but he doesn't want all the hassle," she told the *Los Angeles Times* in 1974.[80]

There were warning signs of an inflating ego. Schuller's church staff included eight ordained ministers, but he wanted to be the only preacher featured on *Hour of Power*. Schuller took ten weeks of vacation each year and in his absence, stations were directed to run tapes of his old services instead of televising live sermons by the other ministers.[81] "Dr. Schuller has been very aware of his mortality and the church drastically suffering if he were removed from the scene," said the Reverend Raymond Beckering, a copastor at the church said prophetically in 1975. "It would be difficult to replace him."[82]

Schuller's relationship with Peale turned frosty when *Hour of Power* entered the New York market—Peale's territory. It was a signal that the protégé was eclipsing his mentor. (They publicly reconciled years later.) Schuller was keeping heady company, befriending celebrities such as John Wayne and Doris Day. He secretly traveled to the Soviet Union in 1972 to visit underground churches in the officially atheist country.[83]

Schuller felt the itch to build big again. This time, he had the vision of an all-glass cathedral that would be in harmony with nature. Neutra died in 1970, so Schuller contacted architect Philip Johnson, whose most famous work was his modernist Glass House in New Canaan, Connecticut. Schuller blanched when Johnson said it was impossible for a building to have a roof of glass in an earthquake zone. He insisted there must be a solution without making even the smallest compromise. "God is in the details—right, Philip?" the minister quipped during a meeting with the non-churchgoing architect.[84] Johnson regrouped and provided renderings of a church larger than Notre-Dame in Paris with a sanctuary that could seat nearly three thousand worshippers. The design was based on the four-pointed star of Bethlehem and a lacework of steel supported more than ten thousand panes of mirrored glass.[85]

It perfectly matched Schuller's vision for what he called the Crystal Cathedral, and now he had to pay for it. He landed a $1 million leadoff gift from John Crean, an Orange County businessman.[86] Schuller wrangled donors to give at least $500 each to sponsor a window. Runaway inflation rates and high construction bids pushed the project's estimated price tag from $10 million to $15 million, enraging Schuller.[87] When contractors threatened to shut down construction, Schuller appealed directly to his congregation on June 18, 1978, and tallied a $1.4 million collection.

Schuller needed the support of more deep-pocketed philanthropists just to keep the cranes in motion. Foster G. McGaw, the founder of the American Hospital Supply Corporation, donated $2 million; Hazel Wright, an *Hour of Power* viewer from Chicago, contributed $2 million to build an organ with sixteen thousand pipes, one of the largest in the world; and W. Clement Stone, a benefactor of Peale's clinic, gave $1 million.[88] Stone, an insurance magnate, had purchased two hundred fifty thousand copies of Schuller's book on self-esteem to send to ministers and asked him to be a motivational speaker at his popular "success" rallies.[89]

To push the project over the finish line, Schuller orchestrated a gala fundraiser featuring retiring opera star Beverly Sills in May 1980. Seats sold at $1,500 each and attendees included stars such as Mickey Rooney and Frank Sinatra, but the evening was marred by the unfinished church's acoustic problems, drawing a barbed review in the *Los Angeles Times*.[90] Two weeks later, Sills told Johnny Carson on *The Tonight Show*: "If you walked in today, you'd still hear my voice." Carson quipped, "I'm all for the Crystal Cathedral—I've got stock in Windex."[91]

The glittering $18 million Crystal Cathedral hosted its first service on September 14, 1980, for its ten-thousand-strong congregation, among the largest Protestant churches on the West Coast. The striking church created made-for-television visuals for the nationally broadcast *Hour of Power*. Schuller mounted annual spectacles such as Easter pageants and *The Glory of Christmas*, a Broadway-style reenactment of the Nativity story that included live camels and flying angels suspended on cables. He invited notable people such as Billy Graham, Ray Kroc, and Coretta Scott King to share their stories of faith on *Hour of Power*.

There were grumbles that Schuller had built the Crystal Cathedral to satisfy his vanity. The Reverend Wendell Karsen, a Reformed Church missionary, charged that Schuller cared more about expensive building projects than the plight of the poor.[92] Dennis Voskuil, a professor at Schuller's alma mater, wrote a book portraying the minister as a shallow purveyor of "inspirational nonsense."[93] Schuller countered that his church's vast assets allowed it to serve up thousands of free meals each week and run other charitable programs. As for spending millions on high-end architecture, Schuller pointed out that monuments to faith such as Notre-Dame and St. Peter's have been sources of inspiration for centuries.[94]

Schuller's son, Robert Anthony, classifies his father as an entrepreneur who intentionally crafted "possibility thinking" to be a marketing message. "He was a huge marketer; that was one of his great gifts," he said in a 2021 interview with the author. "One of his marketing tools was that everything had to have a superlative on it. . . . It had to be the finest worship service on TV. It had to be the biggest pipe organ in the nation. It had to be the best architecture available, period."[95]

Superlatives are newsworthy, and that drove growth into the 1980s, with the elder Schuller always at center stage with a winning smile. About $4 million each year came from Sunday collections, and another $30 million arrived through the mail from *Hour of Power* viewers, the most-watched weekly religious program in the country.[96] The campus was indeed a "shopping center for Christ," complete with a "Possibility Thinkers Bookstore," a thrift store, seminars for pastors, Bible study classes, and at least forty programs. In 1983, the church received thirty-five thousand pieces of mail every week and dispatched fifteen thousand pieces daily. About four hundred employees and hundreds of volunteers kept the machinery running.[97]

But cracks started to form in the gleaming veneer. *Hour of Power* viewership declined in the late 1980s amid a spate of televangelist scandals, and growth would never return. Schuller maintained his appetite for construction. A 234-foot reflective steel spire housing a carillon and chapel—paid for by another million-dollar gift—opened in 1990.[98] He hired Richard Meier, designer of the Getty Center in Los Angeles, to build a welcoming center as the final jewel in Schuller's crown of architectural masterworks. By the time it was complete, in 2003, Schuller had reached his late seventies, his mane of hair now fully white, with grandchildren to dote on. But instead of a long twilight to savor his achievements, Schuller's final years were filled with heartbreak for him and his church.

Schuller had long tapped his only son, Robert A. Schuller, as his successor. The younger Schuller had the right pedigree, with degrees from Hope College and Fuller Theological Seminary. He founded an Orange County church on ranchland donated by Crystal Cathedral megadonors John and Donna Crean. The younger Schuller preached earnestly about linking healthy living to spirituality, but he lacked the flamboyance of his father. "Robert's delivery is slower, more thoughtful," Robert H. Schuller said in 1996. "I am more ebullient and impertinent in my spontaneity. He gets the highest marks from some of my most powerful friends. Three are billionaires. Billionaires. With a B."[99]

In an interview with the author, Robert A. Schuller said that his father's diminishing mental capacity was taking a toll on the Crystal Cathedral's management. "By 2000, his dementia had set in and he couldn't remember a whole lot. He had trouble following the program and knowing when it was time for him to go up. My mother was writing most of his sermons by then," Schuller said.[100] The elder Schuller continued to chair board meetings that would take all day but accomplish little. The son was named copastor in 2000 and fully took over in 2006.

The ministry looked impressive on the surface but it was tottering under severe financial pressures. The costly *Hour of Power* broadcasts were no longer bringing in the audiences or donations that they had for decades. The church was having trouble paying off the more than $40 million welcoming center. The elder Schuller's insistence on mounting a disastrous theatrical production called *Creation* cost the ministry millions of dollars.

The Crystal Cathedral's style of worship also had fallen out of step with modern tastes. A new generation of megachurches featured casually dressed pastors and contemporary bands rather than the cathedral's traditional organ hymns and robed ministers. Startup evangelical churches embraced the digital world and rented buildings rather than taking on the expenses of a television ministry and construction projects. They were as focused on church growth as Schuller had been, but they were doing it for much less money and for a younger audience.

Meanwhile, power struggles were splintering the Schuller family. Robert A. Schuller conducted an audit of the Crystal Cathedral's membership rolls and discovered only about a thousand regular congregants—far below the ten thousand it claimed.[101] He attempted to impose standard practices for governing nonprofits. That meant removing some family members and in-laws from the board who had conflicts of interest because they were also employees.[102] They rebelled and diminished his role, forcing him to resign. In 2009, the board announced the family's eldest daughter, Sheila Schuller Coleman, would become senior pastor.

The Crystal Cathedral buckled under the weight of its legacy costs and the effects of the Great Recession. In 2010, it filed for bankruptcy protection, reporting a $43 million debt. The filing revealed hefty salaries and benefits for Schuller family members on the church's payroll.[103] Sheila Schuller Coleman broke away to found her own church. The elder Schullers cut their ties with the Crystal Cathedral, leaving them with few assets and little income. The Roman Catholic Diocese of Orange purchased the forty-acre campus and converted the Crystal Cathedral into Christ Cathedral.

Arvella Schuller died in 2014, and Robert H. Schuller died the following year at eighty-eight. Schuller's daughter, Carol, issued an appeal through a GoFundMe account to help pay for the funeral on the plaza outside the church he had built. The campaign raised about $6,100 from forty-four donors.[104] Arvella and Robert are buried together on the cathedral's grounds. Their gravestone is inscribed with the words, "God loves you and so do we."

Robert A. Schuller stepped aside from ministry to pursue business projects and to host a daily radio show. When the pandemic shuttered churches in March 2020, he conducted drive-in Sunday services in Newport Beach. In a nod to family history, he encouraged people to "come as you are!" Schuller, who was never overtly political, now preaches against pandemic-related restrictions and mandates. He claims there is no science to support wearing face coverings, and warns that the vaccine's dangers have been underplayed. He says the government and news media are following an agenda of control. "It's a bad flu season. That's all it is. But it's been manipulated so they can implement these things. That's why I call it COVID-ocracy," he said in August 2021. "The main driver of COVID is not the disease, it's fear. God hasn't given us a spirit of fear. But he's given us a spirit of power, love, and a sound mind. Solid theology says that God is the giver of life. And if he is the giver of life, he'll help us through this thing. And if he's not, then it's time for us to go home, and that's OK, too. Nobody's going to live forever. Everybody's going to die."[105]

His son, Bobby Schuller, now hosts *Hour of Power* from his modest Orange County church, Shepherd's Grove, considered the successor church to the Crystal Cathedral. His program is carried on Trinity Broadcasting Network and is shared on YouTube and social media outlets. The church posts its annual financial statements online. His ministry's mission is "to create a radically hospitable church, that unchurched people love to attend"—words that could have been spoken by his grandfather more than a half-century earlier.

8

THE SEEKERS

The Jesus People, Willow Creek, Saddleback, and the Search for the Unchurched

The unchurched aren't asking for watered-down messages, just practical ones. They want to hear something on Sunday that they can apply on Monday.

—Rick Warren[1]

They came by the thousands to Pirate's Cove at Corona del Mar State Beach to answer the call of a balding, middle-aged minister who saw something in them that most of his contemporaries failed to see. The baby boomers—the largest generation in American history—were coming of age and looking for a direction in a country coming undone. Urban riots, demonstrations against the Vietnam War and the draft, strikes on college campuses, and political assassinations shook the nation to its core. Social movements were redefining the roles of women, gays, and Blacks. Activists elevated the exploitation of Mexican American farmworkers and the plight of Native Americans. Protesters rallied against pollution befouling the air and water, leading to the first Earth Day and the creation of the Environmental Protection Agency. Every assumption was open to question, and many young people found an escape in the rising drug culture and boundary-breaking music scene. Their shambolic style of dress and irregular personal hygiene habits were expressions of the tumult within.

The convulsions reordering society reached into the nation's churches. In 1966, *Time* magazine published a stark cover asking, "Is God Dead?" The very question seemed preposterous in a country where a poll in 1965 found 97 percent of people said they believed in God and the numbers of people joining churches roughly tracked population growth.[2] But the same survey found that of those who professed a belief in God, only 27 percent considered themselves to be deeply religious.[3] That meant most people in

111

churches on Sundays were there out of a sense of obligation. Other believers reserved their visits for holidays or were church members in name only. Weekly attendance dropped from 49 percent in 1958 to 42 percent in 1969, according to Gallup.[4] This wide but shallow religiosity further alienated young people from the conformist attitudes of their parents. In their minds, churches were just another authoritarian, hypocritical institution.

The throngs of seekers who ventured to the Southern California coast week after week were looking for something more authentic, more elemental. They found it in Chuck Smith's nondenominational Calvary Chapel, which used the Pacific Ocean for its baptismal waters. "God wants to bless you. So come, let Him zap you," Smith proclaimed to about a thousand people during a beach gathering in 1970.[5] About two hundred candidates clambered down the ocean cliffs and waded out to ministers to be prayed over and then submerged into the sea. Others pointed their index fingers to the sky to signify Jesus was the "one way" to salvation.

The dramatic mass baptisms in coastal Orange County attracted curious newspaper reporters, national magazine photographers, and film crews. The coverage framed many of the new believers as burned-out hippies trying to "get high on Jesus."[6] It was an irresistible media counternarrative to the excesses of the sex, drugs, and rock 'n' roll lifestyle. Skepticism abounded that this "Jesus movement" with its "Smile, God loves you!" bumper stickers was destined to be just another of the era's groovy fads. But Calvary Chapel offered much more than slogans and appealing visuals of sun-kissed beach baptisms. The church operated a chain of communes in California and Oregon that provided safe harbors for wayward young people and intensive Bible study. They were called the Jesus People—or, less kindly, "Jesus Freaks"—and their innovations left an indelible imprint on evangelicalism.

Chuck Smith was born into a family that believed in miracles. His older sister, Virginia, fell ill with spinal meningitis and her mother, Maude Elizabeth, carried her listless body to a Pentecostal pastor, who had preached about divine healing. Virginia's father, Charles, ran into the church and also prayed for God's intervention. The young girl was healed, and her parents pledged to dedicate their lives to Christian service. Their son, Charles, arrived just two months after Virginia's recovery in 1927. His mother prayed, "Lord, I am going to fulfill my promise to You through my son."[7]

Chuck's boyhood in Ventura consisted of the simple pleasures of fishing, bodysurfing, snorkeling, and enjoying the bounty of the family's walnut orchards. The Smiths moved to Santa Ana while Chuck was in high school, and the family joined a Pentecostal church. During a church-hosted summer camping trip, Chuck felt God's call to serve. He agreed to be a youth pastor and enrolled in L.I.F.E. Bible College, affiliated with the International Church of the Foursquare Gospel. Smith never quite felt at ease with the church's miracles-on-demand teaching. At his ordination, it was noticed that he was the only one who didn't fall to the floor after being "slain in the spirit."[8]

Smith met Kay Johnson, whose family attended the Aimee Semple McPherson–founded Angelus Temple in Los Angeles, and they married in 1947 after a six-week courtship. Kay's older sister directed Foursquare churches in Arizona and invited Chuck to pastor a small church in Prescott. After a year, Smith moved his growing family to run a church in Tucson and then back to California for a pastoral position in Corona. There, Smith struggled for the first time as a pastor. The church's congregation declined, and Smith worked full time at a grocery store to make ends meet. When he fell behind on union dues and couldn't pay the penalty, he lost his job.[9]

Smith accepted Foursquare assignments in Huntington Beach in 1960 and then in present-day Chino Hills. Smith informed members of Los Serranos Foursquare Church that they would be reading the entire Bible—starting with the first ten chapters of Genesis—and that he would key his sermons to what they had read that week. The positive response upended everything he had been taught about ministry. Smith witnessed spiritual growth just from the act of reading through the whole Bible.

The revelation brought into the open the uneasiness Smith felt about the denomination since Bible school. Foursquare leaders asked churches to place two paper thermometers in their sanctuaries: one to measure their attendance, the other to track a rival church's attendance. When the contest ended, the losing church had to perform a service for the winner. Smith ignored the directives. A few months later, he learned that Los Serranos had won. Leaders asked him to address a rally to tell people how he did it. Smith wrote back that his congregation hadn't been aware of the contest.[10]

In December 1965, Smith took command of Calvary Chapel, an independent church with twenty-five members in Costa Mesa. Smith remodeled the shabby building and applied his new theories on Bible teaching. In his autobiography, Smith credits the Six-Day War in June 1967 for supercharging his church's growth.[11] The Arab–Israeli conflict resulted in Israel's capture of the Sinai Peninsula, Gaza Strip, West Bank, and Golan Heights, as well as the Old City of Jerusalem and the rest of East Jerusalem. Smith and other premillennials believed that the restoration of the Jews in

Palestine was a sign that the end-time was near. Israel's stunning victory breathed new relevance into biblical prophecy.

The late 1960s did seem to be an apocalyptic time, particularly in California. College campuses like Berkeley were in upheaval, the gruesome crimes of the Manson Family cult shocked the state, and the violence at Altamont near Oakland jolted the rock scene after the "peace and love" vibes of Woodstock months earlier. The Summer of Love in 1967 blossomed in the Haight-Ashbury neighborhood of San Francisco, home to psychedelic music groups like the Grateful Dead and Jefferson Airplane. LSD guru Timothy Leary told young people to "turn on, tune in, drop out," and many fell into the drug culture and out of society.

Smith and his wife studied hippies on Orange County's beaches as if they were anthropologists doing fieldwork. "Where others seemed to be repulsed by these dirty, long-haired 'freaks,' we could only see the great emptiness of their hearts that caused them to turn to drugs for the answers to life that we knew only Jesus could supply," wrote Chuck Smith, who had been among those repelled by them. "But how to reach them?"[12] The Smiths encountered several hippies who decided to give their lives to Jesus. They invited a few to move into their home and listened to them speak about their "disillusionment with the church and the adult world that they called the Straight Society."[13]

Chuck Smith believed these earnest youngsters were in danger of lapsing into their old habits. A real estate agent in the church had purchased the old Blue Top Motel in Newport Beach with the intention of condemning it and rebuilding on the site. Until then, he offered it to the church as a place for the young people to live.[14] The church dubbed it the House of Miracles. The demand was overwhelming, so the church found a second site, then a third, then a fourth. By 1970 the church sponsored twenty-five communal houses across Southern California, plus a ranch in Oregon. These were not free-love kinds of places. Residents who did not have regular jobs were enlisted in work crews. Smith banned drugs and alcohol at the houses, and sex was forbidden. At Mansion Messiah in Costa Mesa, women were required to take a Bible and a commune elder when they went on a date.[15]

Calvary Chapel's membership consisted of "doomsday prophets" who believed Jesus would return to rescue believers from the coming tribulations and Armageddon. Lonnie Frisbee, a twenty-one-year-old resident of the House of Miracles, told a *Los Angeles Times* reporter in 1970 that he had dabbled with LSD and cults before becoming a youth leader at Calvary Chapel. "The reestablishment of Israel as a nation is a major sign that the end of the world is near," he said.[16] Frisbee looked like the era's typical cinematic image of Jesus, lending authenticity to his words. Frisbee matured into a leader of the Jesus movement through his work with the Vineyard association of churches. (Frisbee's homosexuality later prompted churches to disassociate from him. He died of AIDS in 1993.)

The communes nurtured a core of believers and the mass ocean baptisms created priceless publicity. Calvary's Santa Ana church opened in 1969, and Smith added multiple Sunday services and spillover seating outdoors. Bible study groups and other events kept the church busy all week. The year after opening, membership hit fifteen hundred with about half under the age of twenty-five.[17] Smith's relaxed demeanor went a long way to setting a nonthreatening tone. "We felt the church was pretty much just writing them off . . . and that we should make some effort to reach and understand them," Smith said.[18]

One of the youngsters who took part in the Jesus movement was Larry Osbourne, who started going to Calvary Chapel in the late 1960s. Osbourne grew up in a rigid Baptist environment freighted with rules and traditions. What he encountered at Calvary Chapel was "mind-blowing." No one told him to cut his hair or expected him to wear a suit and tie. Smith stripped away everything except for the Bible. "It was just back to the very simple message of Christianity and Jesus and again just simple Christianity without all of the other things added to it, and I said, 'Man, I've never seen this before,'" he said in an interview with the author. "I've never heard anything where someone just simply taught the Bible and explained it."[19]

Mainline Protestant denominations were suspicious of the Jesus movement. An Episcopal priest called their solutions "offensive to the thinking populace." A Presbyterian noted that churches "are really afraid of them." Theologian Vernard Eller remarked, "I hope people don't stop with just getting high on Jesus," insinuating that the movement was just a fad.[20] The image of Jesus as an icon of the counterculture as portrayed in the hit musical *Jesus Christ Superstar* was too much for an older generation accustomed to a distant, wrathful deity.

The criticism that the Jesus movement was simplistic was precisely why it appealed to young people. "The hardest persons to interest in a vital faith in Jesus Christ are those in the church," said Hal Lindsey, a former Campus Crusade for Christ operative.[21] Lindsey codirected the Jesus Christ Light and Power Company in a former fraternity house near UCLA. The house operated much like Calvary's communes, housing up to forty young people and offering ministry and services to hundreds more. "These kids hate impersonalness, bigness, irrelevance, materialism—and I've just given you a description of the average institutional church," he said in 1971.[22]

Lindsey's 1970 book *The Late Great Planet Earth* put a fresh coat of paint on the premillennialism that had dominated evangelical teaching. The book's incredible success—about 20 million copies in print and a film version narrated by Orson Welles—demonstrated the fertile market for apocalyptic beliefs.[23] Like Smith, Lindsey pointed to current events as evidence that the end times were approaching. Lindsey saw great import in the rise of Europe as an economic and political power, as well as in the foundation of the modern state of Israel in 1948 and its military victory in 1967. Based on his biblical calculations, Lindsey believed the rapture would occur by 1988.[24]

Lindsey's predictions were grim: Widespread famines, increasing drug addiction, and the limited use of nuclear weapons would pave the way for the Antichrist.[25] Accepting Jesus Christ now was the only way to be rescued from the coming tribulations and the battle of Armageddon in the Middle East. His book charged denominational leaders with rejecting these biblical truths and thus losing their congregations with "social action gimmicks."[26] Independent Bible-centered churches like Calvary Chapel appealed to this new, unconventional generation.

Some traditionalists in Smith's church were not so sanguine about allowing the counterculture to seep into their sanctuary. They worried that these new worshippers with their long hair and dirty jeans would be a negative influence on their children. "Our challenge was to overcome what most churches had not, namely their insistence on respectability, conformity, and a judgmental attitude toward anything that departed from the norm," wrote Smith, whose clerical garb consisted mostly of Hawaiian shirts.[27] By then, Smith was in his early forties and hardly a hippie, but he also remembered feeling the scorn of church elders.

When the church installed new carpeting, congregants weary of the hippies and their dirty feet posted a sign reading, "No bare feet allowed." The message upset Smith and he declared to the board, "If because of our plush carpeting we have to close the door to one young person who has bare feet, then I'm personally in favor of ripping out all the carpeting and having concrete floors."[28] The "no bare feet" barrier promptly fell.

The church erected revival-style tents to accommodate worshippers while building a sanctuary in 1973. Thousands of people packed each of Smith's three Sunday services. Calvary Chapel launched *The Word for To-day* radio program and later purchased KWVE-FM, known as K-WAVE, which would be the flagship of a nationwide network of stations. The ten-thousand-member church hosted Bible studies and weekend concerts that drew mostly young people. "It's the music that brings them here and the teaching brings them back," a college student said during a chapel concert.[29]

Calvary's music ministry was one of its most notable contributions to the Jesus movement. The contemporary sounds of acoustic guitars blended with heartfelt songs connected with a new generation raised in the folk-rock music culture. Church members rejoiced at the chance to use their musical talents for a higher purpose. Smith had taught the congregation the Aramaic word *maranatha*—translated as "the Lord comes" or "come Lord"—and it became the name of a record label he founded in 1971.[30] Maranatha! Music thrived, selling more than a half-million records in 1978 alone.[31]

Smith's affable manner belied an uncompromisingly literal view of scripture. He never wavered from his belief in biblical prophecy even after the decades passed and the world didn't end in the 1980s like he predicted. ("Every year I believe this could be the year," he insisted, sounding like an optimistic sports fan. "We're one year closer than we were.")[32] Earthquakes and such events as the 9/11 terrorist attacks were interpreted as divine punishments for a sinful world.

Smith didn't consort with conservative politicians like many of his evangelical peers, but he shared their attitudes. He decried political correctness on college campuses, which were overrun by "lesbian and feminist coalitions and assorted anti-traditional and leftist minorities and causes," he wrote in 1993. "The New World Order they espouse is collectivist, amoral, anti-family, anti-American, and anti-Christian."[33] Smith personified a hyper-masculine Christianity, but he also wallowed in the evangelical tradition of feeling persecuted by the mainstream culture. "If you are a Christian, especially a 'traditional' white male, then you are targeted," he wrote. "The use of insulting terms like 'sexist' and 'racist' will bring all sorts of people into line."[34]

Smith, who died in 2013, at the age of eighty-six, inspired his followers to plant Calvary Chapels across the region, forming a loose federation rather than a denomination. (Smith's son-in-law, Brian Brodersen, is senior pastor at Calvary Chapel Costa Mesa.) The Vineyard movement, which today counts more than six hundred congregations in the United States and twenty-four hundred in ninety-five countries, began as a Calvary satellite before breaking off on its own.[35] Among Smith's most successful protégés is Greg Laurie, who battled addictions to marijuana and LSD before finding Christ. Laurie transformed a Bible study group in Riverside into Harvest Christian Fellowship, one of the country's biggest churches. Laurie's radio programs, books, online outreach, and stadium-size Harvest events have made him among the best-known evangelicals in the nation.

Osbourne, who was at Calvary Chapel from nearly the beginning, took over as pastor at North Coast Church in 1980 when it was an overgrown Bible study meeting in warehouses and high school cafeterias. Osbourne realized that he had a natural aptitude for business and leadership. "Most pastors I know who built a large church could have built a large company. They would have had a different mission, and the reason most churches aren't very large is most are more of a shepherd leader," he said.[36] North Coast, aligned with the Evangelical Free Church of America, steadily grew under his stewardship. By the time he stepped aside as senior pastor in 2019, North Coast had more than thirteen thousand people attending services at its seven campuses in San Diego County. Osbourne is now a teaching pastor at North Coast, and he mentors pastors across the country.

The success of theologically conservative churches like Calvary Chapel and the many churches it inspired was in marked contrast to liberal churches. Starting in the 1960s, mainline Protestant denominations witnessed erosion in their ranks. From 1960 to 1996, the United Methodist Church's membership declined from 10.6 million to 8.5 million while the nation's population increased by 90 million.[37] Other mainline denominations such as the United Church of Christ, the Episcopal Church, and the Disciples of Christ also lost ground. During the same period, conservative denominations such as the Southern Baptist Convention grew from 9.7 million members to nearly 16 million.[38] The Pentecostal Assemblies of God and nondenominational evangelical churches like Calvary Chapel experienced even faster growth.[39]

Many Christian thinkers scrambled to explain the dramatic shift. Religious legal scholar Dean M. Kelley's 1972 book, *Why Conservative Churches Are Growing*, argued that liberal churches had drifted too far from their central purpose. Churches that focused on causes such as promoting civil rights, protecting the environment, or combating poverty were indistinguishable from secular groups that had the same aims. Charitable work has its place in a religious context "but with the recognition that such stopgap measures are a distraction and diversion from their distinctive and indispensable service: making sense of life," Kelley wrote.[40] If a church chooses to engage in social work, the action must help clarify the meaning of life for its members.[41] Otherwise, a church becomes like a Rotary Club or a Chamber of Commerce.

Strong religious organizations expect high levels of commitment from their members, such as at Smith's Calvary Chapel when he taught the Bible chapter by chapter, verse by verse. Being involved in the life of the church meant reading the Bible at home, attending a Bible study group during the week, and then reinforcing those lessons at a Sunday service. "They do not feel any divergence between the group's understanding of right and their own; if they do, they hasten to correct their own (mis)understanding," Kelley wrote. "If they find themselves out of step, they do not blame the group."[42] If churches ask little of their congregants, they will be more likely to drift away, he said.

As early as the 1950s, evangelicals studied how to achieve church growth and built their institutions accordingly. Missionary Donald A. McGavran had decades of firsthand experience of what worked and what didn't. He believed too many churches concentrated on caring for existing members rather than looking for lost sheep. Such a "maintenance mentality" leads to stasis and decline. "Setting goals for membership increase is beyond the thinking of most Christians. They set goals for their business activities, the number of cars they will sell, the amount of steel they will produce, or the number of new buildings they will erect; but not for the number of converts their church will win," McGavran wrote in his book, *Understanding Church Growth*.[43]

In a free-market religious climate such as America, churches must compete to survive. Church growth requires obsessive planning and measurable goals; it will not come as a by-product of "witnessing to Christ by kind deeds." "In the midst of hundreds of good things to do, Christians should be clear that the chief and irreplaceable task of Christian mission is always that of bringing unbelievers to saving faith in Christ and into responsible membership in his church," he wrote.[44] McGavran knew from his work overseas that there were billions of unchurched people who were potentially new recruits for Christ. McGavran founded a church growth institute in Oregon that he later moved to Fuller Theological Seminary, becoming the founding dean of the School of World Mission and Institute of Church Growth.

McGavran's systematic approach to church growth tied into a rising generation of data-driven "pastorpreneurs" who studied the techniques of ministers such as Robert H. Schuller as well as secular management gurus like Peter Drucker. Two of those upstart baby boomer pastors, Bill Hybels and Rick Warren, applied these methods to the churches they founded, which became models for the megachurch movement.

From an early age, Hybels exhibited a gift for business leadership. Hybels, born in 1951, was born and raised in Kalamazoo, Michigan, where his family owned a wholesale produce company. He spent much of his youth sorting produce, loading it onto trucks, and delivering it to restaurants and grocers.[45] His future wife, Lynne, recalls him arriving sweaty and dirty at her house for a date after long summer days directing crews to plant and harvest vegetables. The hard work instilled in him "an entrepreneur's love for challenge and risk taking," she wrote.[46] The family's labors bore much fruit: a summer cottage, a forty-five-foot sailboat, a Harley-Davidson, and ample travel opportunities for Hybels as a teenager.[47]

Despite the plenty, Hybels had a nagging feeling that he should be doing something more with his life. Hybels did college coursework in business and economics, but dropped out after a few years. In the summer of 1972, he worked as a counselor at Camp Awana, a Christian camp in Wisconsin. A friend, Dave Holmbo, told Hybels about a music group he had started at South Park Church. The evangelical church in the Chicago suburbs tapped into the energy of the Jesus People movement. Hybels took a position at the Awana Youth Association and joined Holmbo's band, Son Company.

Hybels led a Bible study group on Wednesday nights called Son City at the church in Park Ridge. That experience combined with Christian rock concerts awakened an unexpected spiritual passion in the church community. Hybels and Holmbo designed programs to attract unaffiliated young people. They trained core believers and asked them to bring their unchurched friends to outreach events.[48] Week after week, Hybels refined his presentation to appeal to skeptics.

Hybels understood religious discontent. He grew up in the Christian Reformed Church in North America, which he called "unbelievably self-absorbed."[49] When Hybels was in junior high, his father mentioned a business associate who showed an interest in God after undergoing personal setbacks. When his father suggested inviting him to church, Hybels insisted he reconsider. "If there's *any* spark of spiritual interest in him, we'll extinguish it in sixty minutes flat!" the young Hybels remarked.[50] At seventeen, he reluctantly brought an unruly schoolmate to church. Hybels sank in his pew during the listless sermon and lackluster hymns. "The experience *ruined* him. As far as I know, he never darkened the doorstep of another church again," he wrote.[51]

The traditional way of doing church would never reach those kinds of people. Hybels connected biblical teachings to the everyday lives of the hundreds of young people who showed up each week. Some of these unchurched kids were becoming committed Christians.[52] Son City added sports competitions and arts activities. Much like Calvary Chapel, it offered a wholesome alternative to the drug culture.

A signal event in Hybels's ministry occurred in 1974, when he was just twenty-two. One Wednesday night, nearly six hundred young people—many of them nonbelievers—crammed into the church auditorium. Hybels walked out in jeans and a T-shirt and told them that Jesus's sacrifice on the cross demonstrated God's love for all. Hybels invited the crowd to stand if they wanted to receive Jesus, and most sprang to their feet. The young people waited for hours for someone to pray with them individually. Afterward, an emotional Hybels felt the workings of the Holy Spirit and hosted a weekly "seeker service."[53]

Hybels pursued a degree in biblical studies and took every class taught by Gilbert Bilezikian, who believed the modern world needed to recapture the dynamism of the early church. Hybels asked how, and "Dr. B" said to start a church based on Acts 2, which meant building a community fully dedicated to discipleship, fellowship, and prayer. About twelve hundred young people were active in Son City, but Hybels felt reaching adults was the best way to make a difference.[54] In 1975, he resigned from South Park to start a church in Palatine where some Son City members lived. Hybels paid for sound and lighting equipment with the profits from selling baskets of tomatoes door to door.[55]

Hybels and others deployed into their new territory to understand what the community wanted in a church. They mostly fielded complaints: Church was irrelevant to everyday life, services were boring, and pastors were judgmental and always asking for money.[56] Hybels pledged to create a church that would address people's needs. Hybels looked for space to rent and landed on Willow Creek Theatre, which had plenty of parking and a convenient location. Hybels persuaded the manager to let him rent it on Sunday mornings for $250 per month. About 125 people attended the nondenominational church's first theater service on October 12, 1975.[57] It featured contemporary music, a scripture reading from Bilezikian, and an earnest message—not a sermon—from Hybels. The fledgling church barely scraped by and relied on free labor to load equipment in and out of the theater every Sunday.

Hybels read Schuller's peppy guidebook for ministers, *Your Church Has Real Possibilities!* and, in 1976, attended a seminar for pastors at his Institute for Successful Church Leadership in California. "His was the first church I had ever seen that was unashamedly focused toward reaching unchurched people," Hybels said. "In the church I grew up in everything was to reinforce the already convinced."[58] Hybels noticed that Schuller designed his church building and services "to make it visitor friendly and to put the message at a level that a first-timer could understand its relevance."

During the conference, Hybels met with Schuller in his office atop his Tower of Prayer and drank in the sweeping views of his campus. Hybels asked whether buying a hundred acres was too much property for his young church, renamed Willow Creek Community Church. Schuller, remembering his struggles with acquiring land, urged him to buy it all. "If God chooses to do a miracle, you'd better be ready for it. Don't buy a thimbleful of land. Buy a fifty-gallon drum," Schuller counseled. "Make your thinking big enough for God to fit in."[59]

In June 1977, Schuller attended Willow Creek's fundraising banquet, where Hybels announced that the church needed $600,000 to buy 104 acres in South Barrington, an upscale Chicago suburb.[60] The audacious appeal raised $425,000—a vote of confidence in the church. A similar parcel became available later in the year for $660,000, and the church secured it with a partial payment.[61] During construction, Willow Creek continued to meet at the theater, adding services studded with skits and music to satisfy the growing crowds.

Like all evangelicals, Hybels was inspired by Jesus's Great Commission: "Therefore go and make disciples of all nations, baptizing them in the name of the Father and of the Son and of the Holy Spirit, and teaching them to obey everything I have commanded you."[62] Hybels centered his church on finding people who were lost and teaching them. Willow Creek adapted the Great Commission for its mission statement: "To turn irreligious people into fully devoted followers of Jesus Christ."[63]

Willow Creek hosted its first service at the new site in 1981 in what it called an auditorium, not a sanctuary. Some thought it looked more like a civic center, corporate office park, or community college campus instead of a church. That was exactly the intention. Old stone churches with their vaulted ceilings and steeples were cold and intimidating to outsiders, young people told Hybels.[64] Christian iconography and statuary were inscrutable to them. So Hybels ensured that there were no crosses, pews, or stained-glass windows that might turn them off. The seeker services omitted the recitation of creeds that baffle outsiders. There were no collection plates, no hymnals, and certainly no altar calls. The services were designed to allow newcomers to feel comfortable and blend in. Willow Creek emphasized excellent customer service: ushers who were friendly but not pushy, top-notch entertainment, and high-quality facilities.

Willow Creek's target audience was "Unchurched Harry and Mary"—Harry could be a husband who thinks his wife's faith is pointless and Mary could be a dentist who may believe in Jesus but has delayed having a personal relationship with him.[65] Willow Creek desired upwardly mobile baby boomers. "What we want him [Unchurched Harry] to do is just say, 'I was just at corporate headquarters for IBM in Atlanta Wednesday, and now I come to church here and it's basically the same.' Neutrality, comfort, contemporary, clear: Those are the kinds of values that we want to communicate," Hybels said.[66]

A former religious skeptic named Lee Strobel first ventured into Willow Creek in 1980 and was captivated by Hybels and his relaxed approach. Strobel abandoned his career in journalism to become a teaching pastor at Willow Creek. He assembled a demographic profile of the unchurched—wealthier and more educated than average—and tried to understand their needs. Strobel believed these people were not hostile to God and secretly hungered for a spiritual anchor. Many were from the corporate world and responded to a practical message presented in a nonjudgmental setting. "The attitude, 'That's the way we've always done things' needs to become, 'What can we do better to meet more needs and reach more people with the Gospel?'" he wrote.[67]

George Barna, who had experience as a pollster and a political campaign manager, attended about a dozen churches in the Chicago suburbs in the early 1980s. Once he arrived at Willow Creek, he was hooked right away. "It was a welcome relief to us to find a church that was high-energy about ministry and it came along with great teaching and creative worship and that strong leadership component," Barna told the author in an interview. "Politics is all about marketing. So what I was trying to figure out was, 'OK, how do these things blend together.' Willow Creek was lighting a great fire under me to really continue that examination."[68]

Barna founded a marketing research company that has worked with churches and faith-based organizations for decades. Marketing succeeds when there is satisfaction from both parties that their needs are being fulfilled, he said. "Ministry, in essence, has the same objective as marketing: to meet people's needs. Christian ministry, by definition, meets people's real needs by providing them with biblical solutions to their life circumstances," Barna wrote in a how-to book for pastors.[69] Church marketing helps "*to move people into a relationship with Jesus Christ. That relationship is our product*," he stressed.[70] Instead of using money, people pay by committing their life to that relationship.

Churches falter when they stubbornly follow their idea of what church should be without considering if it is relevant to the community. These are product-driven institutions with a "take-it-or-leave-it" attitude.

Market-driven churches are responsive to society. They don't sell their product to existing users; they sell to the unaffiliated. Barna cautioned that should not be an invitation for church leaders to "water-down" the Gospel to play to the crowd. Ideally, he said, churches should stick to biblical principles while following a marketing plan.[71]

Willow Creek's formula worked wonders. Weekend attendance spiked from five thousand in 1985 to nine thousand by the end of 1987.[72] (Weekday services were designed for committed believers.) It was held up as a model of the modern megachurch, defined as a Protestant church that averages more than two thousand attendees at weekend services.[73] Only 50 churches fit that description in 1970, then 150 in 1980, 310 in 1990, and 600 in 2000.[74] A 2020 survey reported that there were about 1,750 megachurches in the United States.[75]

The paradox of megachurches is that their size allows for greater intimacy. On the surface, megachurches appear to be all flash and no substance. What is seen on television are packed arenas, polished pastors, and high-energy bands. What is unseen are the small groups that cater to every conceivable subset of society: People going through divorce, people who are grieving the loss of a child, people who are widowers. Megachurches steer newcomers into a group of ten or so people who meet during the week for Bible study and fellowship. "Megachurches assume that people in this society do not know each other, nor will they make the effort if left on their own," according to a leading study on the phenomenon. "People desire the intimacy of small groups but will seldom seek it out."[76]

The mission is to move people from anonymity to engagement. "We want Willow Creek not to be a church that offers small groups but to become a church of small groups," Hybels said.[77] Willow Creek perfected the process of discerning the spiritual gifts of each person and assigning them tasks in one of the church's more than ninety ministries. Mechanics could repair donated vehicles for the needy, counselors could help people with addictions, and other volunteers could assist with food distribution.

The church instituted a "Participating Member process" for newcomers "through which they come to understand their identity in Christ, their role in the church, and the expectations God places on them in areas such as spiritual development, financial stewardship, and community life."[78] That meant members were expected to tithe the biblically directed 10 percent, and most in the affluent area did. Hybels didn't want to use professional fundraisers or constantly browbeat people to donate.

Nondenominational churches like Willow Creek must succeed or fail on their own—there is no central headquarters to turn to for help, monetary or otherwise. In 1992, Hybels founded a nonprofit consulting arm called the Willow Creek Association that in less than two years worked with nearly a thousand churches worldwide across many denominations. These churches paid a nominal annual fee for access to teaching materials and conferences at Willow Creek. The training got results: From 1993 to 1995, 64 percent of member churches increased their attendance and only 2 percent reported declines with the remainder staying the same. Churches striving for growth flocked to Willow Creek.[79] By 2000, the association boasted five thousand churches, generating millions of dollars in fees.[80]

Meanwhile, the original church was expanding at an astonishing rate. Willow Creek's 4,556-seat auditorium—larger than any theater in Chicago—was filled for a Saturday service and two Sunday services.[81] Giant-screen TVs and state-of-the-art lighting and sound systems ensured people in the balcony could follow the entertaining music and dramatic sketches. Hybels discussed evergreen topics such as how to turn a house into a home and how to face fear. During the services, the church provided free care for infants and classes for children. In 1992, a $23 million building campaign added a gymnasium, food court, and a small chapel to the campus. That same year Willow Creek hit its highest nonholiday weekend attendance: 17,010.[82] A *New York Times* article in 1995 reported that Willow Creek had a $12.35 million budget and 260 full- and part-time employees. Hybels drew a $67,000 salary, plus an $18,000 housing allowance.[83]

The church attracted about fifteen thousand people each week and their contributions averaged more than $225,000 per week. The Harvard Business School held up Willow Creek as a case study for how nonprofit organizations should operate.[84] When a reporter marveled at Willow Creek's size, Hybels replied, "There are 2 million people within a one-hour drive of this place. In business parlance, we've got 2 percent of market share. We've got a long way to go."[85]

Willow Creek was a juicy target for naysayers. *New York Times* architecture critic Paul Goldberger contrasted Willow Creek's utilitarian style with historic Gothic cathedrals and found it lacking. The suburban megachurch is "a neutral container, a place for the large gatherings that are central to the church's way of serving its members. Architecture may have many jobs at the megachurch, but providing spiritual meaning is not one of them," he wrote.[86] Others took shots at Willow Creek's management approach to Christianity. "Having no other compass than their own sense of what the Bible means and what works, they are easily guided by the pragmatism and individualism of American culture itself," wrote sociologist Robert Wuthnow.[87]

Willow Creek's leaders were just the latest generation of evangelical entrepreneurs. They took what had worked, adjusted it to their time and taste, and created something new. In Hybels's case, he borrowed from Schuller a focus on the unchurched (and an appreciation for expansive free parking), applied modern marketing principles, and built an organizational template that thousands of churches followed. Hybels never launched a TV ministry or embarked on crusades. His public persona, if he had one, was that of the mild-mannered MBA next door.

Like Schuller, Hybels tried to stay out of the culture wars of the 1980s and 1990s, but he held conservative views, opposing abortion rights and same-sex marriage. "We're convinced that, ultimately, a person's perspective on social issues won't fundamentally change until his or her heart is transformed by Jesus Christ," Hybels wrote in 1995.[88] Hybels surprised many in the evangelical community by serving as a spiritual counselor to Bill Clinton during his presidency and participating in a prayer service before Clinton's second inauguration in 1997. Hybels conducted a question-and-answer session with the Democratic president at Willow Creek in 2000, where Clinton expressed contrition for the "terrible mistake I made" in reference to his affair with White House intern Monica Lewinsky.[89]

In the 2000s, Hybels shifted his focus from day-to-day church operations to global issues such as poverty and AIDS. "The number of times Scripture mentions God's passionate concern for the poor, the oppressed, the widows, the orphans, those who are incarcerated, and those who have no voice is astounding!" he wrote in 2007.[90] Willow Creek opened a $10 million center providing food and clothing to needy families in 2013. In a nod to repairing evangelicalism's historic racial divisions, Willow Creek partnered with a predominantly Black church in Chicago on bus tours of the major sites of the civil rights movement.[91]

Hybels's Global Leadership Summit was like an evangelical Davos. Hybels played the role of the avuncular elder statesman who quizzed marquee speakers such as Melinda Gates, Bono, Jimmy Carter, and Rick Warren on their leadership secrets as well as their religious faith. Hybels's mastery of management attracted corporate titans such as General Electric's Jeffrey Immelt and Ford's Alan Mulally. Hybels, still fit and handsome into his sixties, looked the part of a confident chief executive smoothly presiding at a shareholders meeting or product launch. The two-day conference in 2014 was shown via live simulcast to more than three hundred church sites filled with people who paid the $109 registration fee allowing them to listen in.[92]

Hybels was transitioning into retirement when the *Chicago Tribune* published a bombshell investigation in March 2018 alleging that Hybels conducted inappropriate relationships with women in his congregation spanning decades.[93] The alleged behavior included unwanted advances, sexually suggestive remarks, and invitations to hotel rooms. Church inquiries had cleared him of wrongdoing, but some of the accusers felt that they had been dismissed and discredited. A few days later at a church "family meeting," Hybels told a packed Willow Creek that "the accusations you hear in the *Tribune* are just flat-out lies."[94] Few in the audience knew that church officials had been investigating the claims for four years.

The report came as the #MeToo movement encouraged women to reveal sexual harassment by powerful men. In early April 2018, Hybels resigned from Willow Creek after forty-two years at the helm. He acknowledged that the controversy was distracting from the church's mission and apologized for his "defensive" response when the allegations became public. "I too often placed myself in situations that would have been far wiser to avoid," he said, stopping short of admitting wrongdoing.[95]

The resignation shook loose more allegations from women telling of uncomfortable encounters with Hybels, and church elders pledged to renew their inquiry. But by then, it was clear that Willow Creek leaders had mishandled the initial claims. In August 2018, Hybels's successor as lead pastor stepped down, as did the entire board of church elders. Churches canceled plans to broadcast the Hybels-free Global Leadership Summit and speakers such as Denzel Washington dropped out. Leaders of the Willow Creek Association, which organized a network of eleven thousand churches worldwide, removed all traces of its founder from its marketing materials. In 2019, an independent council of Christian leaders concluded, "The credibility of the allegations would have been sufficient for Willow Creek Community Church to initiate disciplinary action if Bill Hybels had continued as pastor of the church."[96]

The fall of Bill Hybels is a cautionary tale for megachurches with founding pastors who grow too powerful to truly be held accountable. Hybels oversaw Willow Creek's rise from a ragtag congregation in a rented theater into an evangelical powerhouse. Hybels married management and ministry in a new, appealing way for the MBA-class of unchurched suburbanites. That led to innovations, but also unchecked authority.

The Willow Creek Association continues its work connecting affiliate churches and mounts a much lower-profile Global Leadership Summit. A visit to a Sunday morning service at Willow Creek's main campus in South Barrington in July 2021 revealed a campus footprint far too big for its congregation. Acres of parking lots went unused.[97] Ushers closed the main sanctuary's balcony, but seating was still plentiful on the main floor. The church has a revamped "teaching team" and "executive team" that will need to reckon with the lingering impacts of the pandemic and the Hybels scandal. The new senior pastor, Dave Dummitt, founded 2|42 Community Church, an independent megachurch with seven campuses in Michigan. Dummitt, who was inspired to start an Acts 2 church as Hybels was, now has the challenge of conjuring a second act for Willow Creek.

In 1971, Diane Morgan, a reporter with a newspaper in Santa Rosa, California, traveled to Chicago with teens selected for a national youth conference. Few from the rural towns of Mendocino County had been so far from home or had seen such a big city. They listened to distinguished professors and a United Nations delegate lecture about science and the environment. On the plane back to the West Coast, Morgan asked the teens what they had gained from the heady experience. "For the most part I met with reactions ranging from slight apprehension to downright reluctance," she wrote. "But such was not the case with Ukiah High's blithesome and loquacious Rick Warren, who responded to my question with, 'How much do you want? . . . I could do a whole thesis, you know.'"[98]

At seventeen, he already stood out as a young man in a hurry. The wiry teen with long, shiny blond hair was student body president, co-organizer of his school's ecology club, president of the Christian group Fishers of Men, and youth pastor and music director at his church. Warren saw no contradiction between Christianity and science. "We must take care of the environment. It's a Christian's place to take care of the world," he said. Warren told the reporter he wanted to be a preacher like his father, and Morgan concluded that with "his warmth and social consciousness, he'll probably be a good one."[99]

Richard Duane Warren, born in San Jose in 1954, had preachers, church planters, and Baptist laypeople on both sides of his family tree. His father, Jimmy, was a Baptist minister and irrepressible little Ricky was the center of attention at church.[100] After a stint in Oregon, Jimmy Warren was assigned to churches in Lake and Mendocino counties in 1965. The family settled in Redwood Valley, a tiny town off Highway 101. Visiting pastors and other guests spun through the welcoming Warren home where Jimmy provided the banter and Rick's mother, Dot, whipped up the meals.[101]

Rick felt the call to ministry at a Christian summer camp and lobbied to start a Christian club at his high school in 1970. The principal declared that the school could not sanction the group because of concerns about church and state separation. Rick kicked off a petition drive, pressed the issue with the school board, and won the support of the district attorney and state attorney general. The club, Fishers of Men, conducted weekly rallies and daily prayer meetings. Rick wrote an article about his triumph for the underground *Hollywood Free Paper*, a Jesus People–inspired publication that claimed a circulation of four hundred thousand. Fascinated readers asked how they could start similar clubs, so he typed up a guide that hundreds followed.[102]

Warren received his preaching license at eighteen and enrolled at California Baptist College in Riverside. He immersed himself in biblical studies during the week and lined up speaking engagements at youth events on weekends. Warren's ebullient personality earned him election as president of his freshman class, following the four consecutive years he was voted class president in high school. He met a pastor's daughter named Elizabeth Kay Lewis, known as "Kay," and proposed marriage before their first kiss at an ice cream parlor near campus.[103] The engagement was drawn out because Rick was in love but Kay was not—at least, not yet.

In 1973, Warren and a friend drove 350 miles to a San Francisco hotel to hear a speech by W. A. Criswell, whom Warren considered "the greatest American pastor of the twentieth century."[104] Criswell was the former president of the Southern Baptist Convention and led First Baptist Church in Dallas. Criswell preached biblical inerrancy—one of his dozens of books was titled *Why I Preach That the Bible Is Literally True*—and led a conservative resurgence in the country's largest Protestant denomination.

Warren admired Criswell as much for his organizational skills as for his preaching ability. Criswell built a powerhouse Sunday school program and added family-friendly attractions such as a bowling alley and a skating rink. The people followed, and First Baptist grew into a colossus, consuming five blocks of downtown Dallas and claiming fifteen thousand members. (First Baptist's current senior pastor, Robert Jeffress, was among Donald Trump's earliest and most ardent evangelical supporters.)

As he listened to Criswell speak that night at a hotel ballroom, Warren felt God's call to be a pastor. "Then and there, I promised God I'd give my entire life to pastoring a single church if that was his will for me," Warren wrote.[105] After the speech, Warren approached Criswell, who placed his hands on the student and prayed, "Father, I ask that you give this young preacher a double portion of your Spirit. May the church he pastors grow to twice the size of the Dallas church. Bless him greatly, O Lord."[106]

With that blessing, Warren studied the writings of church-growth advocates such as Donald A. McGavran and C. Peter Wagner. Warren oversaw an expansive youth program at a church in Norwalk, received his ordination there in 1975, and weeks later married Kay. The Warrens headed east to Southwestern Baptist Theological Seminary in Fort Worth, Texas. In 1978, the Warrens attended a church-growth conference in California hosted by Robert H. Schuller. His practical advice for reaching the unchurched made an impression on the young couple. "He had a profound influence on Rick," Kay said. "We were captivated by his positive appeal to nonbelievers. I never looked back."[107]

During Warren's last year at seminary, he wrote to the hundred biggest churches in the country to find out how they were structured. The feedback confirmed his suspicion that most were led by pastors like Criswell and Schuller who stayed in one place for a long time. Warren's next task was to figure out where to plant his church. He eliminated places that were Southern Baptist strongholds, reasoning that the market was already saturated. Warren discovered that the three most unchurched states were on the West Coast: Washington, Oregon, and California. He drilled down further and focused on four metro areas: Seattle, San Francisco, San Diego, and Orange County.[108] Warren spent much of the summer of 1979 examining demographic trends of the four regions. He determined that Orange County's Saddleback Valley was "the fastest-growing area in the fastest-growing county in the United States during the decade of the 1970s."[109]

The Warrens packed up their meager belongings for the drive from Texas to Southern California. Rick and Kay and their newborn daughter had little money, nowhere to live, and no church. Rick pulled off the jammed rush-hour freeway and asked for guidance at a real estate office. The realtor, Don Dale, found the family a condo to rent without having to put down a security deposit. Warren invited Dale to be the first member of his church. Seven people were present for Warren's first Bible study two weeks later.[110]

Warren had to figure out his church's niche in a county that already boasted high-profile ministers such as Schuller and Chuck Smith. "Our focus would be limited to reaching the unchurched for Christ, people who for one reason or another did not attend any existing church," he declared.[111] Like Hybels, Warren had read Schuller's *Your Church Has Real Possibilities!* and spent twelve weeks going door-to-door. If the person said he or she already belonged to a church, Warren moved on to the next house. The survey revealed four common complaints: Church is boring, church members are unfriendly to visitors, churches care more about money than people, and churches don't offer quality child care.[112]

Dwight L. Moody, an internationally famous evangelist in the late 1800s, instilled a business-like approach to his mass revivals. Moody's organization was "as systematic as an astronomer," wrote one journalist. *Library of Congress, Prints and Photographs Division*

To house his boisterous campaigns, evangelist Billy Sunday's team constructed vast tabernacles such as this one in New York City in the late 1910s. No church was big enough to accommodate all who wanted to see him. *Library of Congress, Prints and Photographs Division*

Billy Sunday, a former professional baseball player, brought a live-wire athleticism to his lucrative evangelistic campaigns. He struck a characteristically flamboyant pose during a visit to the White House in 1922. (The man at right is unidentified.). *Library of Congress, Prints and Photographs Division*

Aimee Semple McPherson, shown in 1927, conducted "faith healing" meetings where she honed her distinctive "foursquare gospel" message. Her unlikely rise to fame and her tumultuous personal life made her an object of admiration and ridicule. *Library of Congress, Prints and Photographs Division*

Two radio towers erected on Angelus Temple's roof transmitted Aimee Semple McPherson's sermons far beyond Los Angeles. She was among the first religious figures to become a radio celebrity. *University of Southern California Libraries and California Historical Society*

Oral Roberts prays for a boy in the healing line at a crusade in Pensacola, Florida, in 1957. Roberts said he felt the power of God flowing like a current through his right hand and used it as his point of contact for healing others. *Photo used by permission: © Oral Roberts Evangelistic Association, Tulsa, OK, USA*

Billy Graham, whose courtly demeanor masked a steely ambition, assiduously collected allies at the highest precincts of business and politics throughout his long evangelistic career. *Library of Congress, Prints and Photographs Division*

President Dwight Eisenhower and Billy Graham, shown in 1957, both believed that America needed a spiritual revival to triumph over "godless" communism. Eisenhower, who underwent a personal religious awakening just before becoming president, endorsed overt displays of religion while in office. *White House Albums, National Park Service (Abbie Rowe): Photographs*

Norman Vincent Peale dispensed his "positive thinking" philosophy through popular books, a weekly NBC radio program, his own magazine, and his role as pastor of a prominent church in Manhattan. He also advanced conservative causes for decades. New York World-Telegram *and the* Sun *Newspaper Photograph Collection (Library of Congress)*

The striking Crystal Cathedral in Garden Grove, California, opened in 1980 and was once one of the best-known churches in the country. After the ministry collapsed, the Roman Catholic Diocese of Orange purchased the campus. *Photo by author*

Joel Osteen's Lakewood Church meets in a sixteen-thousand-seat facility formerly used by the NBA's Houston Rockets. When Hurricane Harvey slammed the region in 2017, critics charged the church was too slow in taking in evacuees. *Julian J. Rossig/iStock photo*

Rick Warren founded Saddleback Church in 1980 and followed business management principles to foster the Southern California congregation's remarkable growth. Warren's *The Purpose Driven Life* is one of the top-selling nonfiction books in modern history. *Photo by author*

President Ronald Reagan confers with Jerry Falwell Sr. in the Oval Office in 1983. The pastor fused evangelicalism and conservative politics through the Moral Majority. Evangelicals have evolved into the Republican Party's most loyal voting bloc. *Courtesy Ronald Reagan Library*

President Donald Trump holds a Bible in front of St. John's Episcopal Church on June 1, 2020, following demonstrations in Lafayette Park near the White House. Episcopal leaders condemned Trump's photo-op while evangelicals praised it. *Official White House Photo by Shealah Craighead*

Warren received monthly stipends from several other Baptist churches, but he knew that putting "Baptist" in the name of his church would alienate unchurched people. Warren chose Saddleback Valley Community Church while staying aligned with the Southern Baptist Convention. Warren's move perturbed some lay leaders who questioned his fidelity to the denomination, but he held firm. "Few people choose a church on the basis of the denominational label. They choose the church that best ministers to their needs," he said.[113]

He synthesized all that he had learned into a letter mailed to fifteen thousand households promoting his church's first service on Easter. It began, "At last! A new church for those who've given up on traditional church services!"[114] Then it recited the four complaints from his survey and explained how his church was different. "We're a group of friendly, happy people who have discovered the joy of the Christian lifestyle," it read.[115] The letter concluded with an invitation to give the church a try for its first public service on Easter Sunday.

Some of the letters arrived early and sixty people showed up for Warren's dress rehearsal on Palm Sunday. That day, he outlined his vision for Saddleback. "It is the dream of welcoming twenty thousand members into the fellowship of our church family . . . it is the dream of at least fifty acres of land, on which will be built a regional church for south Orange County," Warren said on March 30, 1980.[116] A week later, about two hundred people gathered for Warren's Easter service at Laguna Hills High School's theater. Few of them were believers, but week after week, more people committed to Christ.

The congregation hopscotched around southern Orange County—schools, bank buildings, recreation centers, theaters—a total of seventy-nine different facilities in its first fifteen years.[117] The constant motion made it all the more imperative for Warren to sharpen his outreach methods, which he did through doctoral study at Fuller Theological Seminary, a center of church-growth teaching. Warren targeted "Saddleback Sam," an affluent baby boomer archetype similar to Willow Creek's "unchurched Harry." Sam was a college-educated, white-collar worker with a young family. Health and fitness were high priorities, but not "organized religion." Sam preferred casual dress and informal meetings. He enjoyed the laid-back Southern California lifestyle, but he was shouldering the burdens of a mortgage and credit card debt.[118]

Saddleback's "seeker-sensitive" services were designed to be nonthreatening to someone like Sam, so no arcane Christian terminology or dogma. Upbeat contemporary music created a celebratory atmosphere. There was no dress code, and Warren himself disarmingly dressed in Hawaiian shirts. He crafted his messages to be relevant to people's needs. "I consider it a compliment to be called a 'simple' preacher. I'm interested in seeing lives changed, not impressing people with my vocabulary," Warren said.[119]

Once Warren enticed Sam to attend a service, he developed ways to deepen his involvement. "Like a research and development center, we've experimented with all kinds of approaches to reaching, teaching, training, and sending out God's people," he wrote.[120] To become a Saddleback member, he required people to take a class and sign on to Saddleback's covenant. Three classes steered members into progressively more demanding levels of commitment. Saddleback's core consisted of lay ministers equipped to win others to Christ. All of this was in service to Saddleback's mission statement: "To bring people to Jesus and *membership* in his family, develop them to Christlike *maturity*, and equip them for their *ministry* in the church and life *mission* in the world, in order to *magnify* God's name."[121]

Warren keenly understood human behavior. Adults—especially men—have difficulty making friends. They yearn for meaningful relationships, but they don't know how to develop them. If a church could be the glue to bring people together, they would stay engaged. "You can't just *hope* members will make friends in the church," Warren said. "You must encourage it, plan for it, structure for it, and facilitate it."[122] Warren directed the formation of small groups around distinctive purposes: to help new parents, to run a ministry, to nurture in-depth Bible study. They connected people who might have otherwise stayed strangers. The bigger the church grew, the greater chance a newcomer could find the right fit.

One of Warren's most important mentors was Peter Drucker, a pioneer of management theory and a corporate leadership thinker. Drucker believed that "increasingly the *noncustomers* of an enterprise—whether a business, a university, a church, a hospital—are as important as the customers, if not more important." The starting point for these enterprises has to be what "customers consider value" because it is the customer who decides what a business is.[123]

He praised fast-growing megachurches for hewing to this principle. "While all the traditional denominations have steadily declined, the megachurches have exploded. They have done so because they have asked, 'What is value?' to a *nonchurchgoer*. And they have found that it is different from what churches traditionally thought they were supplying," he wrote in 1999.[124] Drucker concluded that such churches "are surely the most important social phenomenon in American society in the last thirty years."[125]

He compared it in significance to the rise of the corporation in the first half of the twentieth century.

Drucker told a story about two churches to define quality growth. The first church measured success solely by the number of new members and assumed that God would take care of their spiritual needs. The second church emphasized the spiritual life of its people and eased out newcomers who did not fully embrace it. Drucker said the second church is value-driven and thus will retain more active members than the first church.[126] Committed members lead to dedicated volunteers, which are essential to keep megachurches running.

Drucker said nonprofit organizations often lack a clear mission because they do not have a conventional "bottom line." For that reason, they have an even greater need for good management.[127] Any organization needs a leader with the communication skills to set priorities and the authority to make difficult decisions. Successful enterprises abandon projects that hinder performance and no longer produce results. Change-averse organizations that strive to "maintain yesterday" squander resources and obstruct progress, in Drucker's view.[128]

Warren governed his church according to that ideal. "The goal of a tradition-driven church is to simply perpetuate the past," Warren wrote. "Older churches tend to be bound together by rules, regulations, and rituals, while younger churches tend to be bound together by a sense of purpose and mission. . . . A church without a purpose and mission eventually becomes a museum piece of yesterday's traditions."[129] (Willow Creek's Bill Hybels also counted Drucker as an important influence, calling him "a wisdom figure for me." "He'll sometimes say to me, 'Bill, don't tell me what new things you're thinking of doing, tell me what mediocre ministries you're thinking of ending,'" he said in a *New York Times* series on megachurches in 1995.)[130]

Warren styled himself as a modern management guru, hosting training seminars for pastors as early as the 1980s and writing *The Purpose Driven Church* in 1995, a church-growth manual that sold more than a million copies. Warren founded the Purpose Driven Network, an association of thousands of churches around the world. As Saddleback's founding pastor and CEO, Warren was the undisputed decision maker. "On matters of day-to-day church governance, it was clear from the beginning that Saddleback was no democracy and that Warren had the final say," wrote Warren biographer Jeffery L. Sheler.[131]

But even Warren was at the mercy of the supercharged Southern California real estate market of the 1980s and 1990s. Warren scouted the region for parcels of land that could contain his expansive vision, but lining up financing proved to be a challenge. A few promising deals fell through. In 1987, a 118-acre parcel opened up at $3.5 million—a bargain by Orange County standards—and Warren implored members of his two-thousand-member congregation to donate on top of their tithing commitment. They fell $1 million short and time was running out to close the deal. At the eleventh hour, Warren acquaintance Maurice McAllister, chairman and founder of a savings and loan company, arranged for a loan and personally committed $250,000 for the Santiago Canyon site.[132]

Warren faced years of regulatory headaches familiar to any entrepreneur in California: Planning commission objections, environmental studies, homeowner association complaints, and byzantine permitting processes. The project stalled. Then a developer offered to swap a sixty-acre tract in Lake Forest for Saddleback's land, which had appreciated during the delay.[133] Warren agreed after receiving assurances that he would face far fewer bureaucratic hurdles. Two major thoroughfares and a planned toll road framed the site—perfect for car-centric Southern California. If people thought nothing of driving past dozens of strip malls on their way to a 150-store shopping center with a dozen restaurants, wouldn't they also be willing to drive by small churches to attend a large, full-service church?

Saddleback worshipped under a tent while its permanent buildings were under construction. Warren pushed for a Worship Center with large windows to let in abundant natural light, but had no interest in making a grand architectural statement like the Crystal Cathedral. The church hired the same architect behind the nearby John Wayne Airport to design Saddleback's utilitarian thirty-two-hundred-seat auditorium, which opened in 1995.[134] Throughout the years, Saddleback added a terrace café, administrative headquarters, a children's center, sports fields, sand volleyball courts, landscaped gardens—and, of course, acres of parking lots.

By the turn of the century, Saddleback's average attendance on weekends exceeded ten thousand, and Warren's seminars for pastors were selling out. Warren worked on the second book of his deal with Zondervan, a Christian-oriented publisher owned by HarperCollins, a subsidiary of Rupert Murdoch's News Corp. In 2002, Zondervan published *The Purpose Driven Life* with a pressrun of two hundred fifty thousand copies.[135] Warren's network of fifteen hundred pastors bought the book in bulk at heavily discounted rates and led their congregations through his "40 Days of Purpose" campaign.[136]

Warren divided the book into forty brief chapters to guide the reader on a forty-day spiritual journey. He opened the first chapter with the words, "It's not about you," then wrote, "If you want to know why you were placed on this planet, you must begin with God. You were born *by* his purpose and *for* his purpose."[137] Warren emphasized that "this is not a self-help book" because self-centeredness will never lead to life's meaning. "Life is about letting God use you for *his* purposes, not you using him for your own purpose," he wrote.[138]

The book ignited a fire in the evangelical subculture that spread to the mainstream like no other book in the modern history of publishing. *The Purpose Driven Life* sold 1.7 million copies in its first five months.[139] Warren, who never sought a radio or television ministry, was invited on national talk shows, where he presented a friendly image of evangelicalism. There were no histrionics, no gloomy prophecies, no strident condemnations, no bad hairpieces or dye jobs. He came across as a relatable guy with a goatee who put on a little too much weight in middle age. He did all of this while holding firm that the Bible was the inerrant word of God and that salvation was possible only through Jesus.

A widely reported incident in 2005 brought a wave of attention to Warren's book. Brian Nichols, a fugitive who had shot and killed four people in an Atlanta courthouse, held a young woman hostage in her apartment. The woman, Ashley Smith, read him passages of Warren's book and they discussed the book's deeper meaning. Smith made pancakes for her captor and after seven hours, Nichols let her go and peacefully turned himself over to authorities. *The Purpose Driven Life* was credited for helping to defuse a terrifying situation.

After being struck by the fact that the Bible contained two thousand verses about the poor, Warren discovered a latent passion for social justice.[140] He concluded that he had been blinded by his success and the affluence of his Orange County community. Following his wife's lead, Warren started a foundation to combat HIV/AIDS and assist orphans in Africa. "I have been so busy building my church that I have not cared about the poor," Warren said in a speech to church leaders in Rwanda. "I felt like anyone who was HIV-positive probably deserved to be ill."[141]

Warren launched a global initiative he called the PEACE Plan, which mobilized local churches to be providers of health care, literacy, and leadership training. Warren's worldwide reach earned him slots at schmooze-fests such as the World Economic Forum, Clinton Global Initiative, and Aspen Institute. The gregarious Warren relished hobnobbing with the global elite. In a 2005 *New Yorker* profile, he name-dropped General Electric's Jack Welch and Rupert Murdoch—"I'm Rupert's pastor!"—in a single anecdote.[142] He attended a U2 concert in Los Angeles at Bono's invitation, unabashedly rocking out to the band's hits and praying with the singer and activist backstage.

Warren rarely discussed partisan political issues unprompted, but just before the 2004 presidential election, he sent an email to the hundreds of thousands of pastors in his Purpose Driven Network that defined five "non-negotiable" issues for Christians: abortion, human cloning, euthanasia, gay marriage, and stem-cell research. Warren did not offer an endorsement, but he didn't need to: George W. Bush's positions were perfectly aligned with his views.[143] During the 2008 presidential campaign, Warren hosted Democrat Barack Obama and Republican John McCain in back-to-back appearances at Saddleback. Also on the ballot that November in California was Proposition 8, a constitutional amendment to ban same-sex marriage. Warren publicly backed the measure, which passed. Liberal groups were upset when Obama invited Warren to deliver the invocation at his inauguration.

The Purpose Driven Life made Warren rich as well as a celebrity. In 2006, *Forbes* magazine estimated Warren's annual earnings at $25 million, ranking below Dan Brown and J. K. Rowling among authors.[144] Total sales hit 32 million by 2012 and surpassed 50 million by 2020, making it one of the top-selling nonfiction books ever.[145] The Warrens resolved that they wouldn't let fame and fortune change them. They did not upgrade to a mansion or splurge on private planes and yachts. Warren not only stopped taking his church salary, but he reportedly paid back all of the money he earned as Saddleback's pastor. The Warrens "reverse tithed," meaning that they donated 90 percent of their income and lived off the remaining 10 percent.

Warren had long said he would step aside as Saddleback Church's senior pastor when he hit the forty-year mark in 2020, but he stayed put during the pandemic-dominated year.[146] In June 2021, Warren announced that he planned to retire as lead pastor. He has cited Peter Drucker's advice that a leader should not choose his or her successor, and there is no indication that Saddleback will stay under family control. Many evangelical ministries have suffered when strong-willed founders stay too long or fumble the handoff to the next generation. In a sense, as Warren has said, Saddleback runs itself. Some three thousand small groups are the church's unseen connective tissue and its two hundred ministries are its face to the world. Saddleback's startup ethos lives on in entrepreneurial pastors who hold services in shopping center vacancies or school auditoriums as Warren had done.

Saddleback appears well-positioned for growth, with about a dozen satellite campuses in Southern California and others sprinkled overseas. It fosters engagement through robust social media channels and online services. Before the pandemic, more than twenty thousand people attended weekend services at its main site in Lake Forest. A visit in August 2021 showed a campus in physical as well as pastoral transition. An extensive center for children was under construction and an overhaul of the Worship Center forced services outdoors. Shaded under the intense summer sun, Warren led the congregation in a PowerPoint-style presentation on "strategies for stressful times." He discussed five points to remember and five things to do in times of unwanted change, all connected to biblical passages. The congregation filled in an outline printed on leaflets with three holes punched down the side. "As your pastor, it's my job to help you through the tough times, not just the good times," he said. "Let's get really practical."[147]

9

SEED-FAITH

The Osteens, Oral Roberts, Televangelists, and the Prosperity Gospel

God wants to increase you financially, by giving you promotions, fresh ideas, and creativity.

—Joel Osteen[1]

The strongest hurricane to strike Texas in generations started as a tropical wave off the west coast of Africa. It crawled across the Atlantic and intensified into a tropical storm on August 17, 2017, receiving the name Harvey. The storm picked up steam as it churned through the warm waters of the Caribbean toward the Gulf Coast. By August 24, meteorologists upgraded Harvey to a Category 1 hurricane, defined as a storm capable of snapping trees and overturning mobile homes. On the following day, a Friday, Harvey strengthened to a Category 4—a hurricane with sustained winds of 130 miles per hour and the potential to cause catastrophic destruction— as it made landfall near Corpus Christi. It was the first Category 4 hurricane to hit the United States in thirteen years.

As the eye of the storm barreled toward Texas, authorities sent conflicting messages as to whether people should evacuate. The governor, Greg Abbott, urged residents of the nation's fourth-largest city to flee. "If I were living in the Houston region, as I once did, I would decide to head to areas north of there," he said at a news conference on that Friday.[2] Local officials, including Houston Mayor Sylvester Turner, did not issue mass voluntary or mandatory evacuation orders, reasoning it would be safest for people to stay. They wanted to avoid a repeat of Hurricane Rita in 2005, when an evacuation order gridlocked highways. "You literally cannot put 6.5 million people on the road," Turner said on Sunday. "If you think the situation right now is bad, you give an order to evacuate, you are creating a nightmare."[3]

Harvey dumped more than thirty inches of rain on much of Houston and up to fifty inches in isolated areas, overwhelming waterways and paralyzing the region. An Army Corps of Engineers official remarked that Harvey generated a volume of rain seen once in a thousand years.[4] Houstonians inundated 911 operators as they watched floodwaters swallow their vehicles and rise to their rooflines. Crews conducted thousands of search-and-rescue operations across the state to avoid the epic tragedy New Orleans suffered during Hurricane Katrina in 2005. The American Red Cross emergency shelter at the George R. Brown Convention Center in downtown Houston filled to near capacity by Monday, August 28.

Some wondered why a former NBA arena that was home to one of the largest churches in America hadn't opened its doors to evacuees. Residents claimed that Lakewood Church was in a less-flooded part of the city and pointed to other houses of worship that were helping. Social media users caricatured Lakewood's pastor, Joel Osteen, as a rich man unconcerned with the plight of Harvey's victims. On the day after the storm made landfall in Texas, Osteen tweeted, "Victoria & I are praying for everyone affected by Hurricane Harvey. Please join us as we pray for the safety of our Texas friends & family." To many, the "thoughts and prayers" message rang hollow given the scope of the crisis enveloping the city. "Joel Osteen won't open his church that holds 16,000 to hurricane victims because it only provides shelter from taxes," wrote one Twitter user in a post that went viral.[5]

Other commenters pounced on Osteen's "prosperity gospel," the controversial teaching that links Christian faith to material success. Osteen and his wife and copastor, Victoria, directed a multimedia empire producing bestselling books, a weekly TV program, and "Night of Hope" events that fill arenas nationwide. A *Houston Chronicle* series on Lakewood Church in 2018 reported that the Osteens' 17,300-square-foot mansion in the exclusive River Oaks section of Houston had an assessed value of $12 million.[6] Estimates of their personal fortune ran north of $50 million.

The online vitriol punctured Lakewood's smooth, business-like veneer. The church's associate pastor, John Gray, posted an Instagram comment on the Sunday after Harvey tore into Texas. "For the people spreading lies about my church. If WE could get there WE WOULD OPEN THE DOORS," Gray wrote. "As soon as the highways aren't flooded please know @lakewoodchurch will do all they can alleviate the pain and suffering of as many people as possible. Love y'all! #CantStandLiars."[7] Don Iloff, Osteen's brother-in-law and Lakewood's spokesman, unloaded on the detractors. "You have the haters. . . . There are people who don't like our ministry, don't like Joel, don't like Lakewood church specifically. And then there is a significant portion of the population that hates faith and religion," he said.[8]

The defensiveness heightened the criticism, with some posting photos of clear streets and loading docks to rebut the argument that the church was inaccessible. Other photos shared with news outlets showed floodwaters inside Lakewood's building and garage areas. Iloff said that the church had never closed its doors and would host the displaced once the city's other shelters were full. Finally, Lakewood announced it would start accepting anyone seeking shelter or emergency supplies on Tuesday—four days after the storm hit.

Osteen himself publicly addressed the backlash. The lithe pastor appeared on national news networks on Wednesday, August 30, to show that his church was open to all. "I think somebody created that narrative that somehow we were high and dry, and none of that is true," Osteen said on ABC's *Good Morning America* with donated clothes and baby supplies piled up behind him. "It was a safety issue, and we took people in from the very beginning."[9]

Harvey caused an estimated $125 billion in damage in Texas and Louisiana—second only to Hurricane Katrina in recent American history when adjusted for inflation—and was directly to blame for the deaths of sixty-eight people in Texas. The catastrophic flooding destroyed about forty thousand homes and wrecked a million vehicles in the Houston metro area.[10] After stumbling in the days after the storm, Lakewood found its stride. In addition to providing temporary housing for displaced victims, Lakewood partnered with Samaritan's Purse, a Christian relief organization overseen by evangelical leader Franklin Graham, to collect money for storm victims.

The tempest over Lakewood Church's response to Hurricane Harvey laid bare the skepticism of megachurches and prosperity gospel preachers. For Osteen's critics, the very notion of a wealthy preacher is incompatible with Jesus's teachings of humility and simplicity. It plays into the stereotype of televangelists as money-hungry hucksters who exploit people's faith. But for Lakewood's tens of thousands of weekly attendees and the millions of other Osteen fans, the pastor's personal financial success is something to admire. They find encouragement and hope that with God's help, they can improve their lot in life. Both sides would likely agree on at least one thing: Lakewood's size and influence are impossible to ignore.

The origins of Lakewood Church and the religious journey of the Osteen family illuminate three vital trends in evangelicalism: The emergence of charismatic Christians, the evolution of prosperity theology, and the importance of television in the spread of both. Joel Osteen's father, John, was raised in Depression-era poverty in Texas. He converted to Christianity as a teenager and picked up degrees at John Brown University in Arkansas and Northern Baptist Theological Seminary in Illinois. In his master's thesis, Osteen wrote that people have "a deeply felt need. . . . Some have spent a week of victory; some a week of defeat . . . all have another week to face; all need the voice of God for direction."[11] Osteen served a stint as a military chaplain and assistant pastor at a Baptist church in San Diego before returning to Texas for good.

Several jolts in Osteen's personal life altered his approach to ministry. Osteen's first marriage ended in divorce, threatening his career as a Baptist pastor and revival preacher. Soon after, he married a nurse named Dodie Pilgrim in 1954 at his church in Baytown just east of Houston. Their first child, Lisa, was born in 1958 with severe medical problems. "We thought her neck was broken," John Osteen wrote. "She couldn't hold up her head. She couldn't hold her arms up."[12] Doctors believed that Lisa's condition, an ailment with symptoms similar to cerebral palsy, would permanently limit her mobility and mental development.

Osteen scoured the New Testament for stories of physical healing, and the Osteens prayed for Lisa's recovery. In time, her condition improved enough to allow her to lead an active life. "It was the miracle of her healing that opened my eyes to the miracle-working power of God and the power of the Holy Spirit," he said.[13] Osteen pivoted to Pentecostalism. He received his baptism in the Holy Spirit—what evangelicals consider a divine gift of spiritual power—and spoke in tongues after reading aloud the account of Pentecost.[14] Such experiences ran against Southern Baptist teachings, and Osteen resigned as pastor of Hibbard Memorial Baptist Church in Houston in 1959. One week later, on May 10, he and dozens of others who were born-again met in a converted feed store. It was the beginning of Lakewood Baptist Church. ("Baptist" was later dropped from the name.)

Osteen plugged into the nondenominational but Pentecostal-friendly Full Gospel Business Men's Fellowship International. The organization, founded in 1952 by Oral Roberts associate Demos Shakarian, brought together business leaders and ministers. Osteen preached regularly at the group's national and regional conventions where he criticized denominational churches that believe "the day of miracles is over, tongues are a farce, prophecy has passed away, and the supernatural is gone."[15] Osteen won invaluable connections with healing evangelists such as Roberts and T. L. Osborn. Both featured Osteen in their publications and revival meetings.

The beliefs of "charismatics"—derived from the Greek word *charisma*, meaning "divine gift"—permeated evangelical congregations in the 1960s and 1970s.[16] These "signs and wonders" can include supernatural healing, speaking in tongues, and prophecy. Author Frances FitzGerald wrote that charismatic Christianity can be seen as a companion to the Jesus People: an ecstatic vision of spiritual authenticity in a time of social disorder. As Osteen often put it: "Pentecost is not a denomination, but an experience from God for everyone."[17]

Osteen's ministry, the John H. Osteen Evangelistic Association, collected donations, organized revivals, and published books and a magazine. He and his church captured national attention. A 1971 *Los Angeles Times* article on charismatics opened with Osteen in his study abruptly "speaking in mysterious sounds . . . that appears to be an unknown tongue."[18] Osteen remarked that he once unknowingly spoke in "perfect Chinese" according to a fluent speaker who witnessed it.

The reporter noted clapping, shouting, and outbreaks of speaking in tongues during Lakewood Church's services. An interpreter translated the utterances for the uninitiated. Osteen saw the hand of Satan behind social problems such as "the phenomenal increase in violence, lust, homosexuality and suicide."[19] He warned that "demonic powers have been unleashed upon our children, husbands, and wives. Homes are being wrecked. Preachers are under attack and many are failing."[20]

Oral Roberts, who had swatted at critics of his faith-healing crusades since the 1950s, was seen as the standard-bearer for charismatics. His presence at the 1966 World Congress of Evangelism in Berlin proved to be an important step into the mainstream for him and the movement. At the beginning of the conference, he felt like a pariah among the learned theologians and eminent ministers. Roberts sulked in his hotel room. When a pastor told Billy Graham about the cool reception to Roberts, Graham requested a meeting. They dined together and Graham agreed to speak at the dedication of Oral Roberts University in Tulsa the following year.

The graciousness of Graham and his allies lifted Roberts's spirits. At a panel discussion, Roberts faced pointed questions about his healing crusades. He disarmingly acknowledged that "in the early part of my ministry I made mistakes. I had to learn the hard way."[21] Graham never spoke in tongues or practiced divine healing, but accepted that they could be genuine spiritual gifts.[22] Graham warmly introduced Roberts at the main assembly, and Roberts won over the crowd with his folksy charm and earnest preaching.

Roberts threw himself into building his university and stopped his traveling crusades in 1968—the same year he left the Pentecostal Holiness denomination to be a Methodist minister. The move shocked adherents of both churches. Roberts explained it as a desire to return to the church of his youth, but the reasons ran deeper than that. His independence had long irritated leaders of his home church; the big-tent Methodists would allow him the freedom he craved. Roberts the businessman also grasped an opportunity: Millions of people in a major denomination he could expose to the charismatic movement.[23]

Next, Roberts resuscitated his television ministry. Broadcasting costs had soared since he made his TV debut in the mid-1950s, but so had the medium's influence. Nearly every American household had access to television by the late 1960s. "A whole new generation has come up not knowing God," Roberts said. "To reach them we have to go where they are, because they are not coming where we are."[24]

Roberts asked his "partner network" to defray the $3 million it would cost to produce and air four one-hour specials and a weekly series on Sundays in 1969.[25] Roberts signed up experienced producers, recorded the programs at NBC's studio in Burbank, and offered up his university's World Action Singers for entertainment. The participation of guest stars such as Mahalia Jackson and Pat Boone helped persuade stations wary of religious programming to run the specials in prime time.

About 10 million people watched the first special, triggering a deluge of mail to the ministry and applications to Oral Roberts University.[26] After broadcasting his Easter special in 1970, Roberts received 31,000 responses of which only 114 were negative.[27] Ratings ticked up into the 1970s. His spring special in 1973 boasted a viewership of nearly 38 million, spurring 760,000 letters in just one month.[28] His ministry's staff and IBM computers crafted specific replies to prayer requests, giving people the impression that they were receiving a personal communication from Roberts.[29] The hope was that they would become regular donors.

Among the few who were unhappy were old-school Pentecostals. Some complained that the young singers' skirts failed to cover their knees while others charged that Roberts had compromised his ministry by going Hollywood. Their grievances proved Roberts's point. His programs were targeted at the unconverted, not hard-core believers. "Oral Roberts is reaching more non-church people than any man in America. Because he has taken a new approach and he's not afraid of criticism of church people," said fellow televangelist Rex Humbard.[30]

Roberts disseminated a teaching he called "seed-faith," which would become a foundation of his ministry. It also inspired the "Word of Faith" movement and the "prosperity gospel"—hallmarks of charismatic Christians like Osteen and the controversial televangelists to come.

One of the colorful founders of the prosperity gospel was A. A. Allen, an ordained minister who jumped bail on a drunken driving charge in Tennessee in 1955 and was defrocked by the Assemblies of God. (Allen insisted that he resigned from the denomination before being asked to leave.)[31] The Arkansas native soldiered on as a renegade traveling preacher under his Miracle Revival Fellowship. Allen stirred up bedlam in every town he passed through. Local clergymen largely withheld their support of his "miracle revivals," deeming his claims sensational and emphasis on money unseemly. Allen's tents doubled as busy marketplaces for his books, magazines, songbooks, photographs, and pamphlets. In 1956, he bragged to a revival crowd that he sold $200,000 in books during the previous year. Still, he desperately appealed for donations. "These baskets are passed in faith. I want you to do what God wants. Give a substantial offering; write a substantial check," he urged.[32]

Allen's radio and TV ministry kept the tents full. His hardscrabble headquarters in Miracle Valley, Arizona, handled the onslaught of mail, managed the finances, dispatched a monthly magazine, ran a Bible college, and organized tour logistics for A. A. Allen Revivals, Inc. Employees churned out ad copy billing Allen as "God's man of faith and power!" who provided "miraculous deliverance from symptoms of sickness, disease, demon possession, mental illness, narcotics, etc."[33] His ads featured "before prayer" photos of people in wheelchairs or on crutches, and "after prayer" photos showed the same people healed and happy.[34] Allen, a white Southerner, promoted his services as "inter-racial" and featured the Black gospel singer Gene Martin.

Not all were pleased by Allen's flamboyance. In 1963, the Coral Gables Church of Christ placed an ad during Allen's three-week revival in Florida that condemned him as a fraud for his healing claims. "Among all the crimes of which men are guilty, there is none more despicable than that of making merchandise of human souls, which is the very lifeblood of the faith-healing racket," it charged.[35]

As he aged, Allen explicitly linked faith and wealth. "PROSPERITY! God is actually giving people power to get wealth," read one claim.[36] He taught what became known as "Word of Faith"—the idea that speaking something could make it come true. "You don't have to believe it," he told his audience, but "I believe I can command God to perform a miracle for you financially."[37] Many chose to believe him and sent in money in exchange for a "prosperity cloth" that Allen supposedly blessed.

Allen leaned into his hard-sell approach. In 1970, in Los Angeles, a young assistant spoke in tongues and preached the offering: "Brother Allen's gonna be standin' here in the middle of this ramp. In his hand he's gonna be holding pledge envelopes. They're marked $100. If you want God to make straight what he's made crooked for you, if you want God to put his blessin' on you . . . march right on up this ramp . . . bring your cash offering."[38] Allen concluded his message with an apt summary of his life and work: "And I think if I was a car salesman, I could sell more automobiles than anybody in Los Angeles. I believe it. But God hasn't called me to sell automobiles. He's called me to preach the gospel and He's callin' on you to help us. And He's gonna bless you for being obedient to His call. Raise your envelopes to heaven and let's ask God to bless you."[39]

Allen lost his battle with his own demons. A few months after making that appeal, Allen was found dead in a San Francisco hotel room. A wallet in the room contained $2,809 in cash, police said.[40] A coroner ruled that the fifty-nine-year-old preacher died of "acute alcoholism and fatty infiltration of the liver." A toxicology report found that his blood alcohol content was .36 percent, caused by consuming roughly ten drinks in an hour.[41] It is the equivalent of being under surgical anesthesia.[42]

Roberts and Allen shared similar philosophies, but Roberts possessed tighter control of his personal life. He was a lifelong devotee of exercise and required students and faculty to follow an aerobics program in the 1970s. (Oral Roberts University declares its mission to be "Educating the Whole Man: Mind, Spirit, Body.") Prospective students deemed "excessively overweight" were enrolled in weight-loss programs and signed a contract that they would stay under body-fat benchmarks.[43] More seriously, the university imposed restrictions on admitting students with disabilities. The rules alarmed federal officials, forcing the university to back off.[44]

Roberts ran his university like a one-man theocracy—"If you don't like belonging to me under God, get up and leave," he once thundered to a campus chapel gathering—but took a lighter hand with his national audience.[45] Television is a cool medium, and overheated appeals would have turned off casual viewers (and raised network objections). Instead, Roberts offered his followers a simple, powerful tool that he said could work miracles.

He outlined elements of it in the early 1950s when he was left thunderstruck by 3 John 2—"Beloved, I wish above all things that thou mayest prosper and be in health, even as thy soul prospereth." Roberts had long set up "blessing pacts" with donors, assuring them "that God will especially prosper you in your job, or your business, or your profession."[46] The Bible is full of references to sowing and reaping, and planting and harvesting—both in a tangible sense and in terms of faith. Roberts taught that if a person sows a seed in a time of loss, he or she should expect to reap a benefit as great or greater than what was lost. "It gives people hope and expectation that seed sown to God will be multiplied back in every area of life," he wrote.[47]

Roberts delved deeper into this idea in his 1970 book, *Miracle of Seed-Faith*. He believed Jesus was a seed planted by God, and that every person could become a new person through Jesus. "Jesus is God's covenant of blessing for every man. Through Jesus I can make a covenant of blessing with God. I said, 'I will call it My Blessing-Pact Covenant with God,'" he wrote.[48] The covenant was based on the faith that God is the source of all things. People needed to give in order to receive, just as planting a seed was necessary to produce a plant. "If you want God to supply your financial needs, then give SEED-MONEY for Him to reproduce and multiply," Roberts directed. By having faith and planting a seed, Roberts insisted that "something good is going to happen to you" and that people could "expect a miracle."[49]

Roberts said the concept worked wonders in his life and for other believers. He told a story about a man at a revival who said he wanted to own a home. He read about Roberts in *Abundant Life* magazine, and mailed five dollars to the Roberts ministry to enter into a "blessing pact" with God. Months passed, and nothing happened. He began to doubt. Then one day, a man stopped by, heard his story, and gave him $700. The next week, another man came by and handed him $1,110. More money followed, allowing the man to buy a $27,000 house with no debt. The audience erupted in applause after hearing the tale.[50] Roberts related other testimonials of people landing a dream job, being able to pay their bills, and finding sudden success in business. "Seed-faith" became the centerpiece of his fundraising appeals.[51]

Roberts contemporary Kenneth E. Hagin put his own spin on the teaching and called it "Word of Faith," an amalgamation of the writings of minister E. W. Kenyon and the New Thought movement that inspired Norman Vincent Peale's "positive thinking." The teaching—variously referred to as "name it and claim it" and "health and wealth"—proclaimed that "a Christian through faith could claim healing, good health, and prosperity as an undisputed right."[52] It rejected poverty and physical suffering, suggesting that those who endured such struggles lacked faith. The movement attracted substantial numbers of adherents.

Roberts attended Hagin's annual camp meeting at his Rhema Bible Training Center outside of Tulsa in 1979. Roberts's spirits and finances were low. Hagin introduced Roberts and took up a collection for him that topped $100,000 that night. Among the contributors were John Osteen and Kenneth Copeland, a Word of Faith evangelist who was formerly Roberts's pilot.[53] The gesture moved Roberts, who spoke at future camp meetings and asked Hagin and Copeland to preach at his university.

The movement's message of uplift proved to be especially attractive to African Americans. With God's favor, they were empowered to improve their station on earth as well as in heaven. One of the leading Black preachers of this message was New York's Frederick J. Eikerenkoetter II, popularly known as "Reverend Ike." In 1969, the faith-healing minister purchased an abandoned movie palace in Washington Heights and made it the headquarters of his United Church Science of Living Institute. From the red-carpeted stage, he urged members of his large congregation to close their eyes and visualize incredible riches. "Money up to your armpits, a roomful of money and there you are, just tossing around in it like a swimming pool," he said.[54]

By the mid-1970s, Reverend Ike was spreading his gospel of prosperity and mind power over nearly two thousand radio stations and in major TV markets. "I am the first black man in America to preach positive self-image psychology to the black masses within a church setting," he boasted in 1975.[55] Reverend Ike condemned social welfare programs for keeping people locked in a mentality of victimhood and in a permanent state of subservience to government. His "Science of Living" doctrine taught that God dwelled within each person, so that power could be used to fulfill any personal need or desire. Abundance was there for the taking, and he grabbed plenty for himself, indulging in flashy jewelry and fashionable suits. "My garages runneth over," the multimillionaire once said, referencing his taste for fancy cars.[56] "I ask you not to put change in our envelopes," he told his congregation as the offering buckets were passed around. "Change makes your minister nervous in the service."[57]

On the other coast, Fred Price pastored a predominantly Black church in the Los Angeles area and directed a TV and radio ministry. Price steered hefty checks toward Roberts and his projects, and Roberts welcomed him to preach on campus in 1980. The charismatic minister outlined his faith philosophy: "I've been down and I've been up, and up is better. . . . If you want to be sick, fine, that's your right to be sick, if you want to. . . . You just be the sick part of the family and I'll be the well."[58] Students were receptive to his presentation, but one professor in the audience shouted, "No!" Roberts chastised the dissenter and demanded an apology. Roberts invited Price back, overriding objectors.

Roberts confessed that he did not fully understand the "faith formula" teachings of people like Price and Hagin, but he sympathized with them as a fellow evangelical entrepreneur.[59] They too had built popular ministries from nothing and deserved the chance to be heard. Even eccentric televangelists like Jim and Tammy Faye Bakker received support from Roberts. "I know Jim Bakker. I know that he loves Jesus and Tammy loves Jesus. . . . It matters not if he's not perfect. . . . I'm flawed and everybody is flawed," Roberts said in 1981, well before the Bakkers were consumed by scandal.[60]

Roberts's ambitious projects stretched even his prodigious fundraising abilities. He pushed for a $250 million City of Faith Medical and Research Center adjacent to his university. Detractors said the complex was unnecessary and blanched at the notion of merging prayer and medicine. In 1980, Roberts sent a fundraising letter to his partners revealing his vision of a nine-hundred-foot-tall Jesus that directed him to finish the City of Faith. Roberts said his partners needed to give "a precious seed this week" to help complete the project.[61] City of Faith opened the following year.

The complex's three triangular towers—a sixty-story medical center, a thirty-story hospital, and a twenty-story research facility—were absurdly out of scale with the rest of the modest city on the rolling Oklahoma plains. An architectural grace note was a sixty-foot-high bronze sculpture of a pair of praying hands at the entrance of the City of Faith. One of the hands was based on a casting of Oral's hand, the other from his son, Richard. They are visible when flying over Tulsa.[62]

City of Faith resembled a Potemkin village: Gleaming buildings on the outside masking the mostly vacant hospital beds and unfinished floors on the inside. Costs spiraled out of control and threatened to sink Roberts's sputtering ministry. His fundraising appeals cast him in the role of a warrior fighting the forces of Satan. Partners received vials of healing oil and prayer cloths that he said had brought miracles to millions. In 1983, the ministry mailed paper napkins printed with outlines of Roberts' hands and the words, "I anoint you, in Jesus' name with my hands. Be healed! Prosper in all your needs being met. . . . Your partner, Oral Roberts."[63] In response to Roberts's methods, leading Tulsa businessman and Roberts confidant John

Williams said, "The endorsement that I gave him was that while he may be a charlatan, he is our charlatan."[64]

City of Faith continued to hemorrhage money, and Roberts turned to an act of desperation. On January 4, 1987, he revealed to his nationwide TV audience that the Lord told him he needed to raise $8 million by March 31 or else "God could call Oral Roberts home." Roberts asked viewers to send in "quick money" to fund scholarships for medical missionaries. He suggested hundred-dollar donations. "I'm asking you to help me extend my life," the aging preacher said through tears.[65]

Critics throughout the country slammed the maudlin plea, but the cash and pledges flowed in. His ministry's TV programs turned into grim telethons, counting down the days until the March 31 deadline. Roberts dialed up the dramatics, saying on his March 22 program that he would not come down from his campus's golden-mirrored Prayer Tower until he reached his $8 million goal. "I've never been this persecuted in four decades. Now I want the hundred-fold return. And I intend to get it," he said from his prayer room in the Space Age tower.[66] He exceeded his goal. "It's April, and I'm alive!" Roberts exulted during his televised "victory report" on April 1.[67] The gambit only delayed the inevitable; City of Faith closed in 1989 and is now used as commercial office space.

Roberts's ministry was fighting for its financial life, but he and his family were not. He lived in a spacious "president's cottage" and his son and heir apparent, Richard, had recently moved into a seven-thousand-square-foot residence on the Tulsa compound.[68] Oral and Evelyn Roberts had a home in Palm Springs and a $2.4 million house in Beverly Hills paid for by university endowment funds in 1982.[69]

Roberts had long been a member of Tulsa's business elite, so it stood to reason he would live like them. Roberts sat on the boards of the National Bank of Tulsa and the Oklahoma Natural Gas Company. He honed his golf game at the prestigious Southern Hills Country Club where he palled around with the Chamber of Commerce set. Roberts's stature allowed him to cut through bureaucratic hurdles and secure the large loans he needed to build the university.[70]

Roberts welcomed captains of industry like Amway cofounder Richard DeVos to campus and showered them with honorary degrees. "He exemplifies a Christian who's operating under a free enterprise system that permits a person who dreams dreams to start with virtually nothing and build," Roberts said of DeVos. "I'm a public enterprise man myself and I'm pretty tired of all the knocks it's getting in the world and the business world is getting."[71] (The DeVos family is among the richest in America and is a major donor to evangelical and conservative causes. Among the family's members is Betsy DeVos, the Trump-era secretary of education.)

Despite Roberts's dubious claims of healing and high-pressure fund-raising appeals, he never faced credible accusations of malfeasance or personal misconduct.[72] (Roberts died in 2009 at ninety-one.) The same could not be said of other televangelists. The most notorious scandal involved the Bakkers, hosts of *The PTL Club* (for "Praise the Lord" or "People That Love") and developers of the Heritage USA amusement park near Charlotte, North Carolina. The Bakkers were a made-for-TV spectacle. Tammy Faye's over-the-top makeup and high-strung emotionalism were godsends for late-night comedians. Jim's shameless appeals for money were based on Roberts's seed-faith teaching.[73] Their odd, up-and-down marriage resembled a long-running soap opera. The Bakkers flaunted their lavish lifestyle in keeping with the go-go 1980s. They boasted flashy residences with gold-plated bathroom fixtures and even an air-conditioned doghouse.[74]

In 1987, the *Charlotte Observer* reported that Jim Bakker had a sexual encounter with church secretary Jessica Hahn in 1980 and used PTL funds to buy her silence.[75] Hahn claimed that she was drugged and raped. Televangelist and fellow Assemblies of God minister Jimmy Swaggart amplified the accusations and condemned Bakker, who resigned and was defrocked. Bakker temporarily ceded control of his South Carolina–based ministry to televangelist Jerry Falwell even though they didn't know each other well. (In an unintentionally humorous fundraising gambit, Falwell gamely plunged down Heritage USA's giant water slide while dressed in his dark preacher's suit.)

Investigative reports revealed that the PTL ministry lacked any semblance of financial accountability. For years, the Bakkers had tapped PTL funds for excessive bonuses and personal expenses, records showed. The most egregious example of mismanagement was PTL's "lifetime partnership" plan. Donors who paid at least $1,000 received a lifetime guarantee of free annual lodging at Heritage USA. But there were far more memberships sold than advertised and too few available hotel rooms. Much of the $158 million raised between 1984 and 1987 covered debts, paid operating expenses, or went directly into the couple's pockets.[76] With the PTL ministry in bankruptcy, the partnerships were worthless.

Jim Bakker accused Falwell of scheming to seize permanent control of PTL just to shut down a competitor. Falwell responded with a blustery news conference to add lurid details to Hahn's allegation and air accusations from Bakker's associates that he had a history of making "homosexual advances." The PTL ministry dissolved, Jim Bakker was convicted on fraud and conspiracy charges, for which he served nearly five years in prison, and Jim and Tammy Faye divorced. Tammy Faye died in 2007, and Jim Bakker resurfaced as a purveyor of end-time "emergency food buckets" and bizarre conspiracy theories.

Jimmy Swaggart had his own problems. In 1986, he had accused fellow Louisiana preacher Marvin Gorman of adultery, running him out of his ministry. Gorman retaliated by orchestrating a motel stakeout to capture evidence of Swaggart's dalliance with a prostitute. When the story leaked, a tearful Swaggart went before TV cameras and delivered his famous "I have sinned against you, my Lord" confession in 1988. The Assemblies of God defrocked him. In 1991, police pulled over Swaggart in the California desert for driving erratically. His female passenger told reporters that she was a prostitute and claimed Swaggart had asked her to have sex. This time, Swaggart responded with a clipped "none of your business" instead of an emotional apology. Swaggart bounced back as an independent evangelist.

Bakker and Swaggart, now in their eighties, have something else in common besides being defrocked: Both received federal Paycheck Protection Program loans in 2020. The pandemic aid program issued between $2 million and $5 million to Swaggart's Family Worship Center in Louisiana and between $350,000 and $1 million to Bakker's Morningside Church Productions in Missouri.[77]

Bakker received the loans despite receiving a warning letter from the Food and Drug Administration for selling unauthorized products that claim to treat or prevent COVID-19. Missouri's attorney general followed up with a lawsuit against Bakker, claiming he was lying to consumers. Bakker, fearing a return to bankruptcy, turned to his audience and issued a familiar plea: "We're asking people to give an offering, and we need a miracle."[78]

The televangelist scandals of the 1980s damaged the reputations of all television ministries. Viewership and donations took major hits, even for morally upright preachers, like John Osteen, who had a congregation to lean on. Osteen stayed connected to the charismatic community by teaching classes at Hagin's Rhema Bible Training Center and appearing at a Copeland "victory crusade."[79]

Osteen believed in the Word of Faith tenet of "positive confession," which meant finding Bible passages relevant to a person's needs and verbally repeating them. Through that act, miracles could happen. Osteen's wife, Dodie, received a diagnosis of metastatic liver cancer in 1981. She was told she had only weeks to live. The Osteens prayed for divine healing as they had done for their young daughter. Soon thereafter, doctors declared

Dodie to be free of cancer. "I know I would have died if it had not been for the Bible," Dodie wrote in her book *Healed of Cancer.* "I clung to my Bible and its healing promises."[80] She has been a cornerstone of Lakewood's ministry for decades.

John and Dodie Osteen's youngest son, Joel, enrolled at Oral Roberts University but dropped out after a year to help his father launch a TV ministry in 1982. Unlike his father, Joel would never go to seminary or partake in systematic study of scripture. Joel's religious education would be to serve as an apprentice to his father. Week after week, he filmed his father's sermons and edited them into thirty-minute programs.[81] John was in his sixties when his TV ministry began, but he was still physically fit and a lively preacher. Multiple television cameras panned over the cavernous, multiracial church while Osteen told tales of healing and battles with Satan. Osteen learned to alternate between preaching to the congregation and smoothly turning to a nearby camera to address the TV audience.

Starting in the 1980s, John Osteen instructed members of his congregation to hold up their Bibles and declare: "This is my Bible. I am what it says I am. I have what it says I have. I can do what it says I can do. Today I will be taught the Word of God. I boldly confess: My mind is alert, my heart is receptive. I will never be the same. I am about to receive the incorruptible, indestructible, ever-living, seed of the Word of God. I will never be the same. Never, never, never. I will never be the same in Jesus' name. Amen."[82] It became a Lakewood Church tradition.

With John Osteen in the pulpit and Joel Osteen in the control room, Lakewood Church's growth surged in the 1980s. The church, dubbed the "Oasis of Love" on billboards around Houston, opened an 8,200-seat facility in 1988, followed by a children's center serving 2,500 children each week and the 62,000-square-foot Family Life Center.[83]

Slowed by health problems, John Osteen asked Joel to preach for him in January 1999. Joel had resisted his previous requests, but accepted this time. With his father following along from his hospital bed, Joel preached his first-ever sermon. Joel was thirty-five but seemed much younger. He rocked a mullet, donned a suit that looked a size too big, and wore a pair of his father's shoes. Osteen overcame his nervousness and delivered a message shot through with homey family references. Five days later, John Osteen died of a heart attack at seventy-seven.

At Osteen's memorial service at Lakewood on January 27, 1999, Joel spoke about their close relationship. "I knew from a little boy he wanted me to preach, but I always told him, 'Daddy, you're the preacher. Who can preach any better than you? You preach, I'll do the television, I'll make you look good,'" Osteen said with his family members arrayed behind him.[84]

Joel emerged as the consensus choice to lead Lakewood. After all, he had been there for seventeen years in an influential behind-the-scenes role. As pastor, Joel Osteen honored his father's vision while charting his own path. Joel kept the church nondenominational but his uplifting messages leaned closer to Norman Vincent Peale than his father. "I realized I wasn't like my father. He was more of a traditional pastor. I'm more of an encourager," Osteen said.[85]

Soon after taking over as senior pastor, Osteen hired church marketing expert Duncan Dodds to negotiate contracts with TV stations. Dodds, who had handled media for Houston's giant Second Baptist Church, bought airtime in all of the top markets to extend the Lakewood brand.[86] (Lawyers trademarked the names Lakewood Church and Joel Osteen.)[87] Osteen wanted top-notch music and hired contemporary Christian singer-songwriter Cindy Cruse Ratcliff as worship director. Osteen also placed family members and in-laws in key roles.

Osteen realized Lakewood needed more space to fit his ambitions. In 2001, he jumped at the chance to move into an arena being vacated by the NBA's Houston Rockets. After a vigorous lobbying effort and much legal wrangling, Lakewood secured a $12 million deal in 2003 to lease the city-owned Compaq Center for thirty years with an option for an additional thirty years.[88] Lakewood spent $95 million on renovations of the facility for its 2005 opening. The church later took out $20 million in loans to cover cost overruns.[89]

Lakewood Church's weekend attendance surpassed fifty thousand, making it by some measures the country's largest church. A three-part *Houston Chronicle* series in 2018 revealed that Lakewood Church took in $89 million during the fiscal year that ended on March 31, 2017, nearly all of it in donations. (Lakewood expects its tens of thousands of members to tithe 10 percent.) Seventy percent of the budget went to TV broadcasts, weekly services, and the "Night of Hope" events. Only $1.2 million was spent on missions and community service.[90]

Osteen and his wife and copastor, Victoria, reportedly stopped taking church salaries in 2005 and instead live off their ample book royalties. His first book, *Your Best Life Now: 7 Steps to Living at Your Full Potential*, published in 2004, sold millions of copies. More books—and a full range of merchandise such as DVDs and devotionals—followed. Osteen's sermons at Lakewood attract about 10 million TV viewers each week. Joel and Victoria Osteen are ubiquitous presences on social media with tens of millions of followers on Twitter, Facebook, YouTube, and Instagram.

What is the message that people receive from the telegenic pastor with the perpetual smile? Osteen views life experiences through the prisms of victory and defeat, excellence and mediocrity, victor and victim. With God all things are possible, as scripture teaches, but he wrote "you must believe first, and then you'll receive."[91] Osteen says people too often set their standards too low and are content to barely get by. For instance, Osteen says his father once had a poverty mentality but learned that "as God's children, we are able to live an abundant life, that it is okay to prosper; that we should even expect to be blessed."[92]

In *Your Best Life Now*, Osteen told a story about walking through their neighborhood with his newlywed wife and coming upon "a fabulous home, much prettier than any of the other homes in the community." Victoria remarked that they would live in a home like that one day, but Joel doubted that they could ever afford it. Victoria's persistence convinced Joel that it was possible. "We kept on believing it, seeing it, and speaking it," Joel wrote, allusions to his father's "positive confession" and Peale's "mind power." Years later, the Osteens moved into a mansion. "God has so much more in store for you, too. . . . Start seeing yourself rising to a new level, doing something of significance, living in that home of your dreams."[93]

Osteen said people facing challenges should rest assured that God has a plan for them. If you get laid off, don't be bitter but trust that God will open up a better path. "If you want to prosper in your finances, put God first. If you want to prosper in your business, put God first. When you honor God, God will always honor you," Osteen wrote.[94] He does not explicitly ask for money in exchange for God's favor on his television program, but he doesn't need to. "If you want to reap financial blessings, you must sow financial seeds in the lives of others," Osteen wrote, echoing Oral Roberts's "seed-faith" teaching. "In the time of need, sow a seed."[95]

Osteen's critics complained that his guilt-free, feel-good messages reduce God to a fulfillment center for personal needs. The mysteries of faith and reflections on traditional Christian themes of sin, sacrifice, or repentance are sidelined in favor of self-help platitudes: "Don't let your past determine your future," "You can't be everything to everybody," and "Find strength through adversity." "Osteen's God . . . seems less like a savior than like a college buddy with really good stock tips, which are more or less guaranteed to pay off for any Christian bold enough to act on them," wrote author and columnist Ross Douthat.[96]

The emphasis on money raised questions about the propriety of religion-based tax breaks. One of the most significant is the "parsonage exemption," a federal tax deduction for ministers' housing expenses. In 1996, the Internal Revenue Service said Rick Warren's annual housing deductions exceeded the "fair market rental value" of his Orange County home.[97] The Saddleback pastor sued and a tax court ruled that clergy members could deduct any amount used to provide a home. The IRS appealed to a federal court. Legal experts charged that such special tax breaks were an unconstitutional government subsidy for religion. Congress defused the issue by passing the Clergy Housing Clarification Act of 2002. It affirmed previous unlimited deductions like Warren's but imposed the "fair market rental value" cap on future claims. (A *Houston Chronicle* report said that the Osteens did not declare their $12 million Houston mansion a parsonage and paid $247,000 in property taxes in 2017.)[98]

Warren, who has condemned the prosperity gospel as a "heresy," said he fought the battle on behalf of pastors of small churches who rely on the exemption to survive.[99] But wealthy religious figures have also taken advantage of the tax break. Televangelist Kenneth Copeland operates a compound in Newark, Texas, that consists of Kenneth Copeland Ministries offices, Eagle Mountain International Church, a private airport, and a lakeside mansion. The church owns the 18,279-square-foot home appraised at nearly $11 million, according to a 2020 report by the Trinity Foundation watchdog group.[100] The mansion has been designated a church parsonage, which makes Copeland's annual housing allowance about $1.3 million when fair rental value is applied, the group estimated. The federally tax-exempt church owns the entire complex, which is not subject to local property taxes.[101] Another federal benefit, the Religious Land Use and Institutionalized Persons Act, gives churches broad freedom to expand or change sites even where there are zoning restrictions.[102]

News reports of televangelists flying in private jets and owning expensive properties raised flags in Congress. In 2007, Charles Grassley, a Republican senator from Iowa, opened an investigation into six media-based ministries: Kenneth and Gloria Copeland of Kenneth Copeland Ministries; Creflo and Taffi Dollar of World Changers Church International; Randy and Paula White of Without Walls International Church; Bishop Eddie Long of New Birth Missionary Baptist Church; Joyce Meyer of Joyce Meyer Ministries; and Benny Hinn of World Healing Center Church. "Jesus comes into the city on a simple mule, and you got people today expanding his gospel in corporate jets. Somebody ought to raise questions about is it right or wrong," Grassley told the *New York Times*.[103]

Grassley, who was then the ranking member of the Senate Finance Committee, requested detailed information from the ministries to determine if their expenditures ran afoul of their tax-exempt status. The ministries headed by Meyer and Hinn cooperated and promised to reform, but the others provided only partial information or refused to cooperate on the grounds that the inquiries were intrusive and violated their religious freedom. Senate staffers said "almost all of those who spoke with us insisted on complete anonymity while others were too frightened to speak with us even anonymously."[104] Potential informants worried about retaliation from the ministries if they cooperated. Investigators concluded that they didn't have the time or resources to issue and enforce subpoenas.

A final report released in January 2011 showed no evidence of wrongdoing by any of the ministries and recommended no legislative remedies. But Grassley's staffers raised general concerns. "This lack of governmental, independent or denominational oversight is troubling when considering that churches can reach the size of large taxable corporations, control numerous taxable and non-taxable subsidiaries, and bestow Wall Street–size benefits on their ministers," the staff memo said.[105] They received financial statements showing how ministries dissolved charitable organizations into a church to avoid having to file IRS Form 990 required for other nonprofit groups. The report detailed the existence of business entities affiliated with church ministries. For example, at least twenty-one assumed names registered with the state of Texas were related to Kenneth Copeland Ministries. These included non-church enterprises such as music recording companies. "This raises the question of whether church status is being gamed to shield such activities of a tax-exempt entity from public scrutiny," the memo concluded.[106]

That question still hangs in the air today. Unlike other nonprofit groups or charities, churches are not required to file annual disclosures to the IRS. Congress has no appetite to force greater transparency and seems content to let churches police themselves. Grassley recommended that the Evangelical Council for Financial Accountability form a commission to follow up on the Senate report. Members of the council, founded by Billy Graham and others in 1979, appoint independent boards and release financial documents. But churches like Lakewood are ineligible to join because the Osteen family controls the board.[107] Many evangelical churches are husband-and-wife operations that include their children and in-laws in leadership roles. The lines between the family and the church are blurred or nonexistent.

Prosperity-gospel preachers, never shy about flaunting their worldly goods, seemed emboldened knowing that they faced essentially no risk of oversight. In 2015, Creflo Dollar asked for donations to replace his Lear jet with a $65 million Gulfstream G650. The appeal provoked a backlash, and his ministry's board dropped the campaign and purchased the plane. "A long-range, high-speed, intercontinental jet aircraft is a tool that is necessary in order to fulfill the mission of the ministry," the board said in a statement in June 2015.[108]

On an episode of HBO's *Last Week Tonight* in 2015, comedian John Oliver skewered figures like Dollar and Copeland. Oliver sent a twenty-dollar donation to Word of Faith televangelist Robert Tilton and asked to be added to his mailing list. That sparked a correspondence in which Oliver mailed additional payments in exchange for packets of miracle oil, prayer cloths, and promises of blessings. Oliver sent a total of $319 and received twenty-six letters over seven months. It inspired Oliver to set up his own church called Our Lady of Perpetual Exemption. The process showed how easy it was to exploit IRS loopholes to found a phony tax-exempt religious organization. Oliver jokingly asked viewers to call a toll-free number to "sow your seed and ye may prosper."[109] (Any donations were sent to Doctors without Borders and the "church" has since been shut down.)

Copeland is among the oldest, wealthiest, and most aggressive televangelists. Like many prosperity preachers, he reached a national audience through the Trinity Broadcasting Network, founded by Jan and Paul Crouch in 1973. Copeland showcased his "good ole boy" charm on his show, *Believer's Voice of Victory*. He said being saved "instantaneously changed my thinking from that of a poor, in-debt, can't-do anything-right, complete and total failure in life to a wealthy man."[110] Believers who have "the blessing" will have dominion over their money and their health, Copeland said.[111]

Copeland's followers fund his high-flying lifestyle. In 2004, the ministry asked for donations to buy a Cessna Citation X jet valued at $20 million. "When God tells Kenneth to travel to South Africa and hold a three-day Victory Campaign, he won't have to wait to make commercial travel arrangements," his website said. "He can just climb aboard his Citation X and go!"[112] The jet also frequently found its way to Copeland's second home in Colorado and exotic vacation spots like Hawaii and Fiji.[113]

Copeland's ministry took possession of a "debt-free" Gulfstream V jet that it purchased in cash for an undisclosed amount from the actor-producer Tyler Perry in 2018. The luxurious aircraft seats fourteen passengers and used models sell for $12 million and up.[114] "Father, we thank you so. And

I'm asking you now, sir, according to your word, bless our partners beyond measure," Copeland theatrically prayed on the tarmac with his gleaming plane behind him. "For you said in 2002, I'm sending you new partners who are very strong financially and they will obey me. And I will increase your longtime partners and they will obey me. And you will not come short, and you will not fail, and you will not lack, and you will not come behind, and you will not be diminished. Praise God! Isn't that good?"[115]

In a video that went viral in 2019, *Inside Edition* correspondent Lisa Guerrero confronted Copeland about his opulent lifestyle. Copeland re-acted to the questions with dramatic biblical quotations and flashes of anger. He loomed over her while getting into a large black SUV at an aircraft hangar and patronizingly called her "sweetheart" and "baby." Guerrero brought up Copeland's recent statement that he didn't want to fly com-mercial because he would have to "get into a long tube with a bunch of demons." Copeland said he wasn't referring to people, adding that the jet was necessary to fulfill his worldwide duties. Guerrero asked him what he thought of critics who say preachers should not live a life of luxury. "They're wrong," he said flatly.[116]

Younger "pastorpreneurs" fluently speak the language of celebrity and materialism. John Gray, formerly an associate pastor at Lakewood Church, became lead pastor at Relentless Church in Greenville, South Carolina, in 2018. Soon after, he bought a $200,000 Lamborghini Urus SUV as an an-niversary gift for his copastor wife, Aventer. Gray told his congregation that he paid for it from his outside income as an author and TV producer. He received a standing ovation when he professed his love for his wife. The church did pay for his $1.8 million home in a gated community.[117] The 7,247-square-foot mansion is classified as a parsonage. "With anything, it's about offering and attracting a senior pastor of Pastor John's caliber with his presence on the world stage," said Travis Hayes, chief financial officer for Relentless.[118]

The Instagram account PreachersNSneakers showcases photos of pas-tors wearing designer clothes (such as Gray in a $1,145 Givenchy sweat-shirt) and footwear (many Yeezys and Air Jordans). These business-savvy pastors know the power of desirable brands. Making them part of their everyday wardrobe is a selling point, not something to hide or be ashamed of.[119] Zoe Church founder Chad Veach, who makes regular appearances on PreachersNSneakers, said the Los Angeles–based church's online pop-up shop sold $10,000 in merchandise in one hour. There's no need for the traditional collection plate because church members can easily tithe with the Pushpay app on their smartphones. "Zoe" (pronounced "zoh-AY" as in

"Be-yon-SAY," as the celebrity-friendly Veach points out) means "abundant life" in Greek, an expression popularized by Oral Roberts.[120]

Whether one calls it Word of Faith, the prosperity gospel, or seed-faith—they all play into the American spirit of optimism. These ministries promise that people have the power to improve their health and financial status directly through God. Even the downtrodden can change their destinies through this faith. Dynamic preachers point to their own stories of upward mobility as compelling examples. But their many critics charge that they exploit the vulnerable by telling people what they want to hear. Their followers keep contributing, faithful that the investment will someday pay off. Meanwhile, the wealthy receive reassurance that their prosperity is divinely ordained.

These attitudes play into the evangelical hallmarks of individualism and free-market capitalism. If a person can improve his or her lot through a personal relationship with God, what need is there for government-run social programs? Followers of media-based ministries consume their messages in the privacy of their homes and some never set foot in a physical church. Many evangelical entrepreneurs and their acolytes are hostile to government intrusion except on their terms and on the issues they care about. Their alignment with the Republican Party reshaped American politics.

10

CULTURE CLASH

Jerry Falwell, Ronald Reagan, and the Rise of Evangelical Political Activism

Preachers are not called to be politicians but to be soul winners.

—Jerry Falwell, 1965

I have become convinced of the need to have a coalition of God-fearing, moral Americans to represent our convictions to government.

—Jerry Falwell, 1980[1]

Evangelicals have harbored politically conservative beliefs for well over a century. They denounced the Social Gospel movement in liberal churches in the late nineteenth century, opposed the New Deal programs of the 1930s, and partnered with Republican Dwight Eisenhower to bring religion more fully into the public square in the 1950s. They have consistently sided with business over labor and favored free-market ideals over public welfare. Evangelicals from Billy Sunday and his flag-waving during World War I to Billy Graham and his broadsides against "godless" communists linked their brawny interpretation of Christianity with patriotism.

But it was the "rights" movements for gay people, women, and Blacks that lit the fuse for the evangelical shift to partisan engagement. Liberal court rulings and the social upheavals of the 1960s and 1970s undermined what evangelicals understood to be America's Christian-based values. The rights of vulnerable minorities had been secured at their expense, they believed. The spirit of sexual freedom sweeping through the culture destabilized their concept of the family. These were assaults on *their* rights. Who would fight for them?

The nation's economy was transforming, too. The Northeast and Midwest were shedding the high-wage manufacturing jobs that sustained the postwar middle class. Foreign competition increased and high inflation eroded buying power. Evangelicals—particularly white heterosexual Christian men whose dominance had been unquestioned since America's founding—felt a loss of control. They believed their country's very soul was at stake.

One of the people who fought hardest to save it was an ambitious pastor from rural Virginia named Jerry Falwell. He shared many traits of other evangelical entrepreneurs: He did not feel bound to denominational strictures, he built a large church from nothing, and he managed a broadcasting empire. Falwell was also a political entrepreneur. He founded an organization, the Moral Majority, that explicitly promoted conservative policies and candidates. Its ascent ran parallel to the rise of the right and Ronald Reagan. The Republican Party and the country have not been the same since.

Jerry Falwell and his twin brother, Gene, were born on August 11, 1933, in Lynchburg, Virginia, then a segregated city along the James River at the foothills of the Blue Ridge Mountains. Their mother, Helen, was a devout Baptist but their father, Carey, was a nonbeliever who profited from both legitimate and illicit businesses. The budding entrepreneur opened a grocery store and later owned a string of service stations, an inn, and bus lines. Carey and his brother, Garland, used oil and gas trucks and even passenger buses to distribute bootlegged liquor. The brothers also sponsored illegal cockfights and dogfights inside a barn on Falwell family property.[2]

Carey drank heavily, especially after his young daughter died in 1931, from a burst appendix. Later that year, Carey shot and killed his brother in an act that authorities judged to be in self-defense. Carey kept busy through the Great Depression, building the Merry Garden dance hall and restaurant with panoramic views of the Blue Ridge Mountains. Big-band acts such as Tommy Dorsey played for up to a thousand patrons who dined and danced into the night.[3]

In his 1987 autobiography, Jerry Falwell related examples of his father's casual cruelty. Falwell said he had a childhood friend who feared Carey's gun-toting reputation. The boys entered the house while Carey read the paper at the kitchen table. Suddenly, he ordered the boys to freeze and aimed his .38 Remington pistol near the visitor's feet and fired. He blew smoke from the pistol and calmly said, "I've been trying to get that fly all day. And finally I got it."[4] Once, Carey got annoyed with a complaining worker who called in sick. He decided to get even and offered to bring the worker a home-cooked lunch. Carey and his friends then caught and killed the worker's tomcat and served it to him as "squirrel stew." Another time, he threw a drunken customer into a cage where he kept a bear.[5]

Carey's alcoholism worsened and his small-town business empire dissipated. He made his religious confession days before dying of cirrhosis of the liver in 1948 when Jerry was just fifteen. Jerry inherited his father's mean streak. He despised his physical education teacher and his "prissy" ways. After witnessing the teacher humiliate a student, Jerry and two other boys wrestled the teacher into a storage room, pulled off the teacher's pants, and tossed him into a bin of basketballs. Jerry pinned up the pants with a note on the school's bulletin board. The boys were called before the principal, who couldn't make it through his lecture without doubling over in laughter.[6] The pranks kept coming. Jerry put a live rat in a Latin teacher's snack drawer and locked his math teacher in a closet so his class could avoid taking a pop quiz.[7] The main punishment for his misadventures was that Jerry was barred from giving his valedictorian address at graduation.

In 1950, he enrolled at Lynchburg College with an eye to being a mechanical engineer. Students were obligated to take courses in the Bible and theology, which made little impression on Falwell. He had stopped attending church despite his mother's pleas. Like millions of Americans, she tuned into fundamentalist preacher Charles E. Fuller's *The Old Fashioned Revival Hour* radio program every week. One Sunday in 1952, Fuller's message moved Falwell in an unusual way. "That morning, I felt Him there but didn't know what I was feeling. He was calling me, but I didn't recognize His voice," Falwell wrote.[8] Falwell and a few friends attended a service that night at Park Avenue Baptist Church where he responded to an altar call. (One of the piano players was Macel Pate, whom Falwell would marry in 1958.)

At eighteen, the born-again Falwell committed to full-time Christian service and transferred to Baptist Bible College, then an unaccredited school in Springfield, Missouri. Falwell received his theology degree with valedictorian honors in 1956. Falwell returned to Lynchburg where his home church was in disarray. Thirty-five members, including Macel and her family, asked Park Avenue's pastor to resign. He refused, and the dissenters pledged to form a new church. They asked Falwell to be their founding pastor. He anguished over the offer and finally agreed. The decision threatened to end his pastoral career before it began. Falwell's denomination, the Bible Baptist Fellowship, excommunicated him. No students from the new church would be accepted at Baptist Bible College, and no one from the school would be permitted to help Falwell's ministry.[9]

Falwell scouted around Lynchburg for a building to house his little congregation. For $300 a month, he rented the abandoned Donald Duck Bottling Company building on Thomas Road in an undeveloped part of the city. Volunteers scrubbed sticky soda syrup off the floors and walls and brought in an upright piano and old theater seats. In July 1956, the preacher conducted the first service at Thomas Road Baptist Church's new location.

Falwell was obsessed with growing his church, likening himself to Eisenhower plotting D-Day. Falwell tacked up a map of Lynchburg and marked his church with a black dot. He put a compass on the dot and drew a radius covering ten blocks and traced it with a black pen, calling it Jerusalem. A twenty-block circle was Judea, a thirty-block radius was Samaria, and the rest of Lynchburg and beyond was "the uttermost part of the earth" as Jesus described it.[10]

Falwell committed to visiting a hundred homes every day, except for Sundays, starting with the smallest circle. The earnest preacher told his neighbors about his new congregation, saying that he added services on Sunday nights to avoid conflicts with other churches. Falwell left behind his card and encouraged people to call whenever they needed spiritual counsel. He assembled lists of names and addresses for follow-up calls and newsletter mailings. Falwell trained others to do door-to-door canvassing as the map's circles expanded. The church's attendance surged.

The next front in Falwell's plan of conquest was broadcasting. The owner of a small radio station let Falwell host a thirty-minute program every morning from the studio. The cost: Seven dollars per broadcast. In December 1956, he walked into Lynchburg's tiny ABC affiliate and signed a contract for a weekly thirty-minute slot for ninety dollars. In his first TV appearance, Falwell promoted the church and asked viewers to come to a service later that night. When Falwell returned to Thomas Road, he found the sanctuary packed with people. "Television made me a kind of instant celebrity," Falwell said.[11]

By the time Thomas Road approached its first anniversary, church volunteers had visited most of the homes in Lynchburg. The publicity from Falwell's TV and radio shows, which he called *The Old Time Gospel Hour* in tribute to Fuller, put pressure on the church to add space. Falwell leveraged his father's old business contacts to secure a loan to build an annex behind the old bottling company. Falwell relied on cheap or volunteer labor to build it.

Thomas Road was not a "come as you are" kind of place. There was a dress code and an emphasis on personal morality: No liquor, no smoking, and no sex outside marriage.[12] Falwell preached a strict Baptist fundamentalism that the Bible was literally true in all aspects. He did not believe in the Pentecostal "gifts of the spirit"—no speaking in tongues or faith-healing exercises at Thomas Road—and condemned liberal churches for their emphasis on social reform.

Like most white men of the South, Falwell did not question the injustices of segregation. He went further by preaching that the Bible justified it. He told his all-white Thomas Road congregation in 1958 that integration was "the work of the Devil" and that "the true Negro" didn't want it.[13] But many of the civil rights movement's leading figures were also Protestant ministers: Martin Luther King Jr., Ralph Abernathy, C. T. Vivian, Joseph Lowery, Fred Shuttlesworth, James Lawson, Hosea Williams, and Andrew Young, among others. They read the same Bible and arrived at the opposite conclusion.

King's famous "Letter from Birmingham Jail" in 1963 was a direct response to eight white clergymen in Alabama who called his campaign "unwise and untimely." King had expected white ministers, priests, and rabbis to support his activities, and he always ended up disappointed. He cited the white ministers who "have remained silent behind the anesthetizing security of stained glass windows" and grieved over others who actively fought the movement.[14] "Injustice anywhere is a threat to justice everywhere," King memorably wrote, but many whites didn't agree. It was the Black church that provided the moral authority and organizational structure to fight Jim Crow.

On March 7, 1965, about six hundred demonstrators in Alabama set out for a march from Selma to Montgomery to push for voting rights for Blacks. The marchers crossed Selma's Edmund Pettus Bridge where they faced lines of Alabama state troopers and local police officers. The lawmen moved in on the peaceful protesters, using nightsticks and tear gas to disperse them. Among those assaulted was one of the march's leaders, a young graduate of a Baptist seminary named John Lewis. "It was religion that got us on the buses for the Freedom Rides; we were in Selma that day because of our faith," Lewis told author Jon Meacham.[15] The images from what became known as Bloody Sunday shocked the nation. The march resumed under federal protection and led to the passage of the Voting Rights Act of 1965.

Falwell's public response to Selma and the civil rights movement was a sermon titled "Ministers and Marches" that he delivered at Thomas Road on March 21, 1965. His remarks reflected the long-held evangelical posture that the primary purpose of churches is to win souls. Genuine social change was possible only through individual conversion to Christ, not legislation or government programs. "We are not told to wage wars against bootleggers, liquor stores, gamblers, murderers, prostitutes, racketeers, prejudiced persons or institutions, or any other existing evil as such," he said.[16] Ministers shouldn't have time to do anything other than preach the gospel of Jesus Christ, he insisted. "I feel that we need to get off the streets and back into the pulpits and into the prayer rooms," he said.[17]

Falwell believed that "these demonstrations and marches have done more to damage race relations and to gender hate than to help." That was not just an attitude held by Southern whites. In May 1964, a Gallup poll reported that 74 percent of Americans believed that the mass demonstrations were more likely to hurt the cause for racial equality, with only 16 percent saying they would help.[18] To most white people, the boycotts, sit-ins, and marches were at best a nuisance and at worst a threat to social order. Falwell questioned the true intentions of civil rights leaders such as King "who are known to have left-wing associations."[19] He alleged that communists were exploiting racial tensions for their own evil purposes. Ministers being involved in "riots and mob actions in American streets" undercut public confidence in churches, he said.[20]

Falwell was hardly a neutral observer. He told a newspaper reporter that he opposed the proposed Voting Rights Act as "a terrible violation of human and private property rights," adding "it should be considered civil wrongs instead of civil rights."[21] Writing in his 1987 autobiography, Falwell tried to soft-pedal his segregationist past. It was just the way life was then and no one questioned its injustice, he wrote. Falwell resented outside agitators, some of whom staged protests at his all-white church. He leaned on the "states' rights" argument, saying, "I was determined to maintain the right to decide for ourselves how we would live together, black and white."[22]

For Falwell and some other white evangelicals, that meant starting private schools where they wouldn't be bossed around. In 1954, when *Brown v. Board of Education* declared racial segregation of public schools unconstitutional, there were only 123 non-Catholic church schools in the country; by 1970, there were nearly 20,000.[23] They became known as "segregation academies." In 1967, Falwell founded the Lynchburg Christian Academy at Thomas Road. He claimed there was not a "whites-only" policy, but the student body was exclusively white for its first two years. Other religious leaders in Lynchburg noticed and objected to Falwell calling a school "Christian" that seemed designed to sidestep integration.[24]

Evangelicals also felt under siege by Supreme Court decisions on school prayer. In 1962, the court ruled in *Engel v. Vitale* that reciting a prayer in New York state's public schools violated the Constitution. (The state's Board of Regents composed the nondenominational prayer.) In a case the following year, the court ruled 8–1 that it was unconstitutional for public schools to sponsor devotional Bible readings and recitations of the Lord's Prayer. "We need more religion, not less," Billy Graham protested. "Why should the majority be so severely penalized by the protests of a handful?"[25] Graham correctly judged public opinion: A Gallup poll found that 70 percent of Americans disapproved of the ruling in the case *Abington School District v. Schempp.*[26] Proposals in Congress to add a school-prayer amendment to the Constitution were frequent but fruitless.

Conservatives fought against sex education in public schools with some success, such as in Anaheim in 1968. Some lobbied for the teaching of creationism as an alternative to evolution. In West Virginia in 1974, conservative pastors and parents rebelled against the introduction of textbooks they found to be un-Christian and unsuitably patriotic. The protests attracted outside groups and spurred a strike, bombings, and death threats.[27] The board relented and allowed conservative-approved textbooks to be taught alongside the officially sanctioned curriculum.[28]

The Lynchburg Christian Academy was just one arm of Falwell's enterprises. There was a facility for alcoholic men, a youth summer camp, one of the country's largest Sunday schools, and a thirty-two-hundred-seat sanctuary modeled on Thomas Jefferson's renderings for a church he never built.[29] The audience for his *The Old Time Gospel Hour* generated bags of mail and buckets of donations. Falwell thought the business world had lessons to teach churches. "Business is usually on the cutting edge of in-novation and change because of its quest for finances. Therefore the church would be wise to look at business for a prediction of future innovation," Falwell wrote in 1971.[30] For example, shopping malls dominated retail by conveniently placing many services under one roof. Churches like Thomas Road that combined multiple ministries could attract the masses and serve many individual needs throughout the week.

In 1971, Falwell hatched an ambitious plan to found a Christian liberal arts college. The school reflected Falwell's fundamentalism in every sense. Students at Lynchburg Baptist College (later Liberty University) were re-quired to join Thomas Road, adhere to a strict dress code—ties for men, long skirts for women—and "refrain from smoking, drinking, dancing, and viewing any motion pictures."[31] They were immersed in the literal inter-pretation of the Bible in the classroom and in the pews.

The school didn't have a formal campus, so students met in Thomas Road's existing buildings and at sites across Lynchburg. Falwell surveyed a large piece of land on a mountain and bought it even though the price tag exceeded $1 million. Falwell sold bonds to his supporters for the school and also to take his TV ministry national, but the campaign raised red flags at the Securities and Exchange Commission. The federal regulators sued Thomas Road in 1973, claiming that the church was insolvent and had no ability to pay back the $6.5 million in bonds sold to investors in twenty-five states.

The charges infuriated Falwell. He fell back on his coterie of powerful businessmen to see him through the crisis. A motel owner loaned money for Thomas Road to buy color television cameras, a trio of business leaders Falwell called "the Three Musketeers" upgraded the ministry's private plane, and a local building contractor took over the mountain land and held it for Falwell.[32] He answered the SEC's charges and denied that any bondholders had been defrauded. Falwell admitted that the church had erred in not issuing a prospectus on the sale of general obligation bonds and lacked proper oversight.[33] He informed the judge, however, that five business executives were willing to serve as the church's independent finance committee. The judge cleared Thomas Road of any intentional wrongdoing.

Falwell never forgot the feeling of being persecuted by government regulators. He was simply trying to spread the message of Christ as far as possible, and anti-Christian forces tried to block him. "I had felt the presence of evil lurking among us as I had not felt its presence before," he wrote of the experience.[34] Falwell and other evangelicals would soon mobilize on the national stage to strike back at these perceived moral evils.

On Monday, January 22, 1973, the Supreme Court delivered a 7–2 decision that overruled all state laws prohibiting or restricting a woman's right to an abortion during the first three months of pregnancy. In the case, *Roe v. Wade*, the court affirmed a constitutional right of personal privacy "broad enough to encompass a woman's decision whether or not to terminate her pregnancy," noting that it was not up to the judiciary to resolve the difficult question of when life begins and concluding, "The unborn have never been recognized in the law as persons in the whole sense."[35]

The ruling made the front pages of the *New York Times, Chicago Tribune,* and *Los Angeles Times* the next morning, but far more space was devoted to the death of former president Lyndon Johnson. News of a peace accord in Paris between the United States and North Vietnam dominated the following day's papers and the remainder of the week. Any follow-ups on the court's abortion decision were pushed inside the papers and then dropped out of sight entirely.

The public reaction to *Roe v. Wade* was surprisingly muted given how large it looms today. There was no public statement from President Richard Nixon, who had appointed the justice who wrote the majority opinion, Harry Blackmun. (Two other Nixon appointees also supported the decision.) The strongest voices against the ruling were Catholic leaders, who had for years lobbied against abortion liberalization bills at the state level. Church doctrine held that human life begins at the moment of conception, thus abortion was a grave moral evil tantamount to murder. Chicago Cardinal John Cody attacked *Roe v. Wade* as a "flagrant rejection of the unborn child's right to life."[36] New York Cardinal Terence Cooke said it was a "horrifying decision," and Philadelphia Cardinal John Krol declared it "an unspeakable tragedy for this nation."[37]

Protestant leaders were less absolutist on the issue. The National Association of Evangelicals disapproved of *Roe v. Wade*, but also said, "We recognize the necessity for therapeutic abortions to safeguard the health or the life of the mother."[38] Abortions may also be called for in cases of rape and incest, the group said. W. A. Criswell, the conservative pastor of First Baptist Church in Dallas and former president of the Southern Baptist Convention, supported the ruling. "I have always felt that it was only after a child was born and had a life separate from its mother that it became an individual person, and it has always, therefore, seemed to me that what is the best for the mother and for the future should be allowed," he said.[39]

Falwell said that he opposed *Roe v. Wade* from the beginning, but he did not preach about it for years. He still believed that ministers shouldn't get involved in politics, so he steered clear of marches and lobbying. Falwell felt that he was too busy with his church and university to study policy matters. But the more Falwell thought about it, legalized abortion seemed to be symptomatic of an overall decline in morality. He brought his concerns to his family and said, "Kids, it is doubtful that you will be living in a free America when you are the same age as your parents."[40] Falwell resolved to take a public stand against abortion rights as well as other issues such as pornography. He encouraged Christians to register voters, support candidates, and get people to the polls.

For the nation's bicentennial in 1976, Falwell organized "I Love America" rallies that featured musical performers from his college. "We were calling America back to God," Falwell wrote of the events staged on the steps of state capitols. "We warned them that our leaders were making decisions that could destroy the moral foundations upon which our country was built. And we challenged them to do something about it in their towns, in their states, and in their nation."[41] The ministry's private planes whisked Falwell between the rallies and Lynchburg. Falwell met with local pastors and accepted speaking engagements and media appearances. The response confirmed to Falwell that there was a demand for political action to promote his vision of Christian morals.

The so-called "year of the evangelical" also featured a presidential election. The Democratic nominee, Jimmy Carter, was a born-again Christian who spoke openly about his Baptist faith. Carter's outsider status and humble demeanor appealed to voters weary of the lies of Vietnam and Watergate. Gerald Ford, the Republican president, survived a fierce primary challenge from Ronald Reagan. Ford, an Episcopalian, was more reticent than Carter about publicly discussing his faith. Still, he reached out to the growing bloc of evangelical voters. A Gallup poll that year reported that 34 percent of American adults considered themselves born-again Christians and 48 percent of Protestants did. Thirty-eight percent of Americans believed that the Bible "should be taken literally, word for word."[42]

Three years after *Roe v. Wade*, partisan positions on abortion were not quite locked into place. Carter did not personally approve of abortion, but he accepted the court's ruling. The 1976 Democratic Party platform said, "We fully recognize the religious and ethical nature of the concerns which many Americans have on the subject of abortion. We feel, however, that it is undesirable to attempt to amend the U.S. Constitution to overturn the Supreme Court decision in this area."[43] The Republican platform acknowledged that there were sincere people in the party on both sides—and even some still in the middle or undecided. The handwringing produced a carefully worded position: "The Republican Party favors a continuance of the public dialogue on abortion and supports the efforts of those who seek enactment of a constitutional amendment to restore protection of the right to life for unborn children."[44]

After the conventions, a furor arose over an interview Carter gave to *Playboy* magazine. The candidate confessed that he had looked with lust upon women other than his wife. "I've committed adultery in my heart many times," said Carter, who believed that God forgave him for his faults. "But that doesn't mean that I condemn someone who not only looks on a woman with lust but who leaves his wife and shacks up with somebody out of wedlock," he continued. "Christ says, Don't consider yourself better than someone else because one guy screws a whole bunch of women while the other guy is loyal to his wife."[45]

Carter's frankness appeared to be an awkward attempt to convince voters that he would not impose his moral standards on others. Falwell pounced on Carter for using "vulgarity, profanity and obscenity" in the interview. "A man who claimed the intelligence to run this country should be intelligent enough to not use that kind of language," he said.[46] Falwell attacked Carter during his *The Old Time Gospel Hour* program broadcast on 260 TV stations nationwide on October 10, just weeks before the election.[47]

To conform with the Federal Communications Commission's equal-time rules, Falwell offered Carter four minutes on his next program for a reply. Falwell edited out criticism of Carter from the October 17 program to allow time for the campaign to respond but declared that he would leave in an anti-Carter segment planned for the following week. The Carter campaign objected to Falwell's "personal attack" and declined his offer. About a hundred stations played it safe and didn't show the program. If they were found to be in violation of FCC standards, the stations could lose their broadcast licenses. Falwell accused the Democrat's operatives of intimidation. "This is a blatant attempt by the Carter organization to muzzle a preacher of the gospel and to deprive him of his freedom of religion and freedom of speech in speaking out on his moral convictions," Falwell said.[48] Despite the controversies, Carter won and roughly split the evangelical vote with Ford.

Falwell ramped up his political activism. In 1977, singer-turned-activist Anita Bryant and her Save Our Children campaign fought a Dade County ordinance in Florida that banned discrimination against gay people in employment and housing. Bryant asked for Falwell's help to repeal it. The pastor invited Bryant, a Baptist, to Thomas Road and said he would speak at a "Christians for God and Decency" rally at the Miami Beach Convention Center. Falwell appeared at the May 22 event with other "Bible-believing" preachers and ten thousand attendees. Falwell insisted that he loved homosexuals but hated the sin of homosexuality. He said it was wrong for government to force "property owners and employers to open their doors to homosexuals no matter how blatant their perverted lives may be."[49]

The county voted by a 2–1 ratio to repeal the gay rights ordinance. "The people of Dade County—the normal majority—have said, 'Enough! Enough! Enough!'" an exultant Bryant said on election night.[50] She later credited Falwell's support as one of the keys to victory. "Dr. Jerry Falwell was among the few preachers in the country who openly rallied to our cause," she said. "He stood up and was counted at a critical time."[51] (The oft-used courtesy title was not due to any advanced coursework Falwell had completed, but from a few honorary doctoral degrees he had received.)

Another front in the gay rights battle opened the following year in California. State Senator John Briggs, an Orange County conservative and a born-again Christian, sponsored Proposition 6 to ban homosexuals from working in the state's public schools. At first, the Briggs initiative appeared to be on track for passage. But public opinion swung against it. San Francisco Supervisor Harvey Milk, the state's first openly gay elected official, led the resistance. Milk encouraged people to come out of the closet, reasoning that people would be less likely to be bigoted if they personally knew someone who was gay. The initiative went too far even for some conservatives. Reagan, a former California governor, opposed the Briggs initiative on the grounds that it would infringe on privacy rights. Voters soundly defeated the measure on November 7, 1978.

Less than three weeks later, disgruntled former supervisor Dan White slipped into San Francisco City Hall and assassinated Milk and Mayor George Moscone. Falwell, who spoke at rallies supporting the Briggs initiative, took stock of the events in California and concluded: "Without question, San Francisco is undergoing a judgment of God today. . . . Do you know that the homosexuals in San Francisco jokingly call Frisco 'Sodom and Gomorrah'? This is a way of flaunting their arrogance in the face of almighty God."[52]

Falwell had kicked off his "Clean Up America" campaign earlier that year with a national advertising blitz. Sample ballots were placed in newspapers and magazines asking three yes-or-no questions: "Do you approve of known practicing HOMOSEXUALS teaching in public schools?" "Do you approve of the present laws legalizing ABORTION-ON-DEMAND?" and "Do you approve of the laws of our land permitting the open display of PORNOGRAPHIC materials on newsstands, TV, and movies?"[53] Falwell encouraged readers to send him the completed ballots and he would share the results with elected leaders. Ministry headquarters received more than 1 million ballots that overwhelmingly supported Falwell's positions.

In April 1979, he led a rally from the steps of the U.S. Capitol. Falwell packaged the event into a *The Old Time Gospel Hour* program that he promoted with another ballot campaign on the same three issues. *The Old Time Gospel Hour* was carried on 325 TV stations and 300 radio outlets, his church claimed seventeen thousand members and took in about $1 million per week, and his university continued to grow. As a television character, Falwell exuded a supreme confidence. "I have never been associated with anyone as easy to work with as Jerry," said ABC veteran Bruce Braun, who directed *The Old Time Gospel Hour*. "He is quick and has a keen understanding of technique."[54] Falwell thickened in middle age, his girth lending him an almost jolly quality on camera, and his calm baritone unnerved his opponents.

Cultural issues such as school prayer, gay rights, and abortion undoubtedly gave shape to evangelicals' political activism. But the true spark was a lesser-known issue that hit evangelicals where they lived. For years, the federal government had been pushing for all schools to comply with racial desegregation policies outlined in the Civil Rights Act of 1964. The Nixon administration in 1970 ordered the Internal Revenue Service to deny tax exemptions to all segregated schools. In 1971, a federal court upheld the IRS policy, ruling that nonprofit private schools that practiced racial discrimination did not qualify as charitable organizations under the tax code. Without the exemption, the so-called "segregation academies" would be forced to raise tuition, putting pressure on enrollment.

In 1976, the IRS formally rescinded the tax-exempt status of Bob Jones University, a fundamentalist bastion in South Carolina. The university did not admit any African American students until 1971, and even then, they were required to be married. Bob Jones continued to prohibit interracial dating and marriage under penalty of expulsion, citing the Bible as justification for its stance against miscegenation. The university sued to preserve its tax exemption, claiming the government violated its religious liberty. (The Supreme Court ruled 8–1 against Bob Jones in 1983.)

Rick Perlstein, a historian of the modern conservative movement, has written that its leaders had become sophisticated at "organizing discontent."[55] The battle over tax exemptions for Christian schools was a prime example. Conservative activists grasped that the standoff could be used to galvanize the evangelical community, even though two Republican administrations had tried to enforce the policy. Carter's IRS commissioner, Jerome Kurtz, provided a helpful assist. In August 1978 he issued guidance that private schools needed to show they were sufficiently desegregated by passing five "affirmative action" tests. For example, a nearly all-white school run by Falwell would have to add sixty-eight more black students, prove that it was making a good-faith effort to recruit minorities, or else face the possible loss of the tax exemption.[56]

Pastors insisted that they should be free to run their schools without government interference, and conservative groups and politicians agreed. Congressman Phil Crane, an Illinois Republican, wrote to Kurtz and accused his agency of imposing racial quotas. Then he introduced legislation to strip the IRS of the authority to adopt any rule related to private school admissions.[57] Religious leaders, including Falwell, mobilized their flocks and flooded the IRS and politicians with hundreds of thousands of protest letters. The IRS held hearings where members of Congress commented on the proposed regulations. Ministers, school headmasters, and concerned citizens testified and packed the hearing rooms for the four days of proceedings. Two months later, Kurtz issued a watered-down proposal that did nothing to quiet the objectors. He requested Secret Service protection because of the death threats.[58] (The Reagan administration revoked the IRS policy.)

Conservative activist Paul Weyrich said years later that the tax-exemption fight had more do with creating the "Religious Right" than any other issue, even abortion. "What caused the movement to surface was the federal government's moves against Christian schools," he said.[59] It was telling that the issue that most roused evangelicals directly related to their finances and put them in the position of defending racial segregation.

Evangelicals grew ever more assertive lobbying for their interests in the public arena. They rallied to the defense of televangelist James Robison in 1979 when TV station WFAA in Dallas–Fort Worth suspended his show for his attacks on homosexuality. His sermon referred to the gay rights movement as a "perversion of the highest order," among other slurs.[60] The ABC affiliate argued that FCC rules required equal time for a response from the gay community because his statement touched on a political issue. To evangelicals, the suspension amounted to censorship. Robison invited Falwell, Criswell, and others to speak at a rally that filled the Dallas Convention Center. "We want to let people hear from the Christians—the moral majority," said Robison, who was let back on the air.[61]

The pastors were struck by the crowd's intensity and wondered how they could build on that momentum. Weyrich agreed to commission a poll of religious Americans on their attitudes about religion and politics. The results showed that evangelicals wanted preachers to be more active in public policy debates. "And moreover, they said, 'Yes, we will financially support both organizations. We won't stop giving to your church.' That was a life-changing experience, because all these guys who had been saying, 'We can't get involved,' all of a sudden saw their people wanted them involved. By the end of the meeting, I had people tripping over themselves to come to me and say, 'What do we do? Tell us what to do,'" Weyrich said.[62]

Weyrich and other conservative activists such as Richard Viguerie and Howard Phillips had been in touch with Falwell about heading a national political organization. They founded a group called Moral Majority, Inc., in June 1979 to influence legislation and promote conservative values. (A separate education foundation and political action committee were also established.) They surmised that the movement had to reach beyond Falwell's base to succeed. Other Protestants, Catholics, Mormons, and even Jews were welcome to march under the Moral Majority's banner. The Moral Majority's leadership ranks were mostly stocked with Baptists, however.

Falwell's new political machine marked the final repudiation of his 1965 "Ministers and Marches" sermon. He mounted "I Love America" rallies at statehouses to support "pro-life, pro-family, pro-Bible morality" politicians like Jesse Helms, the conservative Republican senator from North Carolina.[63] Falwell bashed liberal leaders and celebrities he judged to be un-American. "When I hear Jane Fonda and some other disgraces to America give comfort to the enemies of this land and put down every high holy thing about this land, as a Christian pastor I'm tempted to buy her a one-way ticket to Moscow," Falwell said to applause in Raleigh, North Carolina, in November 1979.[64]

At a Moral Majority fundraising luncheon in the same city, Falwell told pastors that his church interviewed candidates and preached about what was at stake in elections. "I say, 'These two are totally with us and these two are totally against us. Now you go out and vote your conscience, and we'll give you transportation if you need it,'" he said.[65] Falwell had preached for years about the eternal battle between Satan and God, and now he framed political issues as questions of good and evil.

Evangelical theologian Francis A. Schaeffer provided the intellectual justification for Falwell and others to mix with people of other faiths in common cause. Schaeffer theorized that legalized abortion would lead to euthanasia, infanticide, and the murder of other unwanted members of society. The threat to civilization was so dire that evangelicals must find allies wherever they could to defeat it, he said.

Schaeffer worked with Dr. C. Everett Koop, an evangelical pediatric surgeon, to produce a book and film series in 1979 titled *Whatever Happened to the Human Race?* The film includes graphic descriptions of abortion procedures and striking visuals such as a scene of broken plastic dolls littered along the salt flats of the Dead Sea.[66] Schaeffer and Koop took the film on a nationwide tour of churches and it acquired a following among evangelicals. In 1981, Schaeffer published *A Christian Manifesto*, which was heavily promoted by Falwell for its call to Christians to defeat the secular humanist worldview. (Among those inspired by Schaeffer's works was Randall Terry, founder of Operation Rescue. The confrontational group became best known for blocking entrances to abortion clinics in the 1980s and 1990s.)[67]

Falwell and other evangelicals were revving up for the 1980 presidential election. Their appraisal of Carter diminished further as his administration dealt with the Iran hostage crisis and oil shocks. He may have been a born-again Christian, but his policy positions were out of sync with the evangelical movement. Carter was content to let court rulings stand on abortion rights and school prayer. He supported the Equal Rights Amendment and convened a White House Conference on Families attended by gays and lesbians. Evangelicals accused Carter and the Democrats of trying to strip religious schools of their tax-exempt status.[68]

Falwell believed that Carter's policies had led America to the brink of catastrophe. Unelected courts had expelled God and the Bible from public schools and made abortion-on-demand the law of land, he said. "We are fighting a holy war," Falwell declared during the primaries. "We have to lead the nation back to the moral stance that made America great."[69] Falwell audaciously adopted the language of the civil rights movement that he had opposed. "It's like the blacks said in the '60s, 'we shall overcome.' And this time, we are going to win."[70]

Falwell had plenty of fellow warriors. The Christian Voice, a lobbying group that sprang from the anti-gay movement in California, claimed one hundred twenty-six thousand members and two thousand ministers by early 1980.[71] The group issued a "moral report card" for members of Congress based on their stances on a range of issues.[72] Pat Robertson, founder of the Christian Broadcasting Network, said it was time for Christians to act. "We used to think that if we stayed home and prayed it would be enough," he said. "Well, we're fed up. We think it's time to put God back in government."[73] Robertson and Campus Crusade for Christ's Bill Bright orchestrated a gathering of conservative Christians on the National Mall in April 1980. Speakers condemned the acceptance of abortion rights and homosexuality in American life. "Unless we repent and turn from our sin, we can expect to be destroyed," Bright told the crowd.[74]

Falwell wrote a book titled *Listen, America!* that outlined the emerging Christian right's stance on a wide spectrum of issues. In the 1980 book, Falwell said the United States needed to increase defense spending as a show of strength against the Soviet Union. He attacked disarmament treaties as suicide. "The Soviets have always had only one goal, and that is to destroy capitalistic society. They are a nation committed to communism and to destroying the American way of life," he wrote.[75]

To Falwell, that meant less government spending, which was piling up deficits and debt, fueling inflation, and driving up interest rates. Falwell pilfered these precepts from the economist Milton Friedman, but he also harkened back to Dwight L. Moody in his church-based vision of America. "Until the early days of this century, it was widely recognized that churches and other private institutions carried the primary responsibility, not merely for education, but also for health care and charity," he wrote.[76] He suggested that people should tithe and let churches perform those roles, not government.

Falwell believed in the gospel of capitalism, given his own experience as a successful entrepreneur. "The free-enterprise system is clearly outlined in the Book of Proverbs in the Bible. Jesus Christ made it clear that the work ethic was a part of His plan for man. Ownership of property is biblical. Competition in business is biblical. Ambitious and successful business management is clearly outlined as a part of God's plan for His people," he wrote.[77]

Falwell declared that America needed government leaders who would take a stand for morality. He encouraged Christians to register to vote, get educated, and mobilize. They should know their elected officials, attend party meetings, and even run for office. "We cannot be silent about the sins that are destroying this nation. The choice is ours. We must turn America around or prepare for inevitable destruction," he wrote.[78]

Falwell's catalog of national sins included abortion, homosexuality, pornography, secular humanism, and the fractured family. God's plan is for "men to be manly" and "the woman to be submissive," he said.[79] He condemned the Equal Rights Amendment to the Constitution that proposed a guarantee of equal rights for all Americans regardless of sex. Both houses of Congress approved the amendment and sent it to the states for ratification in 1972. The ERA's leading opponent was Phyllis Schlafly, a devout Catholic who found common ground with evangelicals on that and other conservative causes.

Evangelicals perused the Republican field and rallied around Ronald Reagan. On the surface, Reagan seemed to be an improbable vessel: a divorced and remarried actor from unholy Hollywood, a one-time New Deal Democrat and union president, a former governor of liberal California who signed bills that raised taxes and permitted "therapeutic" abortions, and an infrequent churchgoer who saw portents in fate and astrology. But Reagan adroitly shifted with the political winds. His post-acting career as a spokesman for General Electric took him onto factory floors and boardrooms across the country. He preached the verities of free-market capitalism and smaller government as a speaker on the Chamber of Commerce and Rotary Club banquet circuit. Reagan blossomed into a conservative star with his televised "A Time for Choosing" speech endorsing Barry Goldwater for president in 1964. Goldwater lost in a landslide, but Reagan sensed that the party's energy had swung to the right. He quietly reached out to leading evangelicals in 1979 to secure their support.

By 1980, Reagan had hit all of the marks that evangelicals wanted from a candidate. He opposed abortion rights, the ERA, and the IRS policy on private schools. He pledged to slash regulations and cut taxes. He promised a strong national defense, an aggressive posture against the Soviets, and unwavering support of Israel. He spoke of his reverence for the Bible and the power of prayer. He was fascinated by biblical prophecy, asking Jim Bakker on his TV show, "Do you ever feel . . . we might be the generation that sees Armageddon?"[80] Best of all for his supporters, Reagan could hold all of these positions while retaining his personal appeal.

Falwell and other evangelical leaders threw their weight behind Reagan by registering voters, mobilizing precinct workers, and using the media. Reagan cruised to the nomination. Evangelicals directly influenced the Republican Party platform adopted in July 1980. The party dropped its support of the Equal Rights Amendment after supporting ratification for forty years. Activists added a plank declaring "we will halt the unconstitutional regulatory vendetta launched by Mr. Carter's IRS Commissioner against independent schools."[81] There were homey appeals for a return to old-time American values. Three times the party promised to "make America great again."

The GOP toughened its stance against abortion: "We affirm our support of a constitutional amendment to restore protection of the right to life for unborn children. We also support the Congressional efforts to restrict the use of taxpayers' dollars for abortion."[82] The 1980 Democratic platform also hardened its line on reproductive rights: "The Democratic Party supports the 1973 Supreme Court decision on abortion rights as the law of the land and opposes any constitutional amendment to restrict or overturn that decision."[83]

On August 22, 1980, Reagan spoke at a major conference of fundamentalist ministers and other conservatives called the Religious Roundtable. Criswell, Falwell, and Weyrich were among those at a packed Reunion Arena in Dallas. Robison, the televangelist who just a year earlier had been kicked off the air by a local TV station for his attacks on gays, was the warm-up act for the Republican presidential nominee. Robison delivered a high-voltage, Bible-waving order: "You commit yourself to the principles of God and demand those parties and politicians align themselves with the eternal values in this book, and America will be forever the greatest nation on this Earth!"[84] Reagan and others jumped to their feet and cheered.

Reagan began his remarks by saying, "Now, I know this is a nonpartisan gathering, and so I know that you can't endorse me, but I only brought that up because I want you to know that I endorse you and what you're doing."[85] As the speech went on, it was clear that he had the crowd at his command. Reagan believed that the "religious America" that he saw before him had awakened just in time. For too long, people with religious beliefs had been intimidated from political participation. "If we have come to a time in the United States when the attempt to see traditional moral values reflected in public policy leaves one open to irresponsible charges, then the structure of our free society is under attack and the foundation of our freedom is threatened," he said.[86]

Reagan won in a landslide and swept the South, except for Carter's home state of Georgia. He claimed 67 percent of the evangelical vote and carved into traditional Democratic constituencies.[87] The election also flipped twelve Democratic seats in the Senate, giving Republicans control for the first time since the 1950s. Liberal stalwarts such as George McGovern and Frank Church were defeated and conservatives like Dan Quayle and Charles Grassley were voted in.

The Moral Majority and other Christian groups reveled in their victory, but the Reagan years did not fully satisfy them. Some grumbled about the lack of evangelicals in key cabinet and White House posts. Others were unhappy at his nomination of Sandra Day O'Connor to the Supreme Court in 1981 for her support of the ERA and moderate views on legalized abortion. Falwell thundered that all "good Christians" should be worried about the appointment. (An annoyed Barry Goldwater defended his fellow Arizonan: "Every good Christian ought to kick Falwell right in the ass.")[88] Reagan elevated plenty of conservative judges such as Antonin Scalia, but abortion remained legal and public schools weren't suddenly hosting devotional Bible readings. Reagan's rhetoric rarely translated into concrete policy changes. Some in the evangelical movement were frustrated that the administration focused more on the economy and defense than on social issues.

Throughout the 1980s, Falwell continually inserted himself into controversies as the Moral Majority's front man. In 1983, he blamed gay people for the spread of a mysterious disease called AIDS. "I do believe that herpes, AIDS and venereal diseases are a definite form of the judgment of God on society," he said. "He is a loving God, but he makes us pay when we misbehave."[89] At a rally in Cincinnati on the Fourth of July, Falwell said that all gay bathhouses should close and called for the sexual screening of potential blood donors. Falwell labeled gay sexual practices as "very sadistic and bloody and violent." He referenced a bizarre, unverified poll claiming that 22 percent of homosexuals admitted that they ingest human waste.

Falwell's rants against gays and feminists puffed him up into a villain for liberals. He welcomed their hatred. Falwell scheduled his leadership training conference to be in San Francisco just days before the Democratic National Convention in 1984. His presence predictably drew raucous demonstrations. Speakers at the conference riled up the protesters with condemnations of the "homosexual lifestyle." Social psychologist Paul Cameron presented the results of a dubious questionnaire that gay people made up 4 percent of public school teachers but were responsible for up to a third of all sexual advances to students.[90] Another speaker said schools ought to be allowed to dismiss gay teachers just as funeral directors should fire necrophiliacs.

Meanwhile, Falwell's enterprises in Lynchburg were struggling. Moral Majority's travel demands "had taken a tremendous toll on my ministries at Thomas Road Baptist Church," he acknowledged.[91] The fallout from the televangelist scandals also hit him in the pocketbook. In 1987, revenues were $4 million below projections for the year, he said.[92] Falwell decided it was time to concentrate on his core duties as pastor of his twenty-two-thousand-member church and chancellor of Liberty University.

Falwell decamped for Virginia when the Moral Majority and other Christian political action groups were on the wane. The feeling of crisis had passed. America seemed to be on the right course: Reagan carried forty-nine of fifty states in the 1984 election, defeating Democrat Walter Mondale by nearly 17 million votes. Donations to the Moral Majority tumbled, and the organization itself was in disarray. Falwell incorporated it into his Liberty Federation, stepped aside as leader in 1987, and dissolved it soon after the 1988 election. In that race, one of the Republican candidates was another evangelical entrepreneur, Pat Robertson. His candidacy and its aftermath displayed the staying power of evangelicals in Republican politics.

He was a senator's son who was a latter-day convert to politics. In 1966, Robertson believed it was inappropriate for him as a minister to campaign for his father's reelection campaign. "Active partisan politics is the wrong path for true evangelicals," he said.[93] Robertson shared an early reluctance for political activism with his fellow Virginian Falwell, but their backgrounds were vastly different. Robertson came from a prominent family and boasted elite credentials, serving in the Marine Corps in Korea and graduating from Yale Law School. He underwent a religious awakening through Pentecostalism and abandoned a corporate career for the ministry. Robertson earned a Master of Divinity degree in 1959 from the Biblical

Seminary in New York (now the New York Theological Seminary). Although Robertson was ordained a Southern Baptist minister in 1961, he never pastored a church.

Like many Pentecostals, Robertson was drawn to the electronic pulpit. With no cash down, he purchased a defunct TV station in Portsmouth, Virginia, and formally chartered the Christian Broadcasting Network in 1960.[94] In its early years, the network struggled to fill airtime and find donors. Robertson played religious films and some secular programs, talked for hours on theological subjects, and hired Jim and Tammy Faye Bakker to host a children's variety show.[95] Robertson resorted to telethons, asking seven hundred people to pledge ten dollars per month to keep the station on the air. The contributors were called the "700 Club," and it became the name of his flagship nightly program. *The 700 Club*, which made its debut in 1966, marked a breakthrough in Christian programming. It was more like *The Tonight Show* than the typical sermon or revival meeting. Its first permanent host was Jim Bakker, who fielded viewer telephone calls into the night. Robertson later shaped it into a more traditional news program.

CBN moved into new facilities to house its television and radio studios in 1968, and Robertson acquired and operated other stations across the country in the 1970s. CBN bought time on commercial stations to broadcast *The 700 Club* and offered it free to cable TV systems. CBN also showed nonreligious family programs such as reruns of *The Partridge Family* and *The Andy Griffith Show*. Robertson founded a satellite cable service in 1977 that evolved into a separate company that operated The Family Channel, a staple of basic cable. (Rupert Murdoch bought it for $1.9 billion in 1997, a windfall for Robertson and CBN. The channel is now known as Freeform.) By the late 1970s, CBN had three hundred thousand donors who contributed $1.4 million a month.[96] The money opened the gates to further expansion. Billy Graham was the featured speaker for the 1979 dedication of CBN's $20 million campus in Virginia Beach. Robertson followed Oral Roberts and Jerry Falwell by founding his own college, CBN University (later Regent University).

Robertson largely stayed out of partisan politics while building his business. He admired Richard Nixon until Watergate consumed his presidency in 1974. Robertson went on air requesting that the president repent of his sins. "I am not partisan one way or the other. I'm not conservative, liberal, or anything political. I belong to Jesus, and I'm a citizen of Heaven," he said. "But I belong to this nation, and I don't believe this has been anything but a cancer on our society."[97] Robertson cheered the election of the born-again Jimmy Carter in 1976, but their relationship soured before Inauguration Day. In a phone conservation, the president-elect seemed open to Robertson's suggestion to include evangelicals among his appointees. Robertson offered to draw up a list and flew to Plains, Georgia, to hand it to him personally. None of Robertson's recommendations were appointed.[98]

Robertson helped organize a "Washington for Jesus" rally on the National Mall in the run-up to the 1980 election. The event was billed as nonpartisan, but the roster of speakers and their stances on social issues gave the game away. Robertson kept his distance from Falwell and the Moral Majority during the Reagan years, partly because Robertson's charismatic beliefs and Falwell's fundamentalism didn't mix well. Robertson also harbored doubts about the heavy-handed approach of the Christian right-wing groups of the 1980s.[99]

Washington insiders whispered about interest in a potential Robertson presidential campaign.[100] Robertson already had a political organization at his disposal, the Freedom Council, and strategists noted grassroots hunger for a nonpolitician like Robertson. He relinquished his leadership role at CBN in 1987 when he entered the Republican primary campaign, which included Vice President George H. W. Bush and Senator Bob Dole. Robertson finished a surprising second to Dole in the Iowa caucuses, which would be the high point of the Robertson campaign. Bush nearly swept the Super Tuesday contests, including Virginia, and Robertson suspended his campaign before the primaries were over. Still, he could take solace in running a credible race against formidable opponents.

Robertson endorsed Bush, who easily won in November, and looked to fill the void left by the demise of the Moral Majority. Falwell knew how to organize attention-getting rallies, but the Moral Majority lacked the ground game to translate that passion into policy. Robertson asked Ralph Reed, a young political operative from Georgia, to help him set up the Christian Coalition. Reed had just completed his doctorate in American history at Emory University and was a born-again Christian. He felt that evangelicals had mistakenly applied a ministry model to civic engagement. "Most of the state leaders of the Moral Majority were preachers, pastors. And most of them worked like a broadcast national ministry where you just built a big list of supporters and mailed them and phoned them to mobilize them. There was no county-by-county organization, there was no precinct-by-precinct organization," he said in an interview with the author.[101]

Reed built the Christian Coalition like a party organization. He recruited political professionals, hired staff, and contacted Robertson campaign donors to raise money. A parallel program coordinated with church leaders and ministries. Reed, not yet thirty, found himself on the vanguard of a political movement. "Let me tell you something, I went from sitting in a little one-bedroom apartment in Decatur, Georgia, writing a dissertation that nobody was going to read, to directly reporting to Pat Robertson and I say this jokingly, not really, but we were kind of planning the evangelical takeover of the Republican Party. Man, I went from zero to 180 miles per hour pretty fast. It was almost disorienting," Reed said.[102]

Reed portrayed the Christian Coalition as a "pro-family movement" with a broad agenda of supporting "school choice," voluntary school prayer, and tax cuts. Reed's group opposed "minority rights for gays" and supported "the traditional family." He defined opposition to abortion rights as a "compassionate defense of innocent human life." Although Bush lost to Democrat Bill Clinton in 1992, the Christian Coalition ended the year with about two hundred fifty thousand dues-paying members and a thousand chapters in every state.[103]

Clinton's personal scandals and liberal policies opened up many lines for conservatives to attack. The Christian Coalition kept up the pressure on the administration, spending $1.4 million to defeat Clinton's health care plan in 1994. The campaign included 30 million postcards dispatched to tens of thousands of churches.[104] The Christian Coalition rounded up conservatives to run for local offices, serve as convention delegates, and lead state and county parties. "The Christian Coalition did not just back the Republican Party," wrote historian Allan Lichtman. "In collaboration with other conservative Christian groups, it *became* the Republican Party."[105] Those groups included the Family Research Council and Focus on the Family, both founded by evangelical child psychologist James Dobson.

The work paid off in 1994 when Republicans picked up fifty-four House seats, winning control for the first time in forty years. Evangelicals were unquestionably at the core of this ascendancy. Republican affiliation among regular churchgoing white evangelicals soared from 44 percent to 74 percent between 1972 and 1996.[106] By late 1995, the Christian Coalition had 1.6 million members in 1,600 local affiliates.[107] America's right turn prompted Clinton to acknowledge that "the era of big government is over." His ample political skills carried him to reelection against Dole, who never felt fully at ease with the influence of evangelicals on the party. The feeling was mutual. "Religious conservatives and the United States of America deserve better," Robertson said on *The 700 Club* after Dole's loss.[108]

Reed resigned from the Christian Coalition in 1997 to work directly for political candidates. One of them was George W. Bush, a born-again Christian who exemplified the brand of "compassionate conservatism" that Reed espoused. Robertson strongly backed the Texas governor over John McCain in the 2000 primaries. (The Arizona senator's comment that Robertson and Falwell were "agents of intolerance" in the party didn't help his cause.) Bush took 68 percent of the evangelical vote in 2000, a tossup election he won over Democrat Al Gore after a lengthy ballot recount and legal battles in Florida. Four years later, 78 percent of evangelicals supported Bush, constituting 36 percent of his voters.[109]

During his two terms, Bush established an office of "faith-based" initiatives, directed federal grants to abstinence-only forms of sex education, supported a constitutional amendment banning same-sex marriage, signed the Partial-Birth Abortion Act, and advocated the teaching of "intelligent design" along with evolution. He appointed evangelicals to important positions, such as installing Robertson's friend John Ashcroft as attorney general. Two conservative jurists, John Roberts and Samuel Alito, were added to the Supreme Court.

Meanwhile, Robertson tended to his broadcasting empire and Regent University, resigning from the Christian Coalition's board in 2001. (The group suffered from inconsistent leadership and mounting debt, tottering to its end in 2006.) "As one who organizes, manages, and assumes the risks of a business or enterprise, I am more an entrepreneur than a pastor. . . . God has not called me to the ministry. He has called me to be a Christian broadcaster," he said.[110] Robertson continued to speak out on political issues from his perch on *The 700 Club*. He published books warning of secret powers conspiring to create a world government. "A single thread runs from the White House to the State Department to the Council on Foreign Relations to the Trilateral Commission to secret societies to extreme New Agers," he warned in 1991.[111] Robertson's apocalyptic mindset led him to believe that doom was always just around the corner. "It is clearer each day that the world is hurtling toward some type of catastrophe," he wrote a year later.[112]

Two days after the September 11, 2001, terrorist attacks, Falwell appeared with Robertson on *The 700 Club*. Falwell blamed the American Civil Liberties Union and the courts for taking God out of the schools. He cited "the pagans, and the abortionists, and the feminists, and the gays and the lesbians," saying, "I point the finger in their face and say, 'You helped this happen.'" Robertson responded: "Well, I totally concur."[113] Their comments were widely condemned.

Robertson's characterizations of Islam as a "wicked religion" and "not a religion of peace" also irritated the White House.[114] They were deemed to be unhelpful as Bush was prosecuting his "war on terror" with the invasions of Afghanistan and Iraq. Bush fluently spoke the language of evangelicals—the nation was fighting an "axis of evil" and "evil-doers"— and didn't need outside spokesmen to give him credibility. The next Republican president would.

11

BELIEVE ME

Donald Trump and the Enduring Evangelical Influence on Republican Politics

> The support you've given me has been incredible, but I really don't feel guilty because I have given you a lot back.
>
> —President Donald Trump, speaking at an evangelical leadership dinner at the White House in 2018[1]

On the evening of May 25, 2020, Minneapolis police officers arrested George Floyd, a Black man, for allegedly using a counterfeit twenty-dollar bill at a convenience store. While Floyd was in custody, a white police officer, Derek Chauvin, knelt on Floyd's neck for more than nine minutes while three other officers restrained Floyd or stood by. A bystander's cellphone video captured Floyd repeatedly moaning "I can't breathe" while Chauvin pinned him face down on the street. Chauvin continued to kneel on Floyd's neck even after Floyd appeared to slip into unconsciousness. Paramedics arrived and Floyd was pronounced dead at a nearby hospital.

Outrage over Floyd's death kindled protests throughout the country and around the world despite pandemic-related restrictions on mass gatherings. Demonstrators charged that Floyd's death was just the latest example of police brutality against Black people. Two months earlier, Breonna Taylor, a Black woman, was fatally shot by Louisville police officers during a "no-knock" raid on her apartment. Protesters, many marching under the Black Lives Matter banner, demanded wholesale police reform and prompted a reckoning over America's history of racism.

The demonstrations were overwhelmingly peaceful, but there were instances of looting, arson, and rioting. National Guard troops were activated in some states to restore order. In Washington, the unrest reached the perimeter of the White House. Protesters occupied Lafayette Square and some pushed against security barriers. The White House went on lockdown May 29 and President Donald Trump and his family were rushed to an underground shelter. Protesters clashed with Secret Service agents and other law enforcement personnel. On May 31, rioters set fire to the basement of the square's St. John's Episcopal Church, known as the "church of the presidents" because chief executives since James Madison have attended services there.

On June 1, an angry Trump appeared in the Rose Garden and assailed the actions of "professional anarchists, violent mobs, arsonists, looters, criminals, rioters, antifa, and others." The small fire at the church, the vandalized monuments, and the looted small businesses were acts of "domestic terror," he said.[2] Trump ordered thousands of military and civilian personnel to quell the violence in the District of Columbia. He pledged to send military forces into states that did not mobilize their National Guard troops to instill law and order. Trump closed his remarks by mentioning he would pay his respects to "a very, very special place" without saying where.[3]

Just before Trump's speech, mounted police and authorities in riot gear moved in on the peaceful protesters still occupying the square. Flash-bang grenades, rubber bullets, and chemical agents were used to eject hundreds of people. Once Lafayette Square was cleared, Trump surprised the press and even law enforcement leaders by marching from the White House to St. John's. Trump paused in front of the boarded-up church as the cameras whirred. He awkwardly handled a Bible and held it up. A reporter asked if it was his Bible, and Trump replied it was "*a* Bible." (His daughter and senior adviser, Ivanka, retrieved the book from her $1,540 Max Mara bag.)[4] Trump did not open the Bible or meet with anyone from the church. After posing for pictures with top aides, he headed back to the White House.

The divergent reactions from Christian figures revealed the fissures of faith in the Trump era. The Right Reverend Mariann Budde, the Episcopal bishop of Washington, said she received no notice of the visit and resented the president's use of the church as a "prop." "Everything he has said and done is to inflame violence," she said in an interview with the *Washington Post* that day. "We need moral leadership, and he's done everything to divide us."[5] The Most Reverend Michael Curry, the presiding bishop of the Episcopal Church, said Trump's visit and brandishing of the Bible was done "for partisan political purposes."[6] St. John's officials had passed out water and snacks to the protesters before their dispersal.

Such leaders of mainline denominations disliked Trump's policies and his manner even before he was elected in 2016. In contrast, white evangelicals applauded Trump for his photo op, continuing their support shown throughout his campaign and presidency. Robert Jeffress, senior pastor of the First Baptist Dallas megachurch, told the *Atlantic*: "I thought it was *completely* appropriate for the president to stand in front of that church. . . . And by holding up the Bible, he was showing us that it teaches that, yes, God hates racism, it's despicable—but God also hates lawlessness."[7] Ralph Reed, the longtime Republican political operative, said at the time: "His presence sent the twin message that our streets and our cities do not belong to rioters and domestic terrorists, and that the ultimate answer to what ails our country can be found in the repentance, redemption, and forgiveness of the Christian faith."[8]

It is highly doubtful that Trump intended to send such a nuanced message. Trump rarely attended worship services as an adult and has little familiarity with the contents of the book he displayed at St. John's. (His mention of a verse from "Two Corinthians" instead of the proper "Second Corinthians" elicited chuckles from a Liberty University audience during the 2016 campaign.) Trump may have lacked the vocabulary or knowledge of a committed Christian, but he was an expert in transactional relationships. He knew that white evangelicals were the engine that drove the modern Republican Party in terms of voting, fundraising, policy, and passion. But what did evangelicals see in Trump?

Donald Trump attended a Presbyterian church while growing up in Queens, New York, but the religious figure who shaped him the most was Norman Vincent Peale. Trump's parents regularly took him into Manhattan to hear the famous minister preach at Marble Collegiate Church. Peale's teachings about self-confidence, picturing success, and denying negative thoughts were custom-made for the Trumps. Fred C. Trump, Donald's father and a real estate developer, found succor in Peale's business-friendly teachings. Marble Collegiate was the Trump family church: Peale officiated at Donald's marriage to Ivana in 1977, Donald's sisters were also wed there, and his parents' funerals were conducted in the main sanctuary.[9] Trump and his future second wife, Marla Maples, both attended Marble Collegiate. The church's pastor, Arthur Caliandro, performed their marriage ceremony in the grand ballroom of the Trump-owned Plaza Hotel in 1993.[10] (Peale had long been retired and died days after the wedding at the age of ninety-five.)

Peale's prowess at communication and his "positive-thinking" message made a lifelong impression on Trump. "Reverend Peale was the type of minister that I liked, and I liked him personally as well," Trump wrote in 2007. "I especially loved his sermons. He would instill a very positive feeling about God that also made me feel positive about myself."[11] Trump became the living embodiment of Peale's directives. In *The Power of Positive Thinking*, Peale wrote: "Think defeat and you are bound to feel defeated. But practice thinking confident thoughts, make it a dominating habit, and you will develop such a strong sense of capacity that regardless of what difficulties arise you will be able to overcome them."[12] Confidence, domination, strength—all core elements of Trump's public image.

A 1983 profile of Trump in the *New York Times* highlighted his outsized presence in the real estate world, which the writer called the "essence of entrepreneurial capitalism." Trump had by then completed splashy projects in Manhattan that moved him out of the shadow of his domineering father. "The mind can overcome any obstacle," Trump said. "I never think of the negative." Of his accomplishments, he said, "At 37, no one has done more than I in the last seven years." Peale is described in the article as Trump's pastor and appraises him as "kindly and courteous in certain business negotiations and has a profound streak of humility."[13]

In Peale's autobiography, published the following year, he acknowledged how off-base his comment might have seemed considering Trump's brash reputation. Peale expanded on the side of Trump he observed during negotiations in which "Donald was firm but polite and considerate in pursuing the goals he had set. In his quiet, somewhat low-key, but persistent way, he attained for the church one of the greatest assurances of long-term financial stability in its history." The minister listed some of Trump's notable developments—Trump Tower in Manhattan and the Trump Plaza hotel-casino in Atlantic City—and concluded admiringly: "Donald Trump's career has only just begun, but what a beginning. Surely he is one of America's top positive thinkers and positive doers."[14]

When Trump encountered downturns in his business career, such as when his businesses filed for bankruptcy, he clung to Peale's teachings. "What helped is that I refused to give in to the negative circumstances and I never lost faith in myself," he said in 2009. "I refused to be sucked into negative thinking on any level, even when the indications weren't great. That was a good lesson because I emerged on a very victorious level."[15]

Trump toyed with running for president as early as the 1980s, but for which party? Trump contributed to any politician who served his business interests. As a New Yorker, many he supported were liberal Democrats. He evinced little interest in social issues. In a 1999 interview on NBC's *Meet the Press*, Trump said, "I'm very pro-choice" and opposed banning "partial-birth" abortions. He did not take positions on same-sex marriage or gay people serving openly in the military, but neither prospect seemed to disturb him. Trump pointed to his New York background as an explanation, saying "my views are a little bit different than if I lived in Iowa, perhaps."[16] In 2000, Trump briefly ran for the nomination of the Reform Party, founded by former presidential candidate and business magnate Ross Perot. Trump switched his affiliation to the Democratic Party in 2001, jumped to the Republican Party in 2009, declared no party affiliation in 2011, and returned to the GOP in 2012.

His religious interests were also shifting during this period. Trump, confirmed as a Presbyterian, stopped going to Marble Collegiate and often visited Episcopal churches for Christmas and Easter. In 2002, he came across Florida televangelist Paula White while channel surfing. Impressed by her upbeat message, he contacted her and they became fast friends. They were a generation apart and from different worlds. White was born in 1966, in Tupelo, Mississippi, into a troubled family. Her parents separated when she was five and her father committed suicide, casting her mother into poverty and alcoholism. White said she was "sexually and physically abused numerous times in horrific ways" by adult caretakers.[17] In her teenage years, she suffered from eating disorders, had a child out of wedlock, married, and divorced.

White credits a conversion experience in a neighbor's trailer park at eighteen with turning around her life. She married Randy White, a preacher in the Church of God, a Pentecostal denomination. In 1991, they founded the South Tampa Christian Center, an independent church with Pentecostal teachings. (Paula White did not receive a college or seminary degree.) It began as a storefront church with five people. The Whites hunted for the unchurched by converting a truck into a mobile church that ventured into housing projects on Sundays.[18] The outreach worked. South Tampa Christian Center—advertised as "The Perfect Church for People Who Are Not"—had to relocate several times to accommodate its growing multiracial congregation.[19] The couple renamed it Without Walls International Church in 1997 to reflect their spirit of openness. Dallas megachurch leader T. D. Jakes invited White to present at his popular "Woman Thou Art Loosed" conferences, widening her audience.

Paula White started her television ministry in 2001 with a weekly syndicated talk show, *Paula White Today*. White, a slim, fashionably dressed blonde, openly referenced the wounds of her past. If a "messed-up Mississippi girl" like her could pull herself out of the trailer park, so could they. White delivered her blend of self-help advice and religious messaging via Black Entertainment Television, Trinity Broadcasting Network, and big-city stations. Celebrities facing turmoil such as baseball star Darryl

Strawberry and pop singer Michael Jackson began seeking her out for spiritual guidance. White scored a regular gig on *The Tyra Banks Show* as a "life coach."

Trump appeared on *Paula White Today* in 2006 to pitch his latest book, *Why We Want You to Be Rich*, cowritten with Robert Kiyosaki. "The Bible is about empowerment and taking control of your life," White told her audience.[20] The show offered viewers a free copy of the book with every twenty-five-dollar donation to her ministry. Trump returned the favor by writing a blurb for White's 2007 book, *You're All That!*: "Read this and you'll be ready for great success. She is an amazing woman."[21]

The Whites were budding moguls in their own right. They purchased a $2.1 million mansion on Tampa's exclusive Bayshore Boulevard in 2002, trading up from a $1.2 million house in a gated community.[22] They drove high-end vehicles, a Mercedes for her and a Cadillac Escalade for him. Randy White announced their move to the 8,072-square-foot residence to his congregation in a sermon titled "Poverty or Prosperity." "Sow the seed. In due season, reap the harvest. What you sow is what you reap," he preached. "The decision to live in poverty or prosperity is yours."[23] He received a standing ovation.

Without Walls claimed fifteen thousand members—among the biggest and fastest-growing churches in the country—operated dozens of outreach programs and missions, and reported $10 million in annual revenues in 2002.[24] The couple profited from nonchurch business ventures such as a real estate company and commanded large fees as motivational speakers. Like many megachurch founders, they presented themselves as celebrity CEOs as much as pastors. Both underwent rounds of cosmetic surgeries. "We're on television, and you've got to look the part," Randy White said.[25]

Even with success, their lives were not free of tumult. The Whites stunned their congregation in 2007 when they said they were amicably divorcing, the second time for both. Randy White took "100 percent responsibility" for the split, saying he made poor decisions without getting into details. "I think I've let a lot of people down," he told the *Tampa Tribune*.[26] The newspaper had published investigative reports that cast a negative light on the Whites' stewardship of Without Walls. Business leaders complained that the Whites backed out of deals and failed to pay their bills. "Five lawsuits or claims of lien filed against the couple or the church were settled or resolved in court in the plaintiff's favor," the newspaper reported.[27] Church members groused about broken promises and the church's loss of direction. "They grew at an unbelievable speed. It became less about

God and more about self-promotion," said Doreen Fawkes, a former business administrator at Without Walls.[28]

Later that year, Without Walls and Paula White Ministries were among the subjects of a Senate investigation into the tax-exempt status of media-based ministries. The Whites did not fully cooperate, and the overall probe was dropped with no allegations of wrongdoing. The investigation provided an intriguing window into their operations. Audited financial statements of their combined ministries for 2006 revealed $39.9 million in revenue, mostly from tithes and offerings.[29] A 2005 audit showed $22.5 million in long-term debt and $1.2 million for an airplane lease.[30] In August 2008, Without Walls defaulted on a $1 million bank loan and escaped foreclosure the following year.[31]

Insiders told Senate investigators that the Whites chartered jets for personal use and charged the ministry for the trips.[32] The Without Walls credit card and checking account were frequently used for nonchurch expenses, informants said. The Whites purchased a $3.5 million condo in a Trump building in Manhattan with only $2,625,000 financed, according to the report.[33] The Whites did not say whether ministry money helped pay for the condo or their waterfront mansion in Tampa. The audited financial statements did show that the ministry disbursed housing allowances of $713,779 in 2005 and $883,120 in 2006.[34]

The scrutiny of their financial dealings and the Whites' divorce harmed their ministries. Without Walls' attendance plummeted without Paula in the pulpit. She filled in for a few years while Randy White was in rehab before he retook control. The church's bankruptcy in 2014 resulted in the sale of its properties and White's assets. Without Walls continues today with Randy White as pastor and "bishop" of the downsized congregation.

Paula White became senior pastor of the New Destiny Christian Center megachurch near Orlando and married Jonathan Cain, keyboardist for the rock band Journey. Trump's entry into the presidential race in 2015 drew attention to her role as the candidate's spiritual adviser. She has said about her visits to Trump's office, "I would sit like a fly on the wall and be there all day if I had a free day or several hours. . . . I would pray for him, pray for his family, pray for his staff, just talk God, talk life."[35] Trump invited White to a season finale of his NBC reality show, *The Apprentice*, where she prayed with the cast and crew before the taping.[36]

Her business-oriented prosperity gospel outlook meshed well with Trump's worldview. She had survived scandals, and so had he. Both were entrepreneurs, brand-builders, and television personalities. Trump projected an image of wealth and certainty that evangelicals like White value and respect. In him, they saw a flawed, but faithful, mirror.

Trump, a thrice-married former casino mogul not known for his Christian piety, was not at first the top choice of evangelicals for the Republican nomination in 2016. The field was loaded with candidates attractive to the faith community: Ted Cruz, Marco Rubio, Mike Huckabee, Rick Santorum, and Ben Carson. Other high-profile contenders included Jeb Bush, Chris Christie, John Kasich, and Carly Fiorina. Trump's interview with Bloomberg Politics in August 2015 exposed the shallowness of his religious grounding. Asked to identify his favorite Bible passages, Trump demurred. "When I talk about the Bible, it's very personal. So I don't want to get into verses." When an interviewer broadened the question—"Are you an Old Testament guy or a New Testament guy?"—Trump replied: "Probably equal. I think it's just an incredible—the whole Bible is incredible."[37] He then joked that *Trump: The Art of the Deal* was his second-favorite book after the Bible.

Trump's insult-heavy debate performances and outrageous Twitter feed diverted attention from his from less-famous contenders. His anything-goes rallies received wall-to-wall coverage on cable news networks, even though he slammed outlets like CNN as "fake news." He peppered his remarks with the phrase "believe me" so often that he came off like a used-car salesman or someone trying to convince himself of his own reality. (On military officials carrying out his orders, he said: "They're not going to refuse me. Believe me." On a lawsuit against his troubled namesake university: "Believe me, I'll win that case.")[38] Independent fact-checkers strained to keep up with Trump's Gatling-gun spray of falsehoods. The nonpartisan Poynter Institute's PolitiFact examined Trump's claims in 2015 and determined that nearly 80 percent were false.[39]

Trump, the former pro-choice Democrat, rebranded himself as a staunch opponent of abortion rights who would appoint conservative judges from an activist-approved list. He favored restrictive immigration policies, alleging that Mexico was sending people who brought drugs, crime, and rape into America. He declared that Mexico would pay for a wall along the southern border. Under his "America first" approach, Trump the billionaire businessman claimed he would have the know-how to renegotiate trade deals that he asserted had ripped off the country for years. He promised to cut taxes and environmental regulations after two terms of Democrat Barack Obama. Trump had falsely claimed that Obama was not born in the United States and thus was an illegitimate president.

Trump had also fanned rumors that Obama was secretly a Muslim, referring to him at rallies as "Barack Hussein Obama."

Few presidential candidates in history had a narrower, more elite background than Trump—his adult life was a blur of country clubs, private jets, limos, luxury hotels, and high-rise penthouses—but he effectively exploited the grievances of the common man. Evangelicals and Trump shared a feeling of victimization, that they had been laughed at by mainstream culture and treated unfairly by the news media. Trump's campaign slogan, "Make America Great Again," conveyed the message that their country had been seized from them and that it was time to take it back.

Trump won a plurality of the evangelical vote in the early contests that thinned the field to Trump, Cruz, Rubio, and Kasich. Trump racked up victories in winner-take-all primaries, building an insurmountable lead in the delegate count. Pockets of "never-Trump" dissidents remained among the evangelical community and the party, but most accepted the inevitable: Donald Trump would be the presidential nominee. "Trump could not have won the GOP nomination without the Christian vote," wrote Peter Wehner, a longtime Republican Party activist and Trump opponent.[40]

Popular evangelicals like Paula White were useful surrogates for Trump, who included her in a group of evangelical advisers for his campaign. She vouched for Trump's character in interviews where she was described as Trump's "God whisperer." "I found out that he loved God," she said at a Trump rally in Florida in March 2016. "I found a very caring man. I found a man who had more integrity than most people that I had encountered. A compassionate man."[41] White's ties to Trump only strengthened during the campaign. She delivered the benediction on the first day of the 2016 Republican National Convention.

White was not the only high-profile evangelical to back Trump. Jeffress, the senior pastor at First Baptist Dallas, complimented Trump on Fox News during the primaries. That pleased Trump and he invited Jeffress to pray at a Dallas rally and join him on a swing through Iowa. Asked by the author in 2021 why he supported Trump so early in the race, Jeffress said: "It was real easy: It was a political calculation. I felt like he was the only one of that field running that had the power to beat Hillary Clinton."[42]

Jerry Falwell Jr., who succeeded his late father as chancellor of Liberty University, was also an early Trump endorser. "We're not electing a pastor in chief, we're electing a commander in chief, and we can't expect our commander in chief to have the same qualities as our pastors," Falwell said on CNN during the campaign.[43] The family's moral standard for political candidates had shifted considerably. In 1976, Jerry Falwell Sr. condemned

Jimmy Carter, a born-again Christian and Sunday school teacher, for even consenting to an interview with *Playboy*. Trump had not only been interviewed by *Playboy* but was featured on the cover with Playmate Brandi Brandt in 1990. When Jerry Falwell Jr. tweeted a picture of him giving a thumbs-up with Trump in his New York office, clearly visible in the background was the framed *Playboy* with Trump on the cover. (A series of personal scandals forced Falwell to resign as Liberty's leader in 2020.)

That was not Trump's only connection to the magazine. In 2016, the tabloid publisher American Media, in coordination with Trump campaign operatives, paid $150,000 to former Playmate of the Year Karen McDougal to suppress her allegation that she and Trump had an affair. American Media agreed to pay a fine to the Federal Election Commission to settle alleged campaign finance violations.[44]

In the 1990s, evangelicals had argued that "character counts" and strongly condemned Bill Clinton for his extramarital affairs and ethical lapses. Trump had faced numerous credible accusations of sexual assault, which his loyalists shrugged off as proof that he wasn't a perfect person. A few evangelicals likened Trump to Cyrus, the ancient Persian king who freed Jews held captive in Babylon. God chose the pagan king to carry out his will; perhaps God was using Trump as an unlikely vessel to serve the faithful.

The character question underwent a stress test when the *Washington Post* obtained behind-the-scenes footage of Trump on *Access Hollywood* and published it in October 2016. During a taping in 2005, Trump bragged about hitting on a married woman and groping other women. "And when you're a star, they let you do it. You can do anything," he said. "Grab them by the pussy. You can do anything."[45] Trump's campaign looked finished, with some suggesting Trump should drop out and be replaced by running mate Mike Pence, an evangelical favorite. Ralph Reed, chairman of the Faith and Freedom Coalition, advised the faith community to stick by Trump. It was impractical to switch candidates so late in the race, he counseled. Reed surmised that the tape, as vulgar as he believed it to be, would be low on the list of voter concerns.[46]

Reed's intuition was correct. In a poll taken after the tape's release, 72 percent of white evangelicals agreed that "an elected official who commits an immoral act in their personal life can still behave ethically and fulfill their duties in their public and professional life."[47] Only 30 percent of white evangelicals said that was true five years earlier, during Obama's presidency.[48] Trump's pastors rallied to his side. Jeffress said at the time that the candidate's words on the tape were "crude, offensive, and indefensible, but they're not enough to make me vote for Hillary Clinton."[49]

Trump narrowly defeated Clinton in November, stunning political observers. Evangelicals constituted his most loyal voting bloc. He won 81 percent of white born-again or evangelical Christians, who made up 26 percent of the electorate, according to exit polls.[50] Trump also won 60 percent of the white Catholic vote, a decisive factor in toss-up states such as Michigan, Pennsylvania, and Wisconsin.[51] A majority of white mainline Protestants also supported Trump, as did every other category of white voters.

Paula White, who delivered the invocation at the inauguration, emerged as the de facto leader of a group of evangelical pastors and leaders who regularly advised the administration. The informal council weighed in on issues such as immigration and nominations. She arranged side meetings between faith groups and administration officials. White, Jeffress, and other evangelicals made well-publicized visits to the Oval Office where they laid their hands on Trump in prayer. The days of Harry Truman being angry at photographs of Billy Graham kneeling on the White House lawn were long gone.

White continued to serve as Trump's personal spiritual adviser. She enjoyed a level of White House access for a religious leader not seen since Graham counseled Richard Nixon. Evangelicals have "an unprecedented opportunity to have our voice and say heard," said Tim Clinton, president of the American Association of Christian Counselors. "God has placed Paula in a unique place for such a time as this."[52] In 2019, Trump hired White to advise the administration's Faith and Opportunity Initiative to find ways for religious groups to partner with the federal government.

Russell Moore, then the president of the public policy arm of the Southern Baptist Convention, said he had worried about Trump as early as 2015. Moore perceived how easily Trump's personality-based appeal could tie into increasing political polarization. Moore's criticisms of Trump stirred discontent among some Southern Baptists. "I remember in one of these meetings I was expecting the primary issue to be Trump, and it actually was the fact that I had called Paula White a heretic," Moore said in an interview with the author. "Well, anybody who holds to the most basic minimum of Baptist theology would say that Paula White is a heretic from historic Christianity, but I wasn't supposed to say it, not because someone disagreed with me theologically but because she was the faith-based leader for the president of the United States and had the access to the president of the United States. That's, I think, upside down."[53]

Nevertheless, Trump's evangelical supporters were delighted as they watched him carry out their wish list. Trump signed an executive order to weaken enforcement of the Johnson Amendment, which bars charitable organizations such as churches from using tax-exempt funds to endorse or oppose political candidates. (Trump's action was largely symbolic given that only one church in sixty years had lost its tax-exempt status for violating the amendment.)[54] Evangelicals appreciated Trump's steadfast support of Israel and applauded his decision to relocate the U.S. Embassy from Tel Aviv to Jerusalem, a fulfillment of their interpretation of biblical prophecy. Born-again evangelicals were well represented in cabinet and White House positions. Most important, Trump nominated three justices to the Supreme Court, swinging it firmly to the right. At last, the tantalizing prospect of overturning *Roe v. Wade* seemed well within reach.

Trump also fought for "religious liberty" by granting employers greater authority to deny free birth control and abortion coverage under the Affordable Care Act if they felt it violated their religious beliefs. Business owners were allowed to deny service to gay people on religious grounds, and the increasingly conservative federal courts were left to hash it out.

Critics accused evangelicals of political opportunism. They gained the world—or at least the ear of the president—but forfeited their soul by marching in lockstep with Trump, they argued. Jeffress said he was well aware of the arrangement and pointed to the results. "People say, 'Don't you realize this is a transactional relationship?' And I say, 'Duh! What do you think politics is? It's a transactional relationship,'" Jeffress said in an interview with the author. "I do count [Trump] as a friend, I think he still believes I'm his friend. But we understood what was going on. And yes, he wanted evangelical support, I think he sincerely believed much of what he said he agreed with us on. But I'm not under any delusion that he just liked hanging around us. . . . I think it was just very clear that there was a way for him to benefit from our support and there was a way for us to benefit from his presidency."[55]

Reed, in an interview with the author in October 2021, said he has known Trump for more than a decade and "found him to be somebody who was a man of his word, someone who kept his promises." Even so, Reed said Trump presented a "difficult choice" for evangelicals. "I've been in the Oval Office with faith leaders. I've seen them speak truth to power. I've seen them tell him in strong terms that they think he ought to do XYZ or not do XYZ and they were firm and they were true to their beliefs," Reed said. "Let me tell you something, I've been to the White House plenty. I was part of George W. Bush's political team. I didn't need

Donald Trump to get access to the White House, I assure you. I told him things and gave him my advice, but I offered that in private. I generally don't criticize in public."[56]

It seemed like nothing could shake the party's support for Trump: His administration's "zero tolerance" family-separation policy at the border, his opposition to admitting immigrants from what he referred to as "shithole countries," the reports that Trump and his surrogates paid $130,000 in hush money to porn actress Stormy Daniels to cover up an alleged affair, and Trump's reluctance to strongly condemn the white supremacist rally in Charlottesville, Virginia, in 2017. Trump's boosters flocked to conservative media outlets and social media to rationalize his positions and statements. Trump and his allies came to believe that asserting that something was true actually made it so. If the facts suggested otherwise or were inconvenient, they could be easily dismissed as "negative thinking" or, in his parlance, "fake news." He never admitted defeat, never confessed doubt, and brushed away investigations into his dealings as "hoaxes."

One of the biggest "witch hunts" in Trump's mind was a lengthy probe conducted by special counsel Robert Mueller. The former FBI director's team investigated reports of Russian interference in the 2016 election and the Trump campaign's possible involvement in it. The investigation produced indictments and a handful of guilty pleas or convictions. It did not conclude that Trump committed a crime nor did it exonerate him. Trump and his allies portrayed it as a victory.

Soon thereafter, an impeachment inquiry opened to examine reports that Trump unlawfully solicited Ukrainian authorities to influence the 2020 election. On December 18, 2019, the Democratic-controlled House approved two articles of impeachment against Trump on charges of abuse of power and obstruction of Congress. Trump's evangelical allies leaped to his defense. "There are millions of Christians who REALLY mean it when they say they are praying for President @realDonaldTrump. Today's impeachment vote will ensure these same Christians turn out in record numbers to re-elect him in 2020! FARCE!!" tweeted Jeffress on December 18. A day later, White posted on Twitter: "Tonight we lift up our President, @realDonaldTrump in prayer against all wickedness & demonic schemes against him and his purpose in the name of Jesus. Surround him with your angels and let them encamp around about him. Let all demonic stirrings and manipulations be overturned!"

A trial in the Republican-controlled Senate acquitted Trump. He celebrated the outcome at the National Prayer Breakfast, traditionally a nonpartisan event. Trump attacked Mitt Romney, the lone Republican in the Senate to vote to convict, for citing his faith in helping guide him to the decision. Romney is a member of the Church of Jesus Christ of Latter-day Saints, which has deep theological differences with evangelicals. "I don't like people who use their faith as justification for doing what they know is wrong," Trump said at the breakfast.[57]

The impeachment would almost be forgotten in the whirlwind to come: a pandemic, an economic crisis, and the reckoning over race and social justice. Two other events—dispute over the presidential election and the insurrection at the Capitol—would shake American democracy to its foundations.

The 2020 campaign was a race unlike any other. Pandemic-related restrictions hemmed in the candidates to an extraordinary degree. Party conventions were downsized and were mostly virtual. Democratic nominee Joe Biden held few in-person events. Trump continued to hold rallies that were notable for a lack of physical distancing and mask wearing. About a month before the election, Trump tested positive for COVID-19. His case required advanced treatments and hospitalization, pulling him off the road and canceling one of his debates with Biden.

A controversy flared up late in the campaign with the publication of a score-settling memoir by former Trump personal attorney Michael Cohen. The fixer, who served prison time after pleading guilty to fraud charges, claimed Trump privately mocked evangelicals. He wrote that White and other faith leaders were summoned to Trump Tower in 2011 to discuss a potential Trump presidential run. The evangelicals laid their hands on Trump in prayer looking for God's guidance. After the meeting, Cohen wrote that Trump remarked, "Can you believe that bullshit? Can you believe people believe that bullshit?"[58] Cohen told the *Atlantic* that Trump admired evangelical leaders for their money-making abilities. When Cohen told Trump that Creflo Dollar, one of the evangelical leaders at the conference, asked his followers to pay for a Gulfstream G650, Trump said Dollar was "full of shit," according to Cohen. "They're all hustlers," Trump concluded.[59]

Trump's approval ratings had taken a hit during the pandemic, but many evangelical leaders and their "MAGA" churches continued to back him. On October 18, weeks after the Cohen book was published, Trump visited the International Church of Las Vegas and listened as Denise Goulet, the senior associate pastor, informed the crowd of her early-morning vision. "At 4:30, the Lord said to me, 'I am going to give your president a second win.'"[60] They believed that Trump stood up for them against Democratic governors who took away their right to worship in person because of the pandemic. "The Democratic Party today has been taken over by the spirit of the Antichrist. It's an evil party," said Richard Lee, founding pastor of the five-thousand-member First Redeemer Church near Atlanta, at a Trump event.[61]

Many states allowed mail-in voting and early in-person balloting in light of the pandemic. Trump warned of the potential of rampant fraud. The high voter turnout put pressure on election officials to process the ballots and to provide timely results. Biden appeared to be headed to victory as election night passed into the early morning, but Trump asserted, "As far as I'm concerned we already have won it." The counting of absentee and mail-in ballots continued through the week as Trump tried to halt the process through legal challenges. On November 7, major news organizations called Pennsylvania for Biden, handing him the Electoral College votes he needed to win the presidency. On the same day, Trump supporters demonstrated at "Stop the Steal" rallies at state capitol buildings. Some were members of far-right militia groups who wore camouflage and openly carried firearms.[62]

The nation remained stuck in a state of suspension. The Biden transition team was not granted full access to government resources and agencies for weeks. Few Republican leaders publicly accepted that he had won, even though most foreign leaders had recognized Biden as the president-elect. Unfounded rumors of widespread fraud lit up conservative media outlets and social media networks. Trump filed lawsuits challenging the results in states he narrowly lost. State election officials of both parties methodically reviewed their procedures, conducted recounts if required, and certified the results.

White evangelical support for Trump was as overwhelming as it was in 2016. The AP VoteCast survey reported that 81 percent voted for Trump and the Edison exit polls put the estimate at 76 percent. About a quarter of all voters were white evangelical Christians, a higher proportion than their population size.[63] Paula White led a post-election prayer service punctuated with her speaking in tongues. "I hear a sound of victory. The Lord says it is done. The Lord says it is done. The Lord says it is done. For I hear victory, victory, victory, victory in the quarters of heaven," she incanted in a video that went viral. "For angels are being released right now, angels are being dispatched right now" from Africa and South America, she said.[64] Kenneth Copeland announced to his studio audience that the Associated Press had called the election for Biden and then laughed maniacally for nearly thirty seconds.

Trump's options narrowed day by day as his legal team racked up dozens of losses in the courts. On December 14, electors in each state formally cast their votes for president and vice president according to the certified results. Trump still refused to concede. His team filed long-shot appeals to the Supreme Court to overturn the results in key states. On January 2, 2021, Trump pressured Georgia's secretary of state, Brad Raffensperger, to "find" the votes that would make him the winner of the state. The Republican official declined, saying there was no credible evidence of fraud. Raffensperger released a recording of the phone call to media outlets.

The final step would come on January 6 when a joint session of Congress would ceremonially count the electoral votes. Some Republicans in the House and Senate said they planned to raise challenges. As vice president, Mike Pence had the task of presiding over the proceeding, which usually consisted of opening sealed certificates and handing them to tellers to read and tally. Trump declared that Pence had the power to reject electors, contrary to the Constitution and custom. Pence, a born-again evangelical Christian, had been exceedingly deferential to Trump during his term. It was not clear what he would do.

On the morning of January 6, Trump hosted a rally near the White House that he had been publicizing on Twitter. He rambled for more than an hour to tens of thousands of supporters at the Ellipse, saying it was up to Pence to "come through for us" and send the election results back to the states to recertify. "We will never give up, we will never concede. It doesn't happen. You don't concede when there's theft involved," he said. "We fight like hell. And if you don't fight like hell, you're not going to have a country anymore."[65] Trump said he would march with them down Pennsylvania Avenue to the Capitol "to demand that Congress do the right thing and only count the electors who have been lawfully slated." (Trump stayed at the White House and followed along on TV.)

The jacked-up crowd—a dangerous brew of QAnon conspiracists, MAGA die-hards, Christian nationalists, white supremacists, and self-styled militiamen—moved toward the Capitol and easily breached the flimsy police perimeters around the complex. The pro-Trump mob included members of violent far-right groups like the Proud Boys, who Trump had said should "stand back and stand by."[66] A mock gallows was constructed outside the building. Armed rioters broke through windows and doors, forcing the House and Senate to suspend their proceedings.

Pence, who had said earlier in the day that he would perform his duties as prescribed in the Constitution, was evacuated just before rioters burst into the Senate chamber. Ten minutes later, Trump tweeted: "Mike Pence didn't have the courage to do what should have been done to protect our Country and our Constitution, giving States a chance to certify a corrected set of facts, not the fraudulent or inaccurate ones which they were asked to previously certify. USA demands the truth!" House members were barricaded in the House chamber and other Capitol offices. Cellphone videos revealed that members of the mob were hunting for Pence and House Speaker Nancy Pelosi, whose suite of offices were ransacked and occupied. Reporters, camera operators, and photographers—members of the "fake news" media whom Trump had repeatedly called "the enemy of the people"—were assaulted and their equipment smashed.

Military leaders and government officials belatedly called in National Guard forces to reinforce the overwhelmed Capitol Police. They retook control of the Capitol, allowing the House and Senate to reconvene in the evening. Republican members of Congress continued to raise objections to counting electoral votes as if nothing had happened. The debate continued into the early morning when Biden's victory was finally confirmed. The rampage resulted in the deaths of four people plus a Capitol Police officer who died of natural causes after clashing with rioters. More than a hundred law enforcement officials were injured. It was the worst attack on the Capitol since the War of 1812.

The evangelical reaction to the insurrection was mostly muted. Albert Mohler, president of the Southern Baptist Theological Seminary and a Trump voter, said the president's actions were an "attempt to subvert the very constitutional order that he took an oath of office to defend."[67] A handful falsely alleged that Black Lives Matter and antifa, a militant far-left movement, had orchestrated the riot. Most stayed quiet or issued "blame on both sides" statements. "There were a few who, when January 6 happened, were rattled by that and asked what have we done in enabling this sort of language about a stolen election, but there were very few and almost no one who would do that in public. And so that's precisely the problem," said Moore, the former official with the Southern Baptist Convention.[68]

The House impeached Trump one week later on a charge of "incitement of insurrection" with ten Republicans joining all Democrats voting to impeach. The Senate acquitted Trump after he left office. Authorities scoured videos and social media posts to track down and arrest people involved in the riot. Trump maintained his hold over his base. In a poll taken after his second impeachment, 62 percent of white evangelical Protestants viewed Trump favorably. Among all Americans, only 31 percent had a favorable opinion of Trump.[69]

As the shock of the insurrection dulled, Republicans retaliated against members of Congress who voted for impeachment. They were censured by state parties, booed at party conventions, stripped of leadership posts, and threatened with Trump-approved primary challengers. Polling later in the year showed 61 percent of Republicans and 57 percent of white evangelical Protestants placed "a lot of responsibility" for the attack on liberal or left-wing activists despite the lack of credible evidence. Only 15 percent of Republicans and 26 percent of white evangelicals put most of the blame on Trump, numbers far lower than any other group surveyed.[70]

In a display of loyalty to Trump, congressional Republicans in May 2021 blocked a House-approved bill to set up an independent commission to investigate the attack. The Democratic-run House appointed a January 6 select committee that included two Republicans who had been ostracized from their party for voting to impeach Trump and continuing to speak out against him. The vast majority of Republicans and their evangelical base may have deplored the violence, but they supported the reason behind it. A survey in August 2021 reported that 61 percent of white evangelical Protestants believed the election was stolen from Trump, an opinion shared by 71 percent of Republicans.[71]

Republican leaders wanted to move on from examining the insurrection, but not the 2020 presidential election. Arizona approved a partisan review of votes in its most populous county, and lawmakers in other states pressed for similar "forensic audits." The efforts did not overturn the outcome, but they normalized the act of officially questioning verified results. Republican-controlled states speedily approved new voting restrictions that they argued would ensure "election integrity." Democrats charged that they were blatant attempts at voter suppression, particularly against people of color. Georgia passed a law in 2021 granting the GOP-dominated legislature greater control over the state's election board. About a dozen other states have taken similar steps to ensure party loyalists have broader authority to decide which ballots to accept and which electors to select, potentially overruling the will of the voters. Many of the guardrails that barely staved off a constitutional crisis after the 2020 vote will be weakened for the 2024 presidential election.

Something elemental had cracked in the country. If more than two-thirds of a political party believed without evidence that the election was stolen, why would their representatives work with a new administration seen as illegitimate? This intransigence thwarted the country's ability to deal with the resurgence of the pandemic in mid-2021. Political polarization had decayed into a poisonous atmosphere of cynicism and bad-faith arguments.

Under Trump's influence, Republicans felt emboldened to embrace anti-democratic means of acquiring and maintaining power. White evangelicals had cast their lot with Trump and most stood with him throughout it all. In doing so, whether they intended to or not, evangelicals helped enable the country's tilt toward authoritarianism.

EPILOGUE

The Last Patriarch

The Death of Billy Graham and the Fate of the Evangelical Movement

> I don't analyze people. I got a son that analyzes everything and everybody. But I don't analyze people.
>
> —Billy Graham, referencing his
> eldest son and heir apparent, Franklin[1]

When Billy Graham died on February 21, 2018, at the age of ninety-nine, his rites took on the trappings of a state funeral. Congress granted approval for Graham's remains to lie in honor in the Capitol Rotunda, making him the first religious figure to receive that distinction.[2] Pastors marveled at the innumerable souls Graham had won—his ministry estimated Graham had preached to 215 million people in 185 countries during his six decades of crusades. Political leaders, perhaps with a tinge of jealousy, cited his enduring popularity—Graham had appeared in the top ten of Gallup's annual "most admired man" list a record sixty-one times.[3]

Graham lived so long and made so few public appearances in his final decade that he seemed like a figure from history when he died. Even when he was a much younger man, Graham had evoked a sense of nostalgia. A *New York Times* article in 1958 included a comment from a father who took his children to a Graham crusade "so that they might experience a phenomenon in American life that will soon disappear."[4] Graham always seemed like the last of his kind, and he almost certainly was.

His funeral took place on the grounds of the Billy Graham Library in Charlotte, North Carolina, which adjoins the headquarters of the Billy Graham Evangelistic Association. The rambling campus resembles a presidential library with its displays of mementos gleaned from international travels. (Three former presidents attended the library's dedication ceremony in 2007.) The complex's most notable feature is a barn-like structure that hearkens back to Graham's boyhood on the family dairy farm. Visitors enter through the foot of a glass cross. The building is filled with artifacts and multimedia presentations on Graham's life and ministry. Graham's restored childhood home is nearby, as is a silo, to complete the rustic tableaux of the preacher's rural roots.

All of this served as a backdrop to Graham's funeral, which was held under an expansive tent to accommodate the mourners, including the Trumps and the Pences. It was a stately affair, with tasteful hymns and praise from an array of pastors. Four of his five children ascended the platform together and each testified to his fatherly guidance and love for his late wife, Ruth. Later in the service, Graham's eldest son, Franklin, rose from his front-row seat and walked up alone to deliver the eulogy. Billy had long ago handed over the reins of his ministry to Franklin, a more astringent version of his father. Franklin alluded to that public perception in his remarks. "When I think about my father, I can sit quietly and I can still hear his voice. A word of encouragement and sometimes a word of caution—there are quite a few of those," he said with a self-aware chuckle.[5]

Father and son's approach to politics diverged as they aged. Billy Graham's exquisite talent for friendship—and unparalleled skill at flattering the powerful—made him easy company. He forged a close alliance with Dwight Eisenhower and congressional leaders of both parties in the 1950s and 1960s. President Lyndon Johnson frequently summoned Graham to the White House and down to his Texas ranch for fellowship and informal prayer services. Graham relished playing the role of "America's pastor," presiding at presidential inaugurations and gamely sparring on TV with the likes of Johnny Carson and Woody Allen.

When Graham's longtime friend Richard Nixon was elected president in 1968, Nixon treated him more like a political asset than a spiritual counselor. "On the political front, it is important to start an early liaison with Billy Graham and his people," the Republican president wrote in a memo to White House chief of staff H. R. Haldeman dated November 30, 1970. "He was enormously helpful to us in the Border South in '68 and will continue to be in '72."[6] The Nixon administration prized Graham's unwavering support, and Graham was happy to oblige. "It is amazing to me that people who made a hero of [Daniel] Ellsberg for stealing the Pentagon Papers are so deeply concerned about the alleged escapade at Watergate," Graham wrote to Haldeman in October 1972.[7]

Graham sank into the administration's deep well of cynicism and paranoia. The secret Oval Office taping system captured Graham commiserating with Nixon and other top aides about the baleful influence of Jews on the news media. "And they're the ones putting out the pornographic stuff," Graham said about Jews on February 1, 1972. "This stranglehold has got to be broken or this country is going to go down the drain. . . . A lot of the Jews are great friends of mine. . . . They don't know how I really feel about what they're doing to this country."[8] (Graham apologized for his comments when the recordings were made public decades later.) The trauma of Watergate and Nixon's resignation burned Graham so badly that he retreated from partisan politics while many evangelicals were jumping into the fray.

While Graham stayed true to his basic message—accept Christ and be saved—he adopted a less judgmental tone as he transitioned into the role of the nation's avuncular patriarch. In the fire of youth, he had warned America to repent immediately or face certain destruction. He pinned down specific dates for the Second Coming and then rescheduled them with the passage of time. He often described heaven's precise physical properties: sixteen hundred square miles with yellow Cadillac convertibles driving on golden streets. Such statements, Graham conceded later in life, "were rather foolish."[9] He confessed to not always having a ready answer to difficult theological or political questions. Graham recognized that the times had changed, and so had he. As he told interviewer David Frost in 1993: "I've tried to be contemporary. I've tried to keep up with what's going on in the world and relate my messages to the world."[10]

To Graham, that meant being flexible on the social issues that galvanized religious conservatives. Graham believed homosexuality was a sin but added "there are worse sins" and considered it to be on par with adultery.[11] Graham did not condemn gay people or storm the ramparts to strip away their rights. He opposed abortion but backed exceptions in cases of rape or incest or if the life of the mother was in danger. Graham strongly supported birth control, especially after witnessing the pressures of overpopulation during his travels to developing countries.[12] He recognized the American free-enterprise system's flaws—the persistence of poverty and the widening income gap—and that it could not be applied to every country. "I don't think it's the only one that Christians can support. We are a socialist society compared to, let's say, the days of Franklin Roosevelt. There has to be a certain amount of socialism," he said.[13]

After Graham's last crusade—his 417th—in New York City in 2005, the wizened preacher rarely strayed far from his mountaintop home in Montreat, North Carolina. Franklin became the family's most visible face through his leadership of the Billy Graham Evangelistic Association and the Christian humanitarian relief organization Samaritan's Purse—in all, a $765 million evangelical empire.[14]

While Billy Graham mellowed with age, his son courted controversy. After 9/11, Franklin Graham repeatedly disparaged Islam as a "wicked" and "evil" religion and joined a chorus of anti-Muslim sentiment among some evangelicals. In a 2011 interview on ABC with Christiane Amanpour, he said he would consider supporting Donald Trump if he ran for president: "The more you listen to him, the more you say to yourself, 'You know, maybe the guy is right.'"[15] Graham also fanned Trump's unfounded "birther" allegations questioning Barack Obama's American citizenship and raised doubts about whether Obama was truly a Christian. Trump contributed hefty sums to Franklin's ministries in appreciation.[16]

Upon Obama's reelection in 2012, Franklin Graham said, "If we are allowed to go down this road in the path that this president wants us to go down, I think it will be to our peril and to the destruction of this nation."[17] During the 2016 presidential campaign, Graham held rallies in all fifty states urging Christians to vote. He did not explicitly endorse Trump, but Graham's strong preference for him was obvious. Graham delivered the benediction at Trump's inauguration. ("Mr. President, in the Bible, rain is a sign of God's blessing. And it started to rain, Mr. President, when you came to the platform," he remarked before his Bible reading.)[18] Graham consistently defended Trump and his administration's policies from the "fake news" media and liberals.

Graham's hard-edged attitudes touched every aspect of his ministries. In April 2020, early in the coronavirus pandemic, Samaritan's Purse sent up medical tents in New York's Central Park to treat overflow hospital patients. Graham drew fire for his group's requirement that employees and volunteers sign a statement that they believe in Jesus Christ and affirm that "marriage is exclusively the union of one genetic male and one genetic female."[19] Episcopal Bishop Andrew M. L. Dietsche told the *New York Times* that the pledge helped derail plans to place Samaritan's Purse tents inside the Cathedral of St. John the Divine. Dietsche said Graham advocated "an exclusionary view and a very narrow view of what constitutes being a Christian."[20]

Graham undoubtedly would have found no fault with that assessment. Unlike his father, Franklin did not strive to be a consensus religious figure. "Jesus tells us that no one comes to the father except through him," Franklin declared at his father's funeral. "The world with all of its political correctness would want you to believe that there are many roads to God. It's just not true."[21]

Billy Graham had done more than anyone to popularize the aspirations of modern evangelicalism. "His lasting achievement was to bring the great variety of conservative white Protestants, North and South, into his capacious revival tent under the name 'evangelicals,'" wrote journalist and author Frances FitzGerald.[22] Scholar David P. Gushee has argued that evangelicalism was "a brilliant social construction, an invented religious *identity*, that over decades yielded something like an actual religious *community*."[23] The "entrepreneurial efforts" of fundamentalist reformers in the 1940s successfully rebranded their movement as "evangelical," he wrote in his recent book, *After Evangelicalism*.[24] As a result, evangelicals and their business allies shaped postwar American religion and politics.

But what does it mean today to be an evangelical? Has the label outlived its usefulness? Is it as much of a political identity as a religious one? In 2017, the Princeton Evangelical Fellowship altered its name of eighty years to Princeton Christian Fellowship because the term had become an "unnecessary hindrance."[25] "I'm old enough to think [evangelical] is a good word, but it's reached a point where there's so much baggage attached around it so that it's no longer a helpful word to identify ourselves," said William Boyce, the student group's executive secretary and associate chaplain.[26]

Russell Moore spoke at Princeton around that time in his role as president of the Ethics and Religious Liberty Commission, the public policy arm of the Southern Baptist Convention. Moore said when people in the university community objected to "evangelical" in the title, they assumed it represented the "political, culture wars sort of movement that they'd seen on television and it just became easier for them to jettison the word. I understand that, I just don't think we should do that across the board."[27]

Moore resigned in 2021 after a tumultuous eight years as the commission's president. He has raised concerns about the powerful denomination's history of racism and criticized its executive committee's handling of sexual abuse allegations. Moore is now the full-time public theologian for *Christianity Today* and leads a public theology project. Moore is striving to build healthier coalitions under the "evangelical" label. "I don't think there's an alternative that communicates the language very well, and I don't want to cede that language to the ideologues and the grifters—it's too good of a word," he told the author. "It's easy to form a coalition around access to power with a political party or candidate, or the ability to make large amounts of money off of direct mail or targeted email fundraising. That's easy to do and it's easy to do that with extreme rhetoric and constantly upping the extreme rhetoric. It's more difficult to form a coalition of sanity, but I think that's what's necessary right now."[28]

The entrepreneurial nature of evangelicalism too often rewards the most strident voices, which are amplified in social media's echo chambers. "The more fearful or angry one is, the more one is seen to be standing for Christ or standing for the truth," Moore said. That impulse extends well beyond the sanctuary on Sunday mornings. In her incisive book, *Jesus and John Wayne*, scholar Kristin Kobes Du Mez argued that "evangelicalism must be seen as a cultural and political movement rather than as a community defined chiefly by its theology."[29] That movement prizes aggressive masculinity—represented by people like John Wayne and Donald Trump—to assert white Christian dominance at home and abroad, in her assessment.[30]

Evangelicals have long portrayed themselves as warriors fighting to save America from perceived enemies. They opposed gay people serving as public school teachers in the 1970s and 1980s, then they lobbied against same-sex marriage in the 1990s and 2000s, and today the battle is against rights for transgender people and unisex public restrooms. They objected to teaching evolution in schools, denounced sex education, and now attack "critical race theory." Some evangelical pastors insinuated that civil rights leaders had communist ties in the 1950s and 1960s, and now they sound alarms about the far-left infiltration of the Black Lives Matter movement. They condemned the New Deal, the Great Society, and the Affordable Care Act as dangerous forays into godless, anti-American socialism.

Pastors understandably feel called to speak out on public policy issues that they believe to be rooted in morality, but they risk straying from what they have always identified as their primary purpose: Winning souls for Jesus and creating disciples. "Evangelicalism has become very political, which is not a good thing," Miles McPherson, pastor of the Rock Church in San Diego, said in an interview with the author. "We need to focus on the Bible and Jesus more. The label 'evangelical' has too much political baggage right now, and we need to get back to Jesus."[31] McPherson, who is Black, leads a multi-campus, racially diverse congregation that is one of the largest in San Diego County. McPherson acknowledges the persistence of racial divisions in society and sees a role for the church in healing them through his Third Option Similarity Training program.

Walter Kim, former pastor of historic Park Street Church in Boston, became the first person of color to be president of the National Association of Evangelicals in 2020. Kim, the son of immigrant parents, sees a diversity to evangelicalism that is often overlooked. "I think we're experiencing a very interesting shift as we are forced to think through what does it actually mean to be an evangelical. And it's a very complicated picture," he told the author.[32] Evangelicals have a strong sense of personal transformation and social engagement, he said, but what has been lacking is a structure to bolster that activism. "Do we have a forum of discipleship and theology that could sustain and develop the Christian imagination for our civic engagement? This is a weak point in evangelicalism," Kim said.[33] He hopes to partner with churches to strengthen it.

George Barna, an evangelical who founded a research company that has worked on church marketing since the 1980s, thinks some pastors have focused too much on physical growth at the expense of spiritual growth. "Here we are forty years later and we're no better at marketing. We're better at filling auditoriums, we're better at raising money, we're better at creating stunning buildings, but we're not better at ministry," he said in an interview.[34]

For instance, almost all evangelical churches use a small group model in which people meet in a home during the week for Bible study and fellowship. It keeps people attached to the church, but it is not usually successful in fostering discipleship, said Barna, who directs the Cultural Research Center at Arizona Christian University. "What I found in our research is that small groups are terrific for establishing and sustaining community. They're not very effective at growing people spiritually because what you wind up having is ignorant people sharing their ignorance. It's kind of a democratic form of education: 'We're going to vote on what the truth is.' That's not actually how biblical truth works," he said.[35] Churches should match people up with a mentor who is further along in the spiritual journey, Barna said, and then translate that discipleship into action.

American evangelicals have reimagined what a church could be, whether it was a humble tent in a rural field, a specially built urban tabernacle, or a multi-site megachurch. They redefined the worship service—out went the musty organs and solemn hymns and in came the electric guitars and high-energy praise songs. They espoused an ecstatic version of Christianity rooted in their interpretation of eternal biblical truths. They received indispensable backing for their enterprises at the highest ranks of business and politics. In turn, they changed the country. Evangelicals must now decide if their movement is primarily about winning souls or winning power.

ACKNOWLEDGMENTS

I count myself as a person of faith, but not as an evangelical. So this book—a four-year odyssey of reading, reporting, arguing, and thinking—is by definition an outsider's view of the evangelical world. Beginning writers are often instructed to "write what you know," but one of the joys of being a journalist is having to cover things we don't know. And even the subjects we think we understand yield constant surprises. This project was no exception. I have always been fascinated by why people believe what they do and the consequences of those beliefs. I have approached this book with a spirit of curiosity and fairness. Any errors or misjudgments are my fault and my fault alone.

As an independent researcher, I never take for granted the San Diego County and City of San Diego library systems. They are also portals into the treasures within the region's university libraries. After pandemic-related restrictions lifted, I was fortunate to spend three delightful days at Wheaton College's Billy Graham Center Archives in the Chicago suburbs. It's a must-visit for anyone researching evangelicalism. I thank Katherine Graber for accommodating my travel schedule, Bob Shuster for staying after hours and directing me to resources I didn't know I needed, and Emily Banas and Keith Call for their good humor and diligence in processing my requests. At the Morgan Library at Grace College in Indiana, Tonya Fawcett and Rhoda Palmer went out of their way to provide access to the archive's extraordinary collection of Billy Sunday papers and memorabilia. They cheerfully located hard-to-find articles and copied them without me asking. Terry White walked me through Sunday's colorful life during my visit to the Winona History Center in Indiana and then took me on a personal tour of the nearby Billy Sunday Home.

I waited until I was fully vaccinated before attending in-person church services. For my visits, which started in June 2021, I attempted to cover the diversity of evangelical worship: a storefront church in a former billiards hall, high-profile megachurches, a Southern Baptist Convention church, a prosperity-gospel flavored church, and a congregation that met in a hotel reception hall. I felt it was essential to experience worship from the inside to meet people where they are. Without exception, the dozens of people I encountered during my visits to nine different churches—plus a Franklin Graham rally—were joyful and eager to discuss their faith journeys. I thank them for taking in a stranger.

I'm deeply appreciative to George Barna, Robert Jeffress, Walter Kim, Jeremy McGarity, Miles McPherson, Russell Moore, Larry Osbourne, Ralph Reed, and Robert A. Schuller for agreeing to be interviewed. They were all thoughtful, patient, and generous with their time.

Many thanks to my literary agent, Anne G. Devlin of the Max Gartenberg Literary Agency, for again finding a good home for my writing. Jake Bonar, acquisitions editor at Globe Pequot Press–Prometheus Books, has championed this book every step of the way. I also appreciate the care the publisher brought to the book's design, production, editing, and promotion.

It's asking a lot of someone to read drafts of a book, so I'm lucky to have family and friends who answered the call. Jim Antenore, Donna Clary, Mark Clary, Sheila Dougherty, David Franecki, Bennett Furlow, Karen Kucher, Dan Murphy, Laura Redford, Marcia Rubin, Holly Trusiak, and Mitch Weinstock offered valuable feedback and encouragement. I thank them and others—especially Alysia Clary and Jay Rubin—for helping me sharpen my thinking on this complicated subject. At the *San Diego Union-Tribune*, managing editor Lora Cicalo enthusiastically granted me the time and space I needed to work on this book.

When I was growing up, we often discussed the two subjects you are told not to talk about at the dinner table: religion and politics. The main initiator of those conversations was my father, Hal Clary, whom I miss dearly. We sometimes disagreed on the issues of the day—at times loudly as I got older—but never disagreeably. I so wish we could have talked about the ideas behind this book. I know his thoughts would have made it better.

Finally, this book is dedicated to my wife, Jackie. She's my best editor, my biggest supporter, my true companion in life's journey. When the pandemic took hold, we were both forced to work from home dorm-room style in our bedroom. As always, she made the best of adverse circumstances. Our children, Sammy and Elliott, have weathered the shocks of the last two years with amazing grace. I am blessed beyond measure.

NOTES

EPIGRAPH

1. "Cheering Singing Throngs Greet Billy Sunday as He Comes to Launch Revival," *New York World*, April 8, 1917.

PROLOGUE

1. Cleve R. Wootson Jr., "Florida Pastor, Others Flout Stay-Home Orders on Easter," *Washington Post*, April 12, 2020.

2. CNBC transcript from January 22, 2020, https://www.cnbc.com/2020/01/22/cnbc-transcript-president-donald-trump-sits-down-with-cnbcs-joe-kernen-at-the-world-economic-forum-in-davos-switzerland.html.

3. "Remarks by President Trump in Meeting with African American Leaders," February 27, 2020, https://www.whitehouse.gov/briefings-statements/remarks-president-trump-meeting-african-american-leaders/. Interviews that journalist Bob Woodward conducted with Donald Trump in February 2020 revealed that Trump knew the novel coronavirus was deadlier than he let on. The interviews were included in Woodward's book, *Rage*, published in September 2020.

4. Bianca Padró Ocasio, "'Demonic Spirit': Miami Pastor Rejects Coronavirus Warning," *Miami Herald*, March 15, 2020.

5. Daniel Burke, "Police Arrest Florida Pastor for Holding Church Services Despite Stay-at-Home Order," CNN, March 30, 2020.

6. Burke, "Police Arrest Florida Pastor for Holding Church Services Despite Stay-at-Home Order."

7. "University Administration Works Tirelessly to Accommodate Students, Comply with New COVID-19 Laws," Liberty University News Service, March 23, 2020.

8. Elizabeth Williamson, "Falwell Focuses on Critics as Coronavirus Cases Near His University Grow," *New York Times*, April 16, 2020.

9. From the beginning, Republican leaders followed Trump in downplaying the threat. Oklahoma governor Kevin Stitt tweeted a cheerful selfie of him with two of his children dining inside a restaurant on March 14, 2020. "It's packed to-night!" he remarked. (In July 2020, Stitt became the first governor to test positive for the virus.) On the same day, Texas senator John Cornyn tweeted a photo of a bottle of Corona next to a glass of beer with a lime wedge on the lip. "Be smart; don't panic. We will get us through this #coronavirus," he wrote, suggesting it was akin to waiting out a hurricane.

10. Lisa Maria Garza, "Despite Coronavirus Concerns, Worshippers Gather at Orlando Church Under Statewide Exemption," *Orlando Sentinel*, April 5, 2020.

11. Jaclyn Peiser, "Megachurch Pastor Who Held No-Mask Services Misses Hearing after Refusing to Wear Mask in Court," *Washington Post*, September 23, 2020.

12. Peter Baker, "Firing a Salvo in Culture Wars, Trump Pushes for Churches to Reopen," *New York Times*, May 22, 2020.

13. Baker, "Firing a Salvo in Culture Wars, Trump Pushes for Churches to Reopen."

14. The Supreme Court, also in a 5–4 vote, rejected a similar challenge by Calvary Chapel Dayton Valley in Nevada on July 24. The dissenting justices were particularly upset that casinos were permitted to open at greater capacity than houses of worship. Justice Ruth Bader Ginsburg, the court's leading liberal, died on September 18, 2020. Her replacement, the conservative Amy Coney Barrett, swung the court in the opposite direction on this issue. With Barrett's vote, the justices ruled Newsom's order was unconstitutional and separately struck down New York state's restrictions on worship.

15. Sara Cline, "Church Tied to Oregon's Largest Coronavirus Outbreak," Associated Press, June 16, 2020; Christian M. Giggenbach, "Pastor Admits Mistakes but Won't Require Masks," *Register-Herald*, June 16, 2020; Kate Conger, Jack Healy, and Lucy Tompkins, "Churches Were Eager to Reopen. Now They Are Confronting Coronavirus Cases," *New York Times*, July 8, 2020.

16. Ruth Graham, "The Phoenix Megachurch Where Trump Is Speaking Says Its Air Purifiers 'Kill 99.9 Percent of COVID,'" *Slate*, June 23, 2020.

17. Trump resisted wearing protective face masks even after evidence made clear that the simple act helped slow the spread of the virus. During a press briefing on April 3, 2020, Trump read a Centers for Disease Control and Prevention guideline urging all Americans to wear face coverings in public. Then he immediately under-cut it by saying, "This is voluntary. I don't think I'm going to be doing it. . . . I just don't see it for myself." See Michael D. Shear and Sheila Kaplan, "A Debate over Masks Uncovers Deep White House Divisions," *New York Times*, April 3, 2020.

18. Jack Graham, the seventy-year-old pastor of Prestonwood Baptist Church, sat next to Laurie at the Rose Garden event. He ignored medical guidelines to

quarantine for two weeks and led an in-person service at his Dallas-area mega-church on October 4, 2020. "I am ridiculously healthy, let's just put it that way. I'm not sick. I'm fine. . . . I don't have COVID," the maskless Graham assured his congregation at Prestonwood Baptist Church, even though the possibility of asymptomatic spread had by then been well documented. A spokesperson said two tests came back negative without giving dates. Graham's sermon on the Sunday after the Rose Garden event was titled, "Socialism: A Clear and Present Danger." Jack Jenkins and Emily McFarlan Miller, "Trump Evangelical Advisers Exposed to COVID-19 Flout CDC Guidelines, Preach in Public," Religion News Service, October 5, 2020.

19. Patricia Mazzei, "The Virus Death Toll in the U.S. Has Passed 400,000," *New York Times*, January 19, 2021.

20. Elizabeth Dias and Ruth Graham, "White Evangelical Resistance Is Obstacle in Vaccination Effort," *New York Times*, April 5, 2021.

21. Alec Tyson, Cary Funk, Brian Kennedy, and Courtney Johnson, "Majority in U.S. Says Public Health Benefits of COVID-19 Restrictions Worth the Costs, Even as Large Shares Also See Downsides," Pew Research Center, September 15, 2021. Among white, nonevangelical Protestants, 73 percent said they had received at least one dose. Among all Catholic respondents, 82 percent said they had been vaccinated.

22. Jeremy McGarity, author interview, October 5, 2021.

23. McGarity interview.

24. Balmer and Winner, *Protestantism in America*, 22–23; and FitzGerald, *Evangelicals*, 637.

25. Luhrmann, *When God Talks Back*, xv; and Kidd, *Who Is an Evangelical?*, 4–5.

26. "The American Religious Landscape in 2020," *PRRI,* July 8, 2021, https://www.prri.org/research/2020-census-of-american-religion/. The survey found that 14 percent of Hispanics identified as evangelical Protestant and 10 percent as nonevangelical Protestant. Among multiracial respondents, 23 percent identified as evangelical Protestant and 18 percent as nonevangelical protestant. Asian or Pacific Islanders had 10 percent in each camp.

27. Pew Research Center, "U.S. Public Becoming Less Religious," November 3, 2015.

CHAPTER 1

1. Stout, *The Divine Dramatist*, 131.

2. Cousins, *In God We Trust*, 39. For ease of readability, I have modernized the spelling, capitalization, and punctuation when quoting from older writings.

3. Lambert, *Pedlar in Divinity*, 174. For more on Whitefield's clash with Vesey, see Stout, *The Divine Dramatist*, 96.

4. Morgan, *Benjamin Franklin*, 59; and Cousins, *In God We Trust*, 37.

5. Stout, *The Divine Dramatist*, 99.

6. Benjamin Franklin letter to George Whitefield dated July 2, 1756. *Founders Online,* National Archives, https://founders.archives.gov/documents/Franklin/01-06 -02-0210. [Original source: *The Papers of Benjamin Franklin,* vol. 6, *April 1, 1755, through September 30, 1756,* ed. Leonard W. Labaree. New Haven, CT: Yale University Press, 1963, 468–69.]

7. Cousins, *In God We Trust*, 42. Benjamin Franklin letter to Ezra Stiles dated March 9, 1790. His letter to Ezra Stiles, a Congregational minister and president of Yale College, is especially moving considering he was eighty-four years old and weeks away from his death. On the notion of Christ's divinity, Franklin wrote, "It is a question I do not dogmatize upon, having never studied it, and think it needless to busy myself with it now, when I expect soon an opportunity of knowing the truth with less trouble."

8. Cousins, *In God We Trust*, 20–21.

9. Stout, *The Divine Dramatist*, 228.

10. Kidd, *Who Is an Evangelical?*, 24–25.

11. Cousins, *In God We Trust*, 38.

12. Stout, *The Divine Dramatist*, 107.

13. Stout, *The Divine Dramatist*, 226.

14. Marty, *Righteous Empire*, 38; and Wills, *Head and Heart*, 7.

15. Thomas Jefferson letter to John Adams dated October 13, 1813, quoted in Cousins, 241–42. Adams also rejected doctrines such as the divinity of Jesus and the Trinity, compelling him to leave his Congregationalist church to become a Unitarian.

16. Cousins, *In God We Trust*, 243.

17. Koch and Peden, *Selected Writings of Thomas Jefferson*, 256. From Jefferson's *Notes on the State of Virginia*, which were written in 1781–1782 and published in 1785.

18. Koch and Peden, *Selected Writings of Thomas Jefferson*, 289–91. Jefferson believed the statute to be among his greatest achievements. On an obelisk monument over his grave, Jefferson's epitaph reads:

"Here was buried
Thomas Jefferson
Author of the Declaration of American Independence
of the Statute of Virginia for religious freedom
and Father of the University of Virginia."

19. Madison's journals, June 12, 1788, quoted in Cousins, *In God We Trust*, 314.

20. The First Amendment did not apply to the states when it was drafted, and many maintained a porous wall between church and state. When the Bill of Rights was ratified in 1791, five states provided tax support of ministers and a dozen maintained religious tests for office. South Carolina's constitution established the

"Christian Protestant religion" because it was the "true religion." Massachusetts, the cradle of Puritanism, became the last state to disestablish in 1833. See Noll, *Scandal of the Evangelical Mind*, 64, and Wills, *Head and Heart*, 184.

21. Wills, *Head and Heart*, 6.

22. Wills, *Head and Heart*, 224–25.

23. Meacham, *American Gospel*, 81–82.

24. Thomas Jefferson letter to Nehemiah Dodge, Ephraim Robbins, and Stephen S. Nelson, committee of the Danbury Baptist Association, Connecticut, dated January 1, 1802. Quoted in Cousins, *In God We Trust*, 135.

25. Meacham, *American Gospel*, 228.

26. James Madison letter to Robert Walsh dated March 2, 1819, quoted in Cousins, *In God We Trust*, 319–20.

27. Wills, *Head and Heart*, 292–93.

28. Mark Galli, "Revival at Cane Ridge," *Christian History*, no. 45, 1995.

29. Wills, *Head and Heart*, 288–89.

30. Noll, *America's God*, 181.

31. Gorham, *Camp Meeting Manual*, 133.

32. Gorham, *Camp Meeting Manual*, 163.

33. Dow, *Writings of Lorenzo Dow*, 38.

34. McLoughlin, *Modern Revivalism*, 16.

35. McLoughlin, *Modern Revivalism*, 27.

36. McLoughlin, *Modern Revivalism*, 73.

37. Finney, *Lectures*, 181.

38. Finney, *Lectures*, 188.

39. Finney, *Lectures*, 212.

40. Finney, *Lectures*, 220.

41. Finney, *Lectures*, 213–14.

42. Finney, *Lectures*, 253.

43. Tocqueville, *Democracy in America*, 341.

44. Tocqueville, *Democracy in America*, 347.

45. Tocqueville, *Democracy in America*, 508.

46. Tocqueville, *Democracy in America*, 338.

47. Tocqueville, *Democracy in America*, 616.

CHAPTER 2

1. From FitzGerald, *Evangelicals*, 90.

2. W. R. Moody, *Life of Dwight L. Moody*, 263.

3. Lefferts A. Loetscher, "Presbyterianism and Revivals in Philadelphia since 1875," *Pennsylvania Magazine of History and Biography* 68, no. 1, 1944, p. 57.

4. Evensen, *God's Man*, 83.

5. Evensen, *God's Man*.

6. Loetscher, "Presbyterianism," 58.

7. Loetscher, "Presbyterianism," 59.

8. Evensen, *God's Man*, 73.

9. Loetscher, "Presbyterianism," 64–65.

10. Evensen, *God's Man*, 85.

11. Moody, *Life of Dwight L. Moody*, 25.

12. Moody, *Life of Dwight L. Moody*, 26.

13. Moody, *Life of Dwight L. Moody*, 29–30.

14. Loetscher, "Presbyterianism," 55–56.

15. D. L. Moody, *Moody's Stories*, 53–54.

16. Moody, *Life of Dwight L. Moody*, 41.

17. Moody, *Life of Dwight L. Moody*, 50.

18. Moody, *Life of Dwight L. Moody*, 47.

19. McLoughlin, *Modern Revivalism*, 174.

20. McLoughlin, *Modern Revivalism*, 174.

21. Belmonte, *D.L. Moody*, xiii.

22. Moody, *Life of Dwight L. Moody*, 108.

23. Moody, *Life of Dwight L. Moody*, 119.

24. Moody, *Life of Dwight L. Moody*, 116.

25. McLoughlin, *Modern Revivalism*, 177.

26. Evensen, *God's Man*, 96. The building was later the site of the first Madison Square Garden.

27. Moody, *Life of Dwight L. Moody*, 281.

28. Loetscher, "Presbyterianism," 59.

29. Loetscher, "Presbyterianism," 59–60.

30. McLoughlin, *Modern Revivalism*, 221–22.

31. Moody, *Moody's Latest Sermons*, 109.

32. Moody, *Moody's Latest Sermons*, 111.

33. Moody, *Secret Power*, 111–12.

34. Moody, *Moody's Latest Sermons*, 110.

35. McLoughlin, *Modern Revivalism*, 259.

36. McLoughlin, *Modern Revivalism*, 246.

37. Moody, *Moody's Stories*, 82.

38. McLoughlin, *Modern Revivalism*, 250.

39. FitzGerald, *Evangelicals*, 80–81. There are many interpretations of the length, number, and nature of these dispensations.

40. Sutton, *American Apocalypse*, 19–20.

41. D. L. Moody, *New Sermons*, 535.

42. FitzGerald, *Evangelicals*, 67.

43. Marty, *Righteous Empire*, 150.

44. Moody, W. R., *Life of Dwight L. Moody*, 128.

45. McLoughlin, *Modern Revivalism*, 258.

46. McLoughlin, *Modern Revivalism*, 258.

47. McLoughlin, *Modern Revivalism*, 273.

48. McLoughlin, *Modern Revivalism*, 369.

49. McLoughlin, *Modern Revivalism*, 371.

CHAPTER 3

1. Sunday and Gullen, *Billy Sunday Speaks*, 14.

2. Moody, *Moody's Latest Sermons*, 106.

3. McLoughlin, *Modern Revivalism*, 403.

4. Wendy Knickerbocker, "Billy Sunday," Society for American Baseball Research, https://sabr.org/bioproj/person/7fae24bc.

5. McLoughlin, *Modern Revivalism*, 405.

6. Martin, *Hero of the Heartland*, 53.

7. McLoughlin, *Modern Revivalism*, 424–25.

8. Loetscher, "Presbyterianism," 88.

9. Papers of Billy and Helen Sunday, Grace College, box 8. Sunday delivered the sermon on the evening of June 3, 1917, in New York.

10. Sunday and Gullen, *Billy Sunday Speaks*, 201–2.

11. Sunday and Gullen, *Billy Sunday Speaks*, 11–12.

12. Ellis, *Billy Sunday*, 122.

13. Sunday and Gullen, *Billy Sunday Speaks*, 19.

14. McLoughlin, *Modern Revivalism*, 428.

15. McLoughlin, *Modern Revivalism*, 409.

16. Loetscher, "Presbyterianism," 89.

17. Unsigned handwritten letter to Billy Sunday dated February 13, 1914. Papers of Billy and Helen Sunday, Grace College, box 1, folder 23.

18. Mrs. Theodore W. Jones letter to Billy Sunday dated December 28, 1915. Papers of Billy and Helen Sunday, Grace College, box 1, folder 23.

19. Bruns, *Preacher*, 95.

20. "Billy Sunday in the Big Cities," *Literary Digest*, April 4, 1914, 761–62.

21. The creed was adopted on December 4, 1908. For full text, see https://nationalcouncilofchurches.us/common-witness/1908/social-creed.php.

22. FitzGerald, *Evangelicals*, 95–96.

23. McLoughlin, *Modern Revivalism*, 416–17.

24. Sunday and Gullen, *Billy Sunday Speaks*, 14.

25. Bruns, *Preacher*, 130.

26. "Cheering, Singing Throngs Greet Billy Sunday as He Comes to Launch Revival," *New York World*, April 8, 1917.

27. Horace J. Bridges, "Mr. Sunday's Doctrines and the Clergy of Chicago," published by the Chicago Ethical Society, 1918, p. 3.

28. "Labor Criticizes Sunday," *New York Times*, May 2, 1917.

29. "50,000 Persons Paved the Way for Sunday's Revival," *New York Evening World*, April 6, 1917.

30. Martin, *Hero of the Heartland*, 59.

31. McLoughlin, *Modern Revivalism*, 415.

32. Martin, *Hero of the Heartland*, 58.

33. "Rector Denounces 'Sunday Circus,'" *New-York Tribune*, February 26, 1915.

34. "Billy Gets Many Presents Besides $46,102.28 in Cash," *Detroit Journal*, November 6, 1916. Sunday received a "thanks offering" of more than $50,000 for his eleven-week revival in Philadelphia in 1915. See Loetscher, "Presbyterianism," 90.

35. "Billy and 'Ma' Sunday with Handsome New Limousine, the Gift of Henry M. Leland," *Detroit Times*, November 4, 1916.

36. Henry M. Leland letter to Billy Sunday dated November 1, 1916. Papers of Billy and Helen Sunday, Grace College, box 2, folder 25.

37. Bruns, *Preacher*, 95.

38. Martin, *Hero of the Heartland*, 63.

39. Lichtman, *White Protestant Nation*, 30.

40. Barton, *The Man Nobody Knows*, 4, 162. Barton later served a stint in Congress as a New York Republican who opposed the New Deal.

41. "The Greatest Man in the United States," *American Magazine*, October 1914, p. 63.

42. "Sunday Talks Prohibition," *New York Times*, May 3, 1915.

43. Okrent, *Last Call*, 97.

44. Okrent, *Last Call*, 2.

45. Wills, *Head and Heart*, 411.

46. Meacham, *American Gospel*, 141–42.

47. McLoughlin, *Modern Revivalism*, 426–27.

48. McLoughlin, *Modern Revivalism*, 444.

49. Bruns, *Preacher*, 128.

50. Sutton, *American Apocalypse*, 13.

51. C. Allyn Russell, "William Bell Riley: Architect of Fundamentalism," *Minnesota History* (Spring 1972).

52. FitzGerald, *Evangelicals*, 114.

53. Sutton, *American Apocalypse*, 69–70.

54. Sutton, *American Apocalypse*, 71–75.

55. FitzGerald, *Evangelicals*, 115–16.

56. Farrell, *Clarence Darrow*, 391.

57. Farrell, *Clarence Darrow*, 394–95.

58. Farrell, *Clarence Darrow*, 395.

59. Sutton, *American Apocalypse*, 169.

60. Farrell, *Clarence Darrow*, 397.

61. "Bryan Is Buried in Soldier's Grave with Simple Rites," *New York Times*, August 1, 1925.

62. "Burn Crosses for Bryan," *New York Times*, August 1, 1925. The Ku Klux Klan supported Bryan's stance against evolution, but its appreciation likely stemmed from his efforts at the 1924 Democratic National Convention to defeat a resolution denouncing the then powerful organization.

63. FitzGerald, *Evangelicals*, 139.

64. FitzGerald, *Evangelicals*, 140.

65. Homer Rodeheaver letter to Billy Sunday dated October 20, 1929. Papers of Billy and Helen Sunday, Grace College, box 1, folder 38.

66. Rodeheaver to Sunday, October 20, 1929.

67. Kanton Klan No. 212 letter to Billy Sunday dated December 4, 1931. Papers of Billy and Helen Sunday, Grace College, box 1, folder 40.

68. Billy Sunday letter to Herbert Hoover dated October 29, 1932. Papers of Billy and Helen Sunday, Grace College, box 1, folder 41.

69. "3,500 at Funeral of Billy Sunday," *New York Times*, November 10, 1935. Obituaries listed his date of birth as November 19, 1863, but later research revised the year to 1862.

CHAPTER 4

1. From "Throng Greets Evangelist at Her Last Healing Service," *San Diego Union*, February 9, 1921.

2. Her star quality is immortalized in the song "Hooray for Hollywood" featured in the 1937 film *Hollywood Hotel*. It helped that her name rhymed with Shirley Temple.

3. Blumhofer, *Aimee Semple McPherson*, 232–33.

4. Blumhofer, *Aimee Semple McPherson*, 232–33.

5. Burgess and McGee, *Dictionary of Pentecostal*, 10.

6. "Great Temple Is Dedicated," *Los Angeles Times*, January 2, 1923.

7. "Great Temple Is Dedicated."

8. "Great Temple Is Dedicated."

9. Mark Kendall, "The House of the Spirit," *Los Angeles Times Magazine*, January 8, 2006, 30. The bungalow at 216 North Bonnie Brae Street in Historic Filipinotown still stands and is an important historical site for Pentecostals. The Azusa Street Mission, in modern-day Little Tokyo, is long gone, but there is a street sign that notes the site as the "Cradle of the Worldwide Pentecostal Movement."

10. "How Holy Roller Gets Religion," *Los Angeles Herald*, September 10, 1906.

11. "Women with Men Embrace," *Los Angeles Times*, September 3, 1906.

12. "Women with Men Embrace."

13. "Churches Aroused to Action," *Los Angeles Evening Express*, July 18, 1906.

14. "Religious Workers Aroused," *Los Angeles Evening Express*, September 28, 1906.

15. McPherson, *This Is That*, 30.

16. Frank B. Schumann, "Converts Flock to Altar When Call Is Sounded," *Oakland Tribune*, July 22, 1922.

17. "Female Billy Sunday Adopts the Motor Car to Spread the Gospel," *Stockton Daily Evening Record*, February 13, 1919.

18. "Miraculous Faith Healing Performed in Philadelphia by Los Angeles Evangelist," *Los Angeles Times*, October 31, 1920.

19. Blumhofer, *Aimee Semple McPherson*, 16.

20. Blumhofer, *Aimee Semple McPherson*, 214–15.

21. "Woman Preacher Continues Talk from Dreamland," *San Diego Union*, January 8, 1921.

22. "Throng Greets Evangelist at Her Last Healing Service," *San Diego Union*, February 9, 1921.

23. "Crippled Little Children Cured by Faith Healer," *San Francisco Chronicle*, September 6, 1921.

24. Darwin J. Smith, "'Miracles' of Mrs. McPherson Prove Myths," *Sacramento Bee*, February 15, 1922.

25. Smith, "'Miracles' of Mrs. McPherson Prove Myths."

26. "Mrs. M'Pherson Says Healing Is Matter of Faith," *Sacramento Bee*, February 16, 1922.

27. "Mrs. M'Pherson Says Healing Is Matter of Faith."

28. Darwin J. Smith, "Fresno Finds 'Miracle' Claims Are Unfounded," *Sacramento Bee*, February 16, 1922.

29. Smith, "Fresno Finds 'Miracle' Claims Are Unfounded."

30. Smith, "Fresno Finds 'Miracle' Claims Are Unfounded."

31. Darwin J. Smith, "'Miracles' Are Attempted on Picked Subjects," *Sacramento Bee*, February 17, 1922.

32. "Mrs. M'Pherson Denies She Has Power of Healing," *Sacramento Bee*, February 17, 1922.

33. "'Miracle Woman' Abandons Plan to Come Here," *Sacramento Bee*, February 17, 1922.

34. "'Miracle Woman' Abandons Plan to Come Here."

35. "'Miracle Woman' Abandons Plan to Come Here."

36. Blumhofer, *Aimee Semple McPherson*, 238–39.

37. Darwin J. Smith, "Investigations Show 'Miracles' Are Not Facts,'" *Sacramento Bee*, February 21, 1922.

38. Frank B. Schumann, "Converts Flock to Altar When Call Is Sounded," *Oakland Tribune*, July 22, 1922.

39. Blumhofer, *Aimee Semple McPherson*, 192; and Burgess and McGee, *Dictionary of Pentecostal*, 462.

40. Blumhofer, *Aimee Semple McPherson*, 192.

41. Blumhofer, *Aimee Semple McPherson*, 244.

42. Blumhofer, *Aimee Semple McPherson*, 244–46.

43. Blumhofer, *Aimee Semple McPherson*, 246.

44. Leona Montgomery, "Organizing Soul Savers," *Los Angeles Times*, February 18, 1923.

45. Blumhofer, *Aimee Semple McPherson*, 266.

46. Hangen, *Redeeming the Dial*, 57, 68.

47. Blumhofer, *Aimee Semple McPherson*, 266.

48. "Value of Radio Reviewed," *Los Angeles Times*, February 10, 1924.

49. Bruns, *Preacher*, 296–97.

50. Evans, *They Made America*, 225.

51. Bruns, *Preacher*, 296.

52. Carpenter, *Revive Us Again*, 127–28.

53. Paul Rader, "Christ or Crime?," National Radio Chapel Announcer, December 1925. Billy Graham Center Archives, Wheaton College, collection 38, box 1, folder 10.

54. "A Radio Message from the Cathedral of the Air," *World-Wide Christian Courier*, January 1928. Billy Graham Center Archives, Wheaton College, collection 38, box 1, folder 11, 7.

55. Billy Graham Center Archives, Wheaton College, collection 38, box 1, folder 11, 8.

56. Billy Graham Center Archives, Wheaton College, collection 38, box 1, folder 11, 8.

57. Carpenter, *Revive Us Again*, 134.

58. Carpenter, *Revive Us Again*, 131.

59. Carpenter, *Revive Us Again*, 139; and Bruns, *Preacher*, 297.

60. Carpenter, *Revive Us Again*, 131.

61. Finke and Stark, *Churching of America*, 221–23.

62. Hatch, *The Democratization of American Christianity* 217.

63. Finke and Stark, *Churching of America*, 221.

64. Blumhofer, *Aimee Semple McPherson*, 257–58.

65. "Thousands at Aimee Rites," *Los Angeles Times*, October 19, 1944.

66. "Thousands at Aimee Rites."

67. Elane Woo, "Evangelist's Son Longtime Leader of Foursquare Church," *Los Angeles Times*, May 28, 2009.

CHAPTER 5

1. From Harrell, *Oral Roberts*, 185.

2. Balmer, *Making of Evangelicalism*, 5.

3. Marty, *Modern American Religion*, 106.

4. Lichtman, *White Protestant Nation*, 123.

5. Marty, *Modern American Religion*, 107.

6. Marty, *Modern American Religion*, 107.

7. Sutton, *American Apocalypse*, 286.

8. Marty, *Modern American Religion*, 107. The Federal Council of Churches merged with other groups in 1950 and was renamed the National Council of Churches.

9. Smith, *American Evangelicalism*, 61.

10. J. Elwin Wright letter to members of the board of administration of the NAE dated February 25, 1944. Billy Graham Center Archives, Wheaton College, collection 20, box 65, folder 21.

11. Marty, *Modern American Religion*, 444–45.

12. Henry, *Uneasy Conscience*, 80–81.

13. Henry, *Uneasy Conscience*, 88–89.

14. Lichtman, *White Protestant Nation*, 125–26.

15. Graham, *Just as I Am*, 26.

16. "Ham Predicts End of Christian Era," *Charlotte Observer*, October 8, 1934.

17. Graham, *Just as I Am*, 37.

18. Martin, *Prophet with Honor*, 69.

19. Bob Jones College is now Bob Jones University in Greenville, South Carolina, and the Florida Bible Institute is today Trinity College of Florida.

20. Graham, *Just as I Am*, 46–47.

21. Graham, *Just as I Am*, 88.

22. Graham, *Just as I Am*.

23. Graham, *Just as I Am*, 94.

24. Graham, *Just as I Am*, 108.

25. C. Allyn Russell, "William Bell Riley: Architect of Fundamentalism," *Minnesota History*, Spring 1972.

26. In his autobiography, Graham tells a story about Hillary Clinton requesting a private luncheon with him when she was First Lady of Arkansas. When Graham demurred, Clinton suggested that they sit together in a hotel dining room in view of others, and Graham agreed. Mike Pence brought renewed attention to the "Billy Graham rule" when it was revealed after he became vice president that he had long followed it. Pence, an evangelical, also reportedly declines to attend functions where alcohol is served without his wife at his side.

27. Graham, *Just as I Am*, 139.

28. Frost, *Billy Graham*, 144.

29. Graham, *Just as I Am*, 144.

30. Gibbs and Duffy, *Preacher and the Presidents*, 5.

31. Kruse, *One Nation*, 35–36.

32. McLoughlin, *Billy Graham*, 51.

33. In his later years, Graham quietly dropped the fraught label "crusade" from his events.

34. Graham, *Just as I Am*, 163.

35. Graham, *Just as I Am*, 172–73.

36. Wacker, *America's Pastor*, 155.

37. Frady, *Billy Graham*, 231.

38. Graham, *Just as I Am*, 179.

39. Graham, *Just as I Am*, 180.

40. Frady, *Billy Graham*, 231.

41. Graham, *Just as I Am*, 182.

42. Frady, *Billy Graham*, 225.

43. Lichtman, *White Protestant Nation*, 215.

44. Martin, *Prophet with Honor*, 217.

45. Billy Graham, "God Before Gold," *Nation's Business*, September 1954, 34–35.

46. Kruse, *One Nation*, 37.

47. Kruse, *One Nation*, 27.

48. FitzGerald, *Evangelicals*, 202.

49. Kruse, *One Nation*, 38.

50. Lichtman, *White Protestant Nation*, 215.

51. Harrell, *Oral Roberts*, 7.

52. Harrell, *Oral Roberts*.

53. Roberts, *Expect a Miracle*, 34–35.

54. Roberts, *Expect a Miracle*, 376.

55. Harrell, *Oral Roberts*, 83.

56. Harrell, *Oral Roberts*, 84.

57. Harrell, *Oral Roberts*, 85.

58. Harrell, *Oral Roberts*, 86.

59. Harrell, *Oral Roberts*, 89.

60. Harrell, *Oral Roberts*, 96.

61. Harrell, *Oral Roberts*, 91.

62. Burgess and McGee, *Dictionary of Pentecostal*, 321.

63. Roberts, *Expect a Miracle*, 153–54.

64. Harrell, *Oral Roberts*, 118, 120.

65. Harrell, *Oral Roberts*, 118.

66. Harrell, *Oral Roberts*, 119.

67. Harrell, *Oral Roberts*, 120.

68. Harrell, *Oral Roberts*, 121.

69. Harrell, *Oral Roberts*, 120–21.

70. Harrell, *Oral Roberts*, 128.

71. Harrell, *Oral Roberts*, 129.

72. Harrell, *Oral Roberts*, 141.

73. Roberts, *Expect a Miracle*, 145–46.

74. Harrell, *Oral Roberts*, 130.

75. Roberts, *Deliverance*, 12. The Bible quotation is how Roberts cites it in his text.

76. Roberts, *Expect a Miracle*, 126–27.

77. Harrell, *Oral Roberts*, 162.

78. Harrell, *Oral Roberts*, 163.

79. Harrell, *Oral Roberts*, 165.

80. Harrell, *Oral Roberts*, 166.

81. Harrell, *Oral Roberts*, 169.

82. Jack Gould, "On Faith Healing," *New York Times*, February 19, 1956.

83. Harrell, *Oral Roberts*, 179. Graham mentions Roberts only once in his long autobiography.

84. Harrell, *Oral Roberts*, 179.

85. Harrell, *Oral Roberts*, 180–81.

86. Harrell, *Oral Roberts*, 181.

87. Harrell, *Oral Roberts*, 176.

CHAPTER 6

1. From Eisenhower's remarks to the "Back to God" program of the American Legion broadcast on radio and television on February 20, 1955. Eisenhower participated in the programs each year. Online by Gerhard Peters and John T. Woolley, The American Presidency Project, https://www.presidency.ucsb.edu/node/233928.

2. Graham, *Just as I Am*, xxii.

3. Frost, *Billy Graham*, 98.

4. Graham writes in his autobiography that he smoothed over relations with Truman after he left office.

5. Graham, *Just as I Am*, xxiii.

6. Soon after becoming pastor at Marble Collegiate Church, Norman Vincent Peale picked a fight with the incoming first lady, Eleanor Roosevelt. She had remarked that young ladies should find out their capacity for drinking and learn to do it in moderation. Peale was furious that she would condone alcohol use at all. "Her knowledge of the United States doesn't go any further than the Hudson River, and yet here is this statement by this child of the rich who doesn't understand anything about American life. I can't say her husband is any better," Peale said at a luncheon of the New York Women's Christian Temperance Union. "Drys Hail Attack on Mrs. Roosevelt," *New York Times*, January 15, 1933; Gordon, *Minister to Millions*, 187–88.

7. Sutton, *American Apocalypse*, 244.

8. Lichtman, *White Protestant Nation*, 79. The critiques veered off into anti-Semitism, with fundamentalist minister William Bell Riley claiming the Roosevelt administration was "a Jewish-controlled regime" and pointing at Jews as scheming to "filch the land of all its gold, take over its cattle and its farms and possess themselves of all its factories, arts and industries." (See FitzGerald, *Evangelicals*, 145) Protestants didn't corner the market on religious-based opposition to Roosevelt. The Roman Catholic priest Father Charles E. Coughlin's conspiratorial screeds against Jews and communism won him a mass radio audience in the 1930s.

9. Lichtman, *White Protestant Nation*, 80–81.

10. "Great Virtue Seen in Individualism," *New York Times*, May 28, 1934.

11. "Defends the Work of Radical Ministry," *New York Times*, March 16, 1936.

12. "C.I.O. Denounced as 'Predatory Mob,'" *New York Times*, June 14, 1937.

13. "U.S. Curb on Labor Urged by Dr. Peale," *New York Times*, April 7, 1941.

14. Gordon, *Minister to Millions*, 200.

15. "Roosevelt Defeat Urged by Dr. Peale," *New York Times*, July 22, 1940.

16. Hoge, Johnson, and Luidens, *Vanishing Boundaries*, 1.

17. Turner, *Bill Bright*, 2–3.

18. Turner, *Bill Bright*, 34.

19. Turner, *Bill Bright*, 52.

20. Turner, *Bill Bright*, 63.

21. Turner, *Bill Bright*, 64.

22. Lichtman, *White Protestant Nation*, 174.

23. See https://news.gallup.com/poll/1690/religion.aspx.

24. Putnam and Campbell, *American Grace*, 87.

25. Herberg, *Protestant-Catholic-Jew*, 2.

26. Putnam and Campbell, *American Grace*, 87.

27. Herberg, *Protestant-Catholic-Jew*, 75.

28. Herberg, *Protestant-Catholic-Jew*, 75–84.

29. Herberg, *Protestant-Catholic-Jew*, 263–64.

30. Niebuhr, *Irony of American History*, 173.

31. Niebuhr, *Irony of American History*.

32. See https://www.loc.gov/resource/mal.4361300/?st=text.

33. Niebuhr, *Irony of American History*, 173.

34. Frady, *Billy Graham*, 237.

35. Kruse, *One Nation*, 55.

36. Public Law 324 (66 Stat. 64).

37. Gibbs and Duffy, *Preacher and the Presidents*, 32.

38. Gibbs and Duffy, *Preacher and the Presidents*, 32.

39. Graham, *Just as I Am*, 190.

40. Graham, *Just as I Am*, 192.

41. "Text of Eisenhower Speech," *New York Times*, December 23, 1952.

42. Graham, *Just as I Am*, 199.

43. Graham, *Just as I Am* (New International Version translation).

44. Inboden, *Religion*, 266.

45. Gibbs and Duffy, *Preacher and the Presidents*, 43.

46. In his book *The Family: The Secret Fundamentalism at the Heart of American Power*, Jeff Sharlet defines Abraham Vereide as the founder of the Family, or the Fellowship, a "self-described invisible network of followers of Christ in government, business, and the military." Other than organizing the annual National Prayer Breakfast in Washington, the Fellowship's activities in the highest precincts

of power are kept in confidence. The book is the basis for a Netflix original documentary. Sharlet, *Family*, 3.

47. Sharlet, *Family*, 138.

48. Vereide also formed the International Council for Christian Leadership, an umbrella group for the national fellowship organizations.

49. Kruse, *One Nation*, 48–49.

50. Graham, *Just as I Am*, 202–3.

51. Sharlet, *Family*, 196–97.

52. Kruse, *One Nation*, 77. Hilton produced hundreds of thousands of copies of the image, and Eisenhower hung one in the Oval Office.

53. Dwight Eisenhower, Remarks at the Dedicatory Prayer Breakfast of the International Christian Leadership. February 5, 1953. Online by Gerhard Peters and John T. Woolley, The American Presidency Project https://www.presidency.ucsb.edu/node/231800.

54. Inboden, *Religion*, 273.

55. Inboden, *Religion*, 274.

56. Kruse, *One Nation*, 88–89.

57. Meacham, *American Gospel*, 177–78. The term *Judeo-Christian* was coined as early as 1899.

58. As an example of his openness, Graham invited Martin Luther King Jr. to deliver a prayer from the platform in Madison Square Garden during his 1957 New York crusade. But Graham's sense of caution—and perhaps fear of aliening his base of white Southerners—appeared to win out as the struggle for civil rights heated up in the 1960s. Graham did not participate in demonstrations such as King's 1963 March on Washington and declined to endorse the decade's landmark civil rights laws.

59. Pollock, *Billy Graham*, 98.

60. Martin, *Prophet with Honor*, 176.

61. Billy Graham letter to Dwight Eisenhower dated March 27, 1956, Eisenhower Presidential Library, box 16. For this and other Eisenhower-era civil rights materials, see https://www.eisenhowerlibrary.gov/research/online-documents/civil-rights-president-eisenhower-and-eisenhower-administration.

62. Dwight Eisenhower letter to Billy Graham dated March 30, 1956, Eisenhower Presidential Library, box 16.

63. Billy Graham letter to Dwight Eisenhower dated June 4, 1956, Eisenhower Presidential Library, box 16.

64. Graham, *Just as I Am*, 201. In 1959, Graham held a crusade in Little Rock and insisted on preaching to an integrated audience at War Memorial Stadium. Graham's stand made an impression on one of the attendees, a young Arkansan named Bill Clinton.

65. Graham, *Just as I Am*, 297–98.

66. FitzGerald, *Evangelicals*, 186.

67. Martin, *Prophet with Honor*, 230–31.

68. Murray Illson, "Graham Crusade to Cost $900,000," *New York Times*, May 10, 1957.

69. Frady, *Billy Graham*, 294–95.

70. Frady, *Billy Graham*, 296.

71. "Billy Graham: A New Kind of Evangelist," *Time*, October 25, 1954.

72. Frady, *Billy Graham*, 285–86.

73. Frady, *Billy Graham*, 278–79.

74. Pollock, *Billy Graham*, 243.

75. Reinhold Niebuhr, "A Theologian Says Evangelist Is Oversimplifying the Issues of Life," *Life*, July 1, 1957.

76. Marty, *Modern American Religion*, 438–39.

77. Martin, *Prophet with Honor*, 187.

78. "Text of Billy Graham's Sermon Opening His Crusade in Madison Square Garden," *New York Times*, May 16, 1957.

79. "Text of Billy Graham's Sermon."

80. Stanley Rowland Jr. "Almost All Garden Seats Full at Opening of Graham Crusade," *New York Times*, May 16, 1957.

81. Stanley Rowland Jr. "City Idolatrous, Graham Asserts," *New York Times*, May 19, 1957.

82. Val Adams, "News of Television and Radio," *New York Times*, May 26, 1957.

83. "Billy Graham Asks for Financial Aid," *New York Times*, June 22, 1957.

84. Graham, *Just as I Am*, 316.

85. Gibbs and Duffy, *Preacher and the Presidents*, 75.

86. George Dugan, "Graham's Impact Termed Fleeting," *New York Times*, January 26, 1958.

87. Dugan, "Graham's Impact."

88. FitzGerald, *Evangelicals*, 198.

89. Dugan, "Graham's Impact."

90. Norman Vincent Peale letter to Billy Graham dated October 22, 1957. Quoted in Pollock, *Billy Graham*, 186.

91. McLoughlin, *Billy Graham*, 219.

CHAPTER 7

1. Peale, *Power of Positive Thinking*, 169.

2. Gordon, *Minister to Millions*, 155. Arthur Gordon's sympathetic biography of Peale was published in 1958 after Peale had risen to national fame.

3. Peale, *The True Joy of Positive Living*, 123–24.

4. Gordon, *Minister to Millions*, 157–58.

5. Gordon, *Minister to Millions*, 167.

6. Peale, *The True Joy of Positive Living*, 124–25.

7. Gordon, *Minister to Millions*, 177–78.

8. Peale, *The True Joy of Positive Living*, 34.

9. Gordon, *Minister to Millions*, 105.

10. Gordon, *Minister to Millions*, 109.

11. Gordon, *Minister to Millions*, 141.

12. "Reshaping the Personality," *New York Times*, February 3, 1936; and Lane, *Surge of Piety*, 11–12.

13. George, *God's Salesman*, 84–85.

14. Eckhardt, *Surge of Piety*, 79.

15. George, *God's Salesman*, 85.

16. George, *God's Salesman*, 87.

17. "Dr. Smiley Blanton Dead Here; Psychiatrist and Author Was 84," *New York Times*, October 31, 1966. Quote from 1953 interview.

18. George, *God's Salesman*, 95–96. Other prominent religious figures tried to apply psychology to spiritual questions. Rabbi Joshua Loth Liebman's best-selling book *Peace of Mind*, published in 1946, transcended Judaism by attempting to link psychiatry and religion as a means of achieving inner peace. The Boston rabbi had undergone psychoanalysis and incorporated it in his teachings. Liebman portrayed God as a reassuring presence rather than an angry hurler of thunderbolts, a message Peale admired. Monsignor Fulton J. Sheen, widely known for his radio and television appearances, appealed to many non-Catholics despite his more orthodox approach.

19. Horowitz, *One Simple Idea*, 182.

20. Paul Hutchinson, "Have We a 'New' Religion?" *Life*, April 11, 1955.

21. George, *God's Salesman*, 92.

22. Horowitz, *One Simple Idea*, 182.

23. Lane, *Surge of Piety*, 68.

24. Horowitz, *One Simple Idea*, 187.

25. Peale, *Power of Positive Thinking*, xii.

26. Peale, *Power of Positive Thinking*, 11.

27. Peale, *Power of Positive Thinking*, 44.

28. Peale, *Power of Positive Thinking*, xiii.

29. Marty, *Modern American Religion*, 320.

30. William Lee Miller, "Some Negative Thinking about Norman Vincent Peale," *The Reporter*, January 13, 1955, 20. Miller cuttingly appraised Peale's repetitious writing style: "The chapters of his books could easily be transposed from the beginning to the middle, or from the end to the beginning, or from one book to another. The paragraphs could be shuffled and rearranged in any order."

31. Miller, "Some Negative Thinking," 21.

32. Peale, *The True Joy of Positive Living*, 144–45.

33. Kenneth A. Briggs, "Dr. Norman Vincent Peale Still an Apostle of Cheer," *New York Times*, January 2, 1978.

34. George, *God's Salesman*, 131; and Paul Hutchinson, "Have We a 'New' Religion?" *Life*, April 11, 1955.

35. Marty, *Modern American Religion*, 326–27.

36. Peale, *Stay Alive*, 97.

37. Peale, *Stay Alive*, 95–96; and Eckhardt, *Surge of Piety*, 80–81.

38. King frequently made this point. Quotation from his sermon at Washington National Cathedral on March 31, 1968, just days before his assassination. Accessed at https://kinginstitute.stanford.edu/king-papers/publications/knock-midnight -inspiration-great-sermons-reverend-martin-luther-king-jr-10.

39. George F. Will, "Mike Huckabee's 'Appalling' Crusade,'" *Washington Post*, May 15, 2015; and Gordon, *Minister to Millions*, 226.

40. Graham, *Just As I Am*, 391–93; Martin, *Prophet with Honor*, 284–87. Graham created an election-year tempest of his own when he tried to help Nixon without formally endorsing him. Publishing magnate Henry Luce asked Graham to write a testimonial about Nixon for *Life* magazine. Graham agreed and Luce scheduled the article to run just before the election. After talking to associates, Graham had second thoughts about taking such a public stand on a political matter. (His article included thinly veiled jabs at Kennedy, though it did not explicitly reference his Catholicism.) Graham asked Luce to pull it at the last minute. Luce agreed and replaced it with a nonpartisan piece by Graham about the obligation of Christians to vote.

41. "Protestant Groups' Statements," *New York Times*, September 8, 1960. Among the attendees at the Mayflower Hotel meeting were prominent evangelicals such as Harold John Ockenga, pastor of Boston's Park Street Church and cofounder of Fuller Theological Seminary, and L. Nelson Bell, executive editor of *Christianity Today* and Billy Graham's father-in-law.

42. George Dugan, "Peale Criticized at Grace Church," *New York Times*, September 12, 1960.

43. "Transcript: JFK's Speech on His Religion," NPR, December 5, 2007. The nation's second Roman Catholic president, Joe Biden, finds himself in a completely opposite situation. He is being criticized for *not* following the Catholic Church's stance against abortion rights when performing his public duties. Some bishops have gone so far as to threaten to deny him communion.

44. Horowitz, *One Simple Idea*, 189.

45. Peale officiated at the wedding of Richard Nixon's daughter, Julie, and Dwight Eisenhower's grandson, David, at Marble Collegiate Church soon after Nixon won the presidency in 1968. Nixon invited Peale to participate in religious services at the White House.

46. "The History of the Crystal Cathedral," *New York Times*, October 23, 2010.

47. Schuller, *My Journey*, 17–19.

48. Schuller, *My Journey*, 28–29.

49. Schuller, *My Journey*, 45.

50. Schuller, *My Journey*, 127.

51. Schuller, *My Journey*, 140–42.

52. Schuller, *My Journey*, 171–72.

53. Schuller, *My Journey*, 183–84.

54. McGirr, *Suburban Warriors*, 25.

55. Starr, *Golden Dreams*, 6.

56. Starr, *Golden Dreams*, 12.

57. McGirr, *Suburban Warriors*, 48–49.

58. McGirr, *Suburban Warriors*, 50–51.

59. Schuller, *My Journey*, 192.

60. Schuller, *My Journey*, 180–181.

61. Schuller, *My Journey*, 206.

62. Schuller, *My Journey*, 207.

63. Schuller, *My Journey*, 212.

64. Schuller, *My Journey*, 216.

65. Schuller, *God's Way*, 114–15.

66. Schuller, *God's Way*, 149.

67. Schuller, *God's Way*, 130.

68. Schuller, *God's Way*, 86.

69. Schuller, *God's Way*, 121.

70. Spencer Crump, "Church Offers First Indoor-Outdoor Rites," *Los Angeles Times*, November 12, 1961.

71. See *Los Angeles Times*, April 17, 1965.

72. Schuller, *My Journey*, 266.

73. Schuller, *My Journey*, 281–82.

74. McGirr, *Suburban Warriors*, 106–7.

75. Schuller, *God's Way*, 27.

76. Schuller, *God's Way*, 100.

77. Schuller, *God's Way*, 102.

78. Schuller, *My Journey*, 293.

79. Russell Chandler, "A Bold Experiment in Modern Religion Arrives at a Milestone," *Los Angeles Times*, March 17, 1975.

80. Shearlean Duke, "Pastor's Wife: 'My Career Is My Husband,'" *Los Angeles Times*, October 23, 1974.

81. Chandler, "A Bold Experiment."

82. Chandler, "A Bold Experiment."

83. In 1989, industrialist Armand Hammer whisked Schuller to the Soviet Union aboard his private plane for an audience with Soviet leader Mikhail Gorbachev. Schuller was cleared to tape a message broadcast on Christmas Day on Soviet TV.

84. Calvin Tomkins, "Forms under Light," *New Yorker*, May 23, 1977.

85. Tomkins, "Forms under Light."

86. Schuller, *My Journey*, 352–53.

87. Schuller, *My Journey*, 358–61.

88. Schuller, *My Journey*, 384–87, 391.

89. Schuller, *My Journey*, 323, 470.

90. John Dart, "Minister's Vision in Glass Built with Mottoes and Millions," *Los Angeles Times*, September 13, 1980.

91. Dart, "Minister's Vision in Glass"; Schuller, *My Journey*, 393.

92. Schuller, *My Journey*, 406–7.

93. Bella Stumbo, "Schuller: The Gospel of Success," *Los Angeles Times*, May 29, 1983. The reporter noted that in private, Schuller "is often surprisingly aloof, stiff and uncomfortable, sullen and sour at times, defensive at others. In conversation, he is perpetually dominant, both condescending and pedantic. He displays not the slightest trace of spontaneous humor, rarely smiles and never seems to laugh."

94. Schuller, *My Journey*, 407.

95. Robert A. Schuller, phone interview with author, August 20, 2021.

96. Bella Stumbo, "Building Schuller's Televised Empire," *Los Angeles Times*, May 29, 1983.

97. Stumbo, "Building Schuller's Televised Empire."

98. Schuller, *My Journey*, 445.

99. Janet Wiscombe, "The Son Also Rises," *Los Angeles Times*, July 21, 1996.

100. Schuller interview.

101. Laurie Goodstein, "Dispute over Succession Clouds Megachurch," *New York Times*, October 23, 2010.

102. Goodstein, "Dispute over Succession."

103. William Lobdell and Mitchell Landsberg, "O.C. Pioneer of the Megachurch," *Los Angeles Times*, April 3, 2015.

104. Kimberly Winston, "Crystal Cathedral Founder's Memorial Covered by Crowdfunding Campaign," *Religion News Service*, April 21, 2015.

105. Schuller interview.

CHAPTER 8

1. Warren, *Purpose Driven Church*, 191.

2. "Toward a Hidden God," *Time*, April 8, 1966, p. 82. Figure from a Lou Harris poll in 1965.

3. "Toward a Hidden God," 83.

4. Putnam and Campbell, *American Grace*, 98.

5. Liz McGuinness, "Church Communes, Services Aim for Drug-Oriented Youth," *Los Angeles Times*, September 6, 1970.

6. McGuinness, "Church Communes."

7. This anecdote is related in Chuck Smith's autobiography, "as told to" his son, Chuck Smith Jr. Smith, *Chuck Smith*, 11–12.

8. Smith, *Chuck Smith*, 42.

9. Smith, *Chuck Smith*, 72–73.

10. Smith, *Chuck Smith*, 129–33.

11. Smith, *Chuck Smith*, 162–63.

12. Smith and Brooke, *Harvest*, 30.

13. Smith and Brooke, *Harvest*, 31.

14. Smith, *Chuck Smith*, 179.

15. McGuinness, "Church Communes."

16. McGuinness, "Church Communes."

17. McGuinness, "Church Communes."

18. McGuinness, "Church Communes."

19. Larry Osbourne, phone interview with author, September 25, 2021.

20. John Dart, "The New Evangelism: Getting High on Jesus," *Los Angeles Times WEST magazine*, September 19, 1971.

21. Dart, "The New Evangelism."

22. Dart, "The New Evangelism."

23. Sutton, *American Apocalypse*, 346.

24. Sutton, *American Apocalypse*, 346.

25. Lindsey, *Late Great*, 184–85.

26. Lindsey, *Late Great*, 182.

27. Smith and Brooke, *Harvest*, 32.

28. Smith and Brooke, *Harvest*, 35.

29. Leslie Berkman, "The Church That Chuck Built," *Los Angeles Times*, May 6, 1973.

30. Smith, *Chuck Smith*, 185–86.

31. McGirr, *Suburban Warriors*, 248.

32. Christopher Goffard, "Pastor Chuck Smith Dies at 86; Founder of Calvary Chapel Movement," *Los Angeles Times*, October 3, 2013.

33. Smith and Brooke, *Harvest*, 80–81.

34. Smith and Brooke, *Harvest*, 81.

35. See VineyardUSA, https://vineyardusa.org/explore/church-planting-multi-sites-missional-communities/.

36. Osbourne interview.

37. Harvey and Goff, *Columbia Documentary History*, 7.

38. Harvey and Goff, *Columbia Documentary History*, 7.

39. Finke and Stark, *Churching of America*, 246.

40. Kelley, *Why Conservative Churches*, 135.

41. Kelley, *Why Conservative Churches*, 139–40.

42. Kelley, *Why Conservative Churches*, 141.

43. McGavran, *Understanding Church Growth*, 266, 268.

44. McGavran, *Understanding Church Growth*, 278–79.

45. Hybels and Hybels, *Rediscovering Church*, 24.

46. Hybels and Hybels, *Rediscovering Church*, 24. This book is divided into two parts. In the first half, Lynne Hybels writes about the origins of Willow Creek; the

second part is written by Bill Hybels, who discusses how his lessons can apply to other churches.

47. Hybels and Hybels, *Rediscovering Church*, 24.

48. Hybels and Hybels, *Rediscovering Church*, 24, 29–30.

49. Hybels, *Holy Discontent*, 55–56.

50. Hybels, *Holy Discontent*, 56–57.

51. Hybels, *Holy Discontent*, 57. These anecdotes are also in Hybels and Hybels, *Rediscovering Church*, 30–32.

52. Hybels and Hybels, *Rediscovering Church*, 16.

53. Hybels and Hybels, *Rediscovering Church*, 39–41.

54. Hybels and Hybels, *Rediscovering Church*, 51.

55. Hybels and Hybels, *Rediscovering Church*, 52.

56. Hybels and Hybels, *Rediscovering Church*, 57–59.

57. Hybels and Hybels, *Rediscovering Church*, 62.

58. El-Faizy, *God and Country*, 36.

59. Schuller, *My Journey*, 341–42; and Hybels and Hybels, *Rediscovering Church*, 69.

60. Hybels and Hybels, *Rediscovering Church*, 70.

61. Hybels and Hybels, *Rediscovering Church*, 72.

62. Matthew 28:19–20, NIV.

63. Hybels and Hybels, *Rediscovering Church*, 133.

64. Loveland and Wheeler, *Meetinghouse to Megachurch*, 123.

65. Strobel, *Inside the Mind*, 13–14.

66. Loveland and Wheeler, *Meetinghouse to Megachurch*, 123.

67. Strobel, *Inside the Mind*, 69.

68. George Barna, phone interview with author, September 24, 2021.

69. Barna, *Step-by-Step Guide*, 21.

70. Barna, *Step-by-Step Guide*, 24.

71. Barna, *Step-by-Step Guide*, 27–32.

72. Hybels and Hybels, *Rediscovering Church*, 101.

73. Thumma and Travis, *Beyond Megachurch Myths*, xviii.

74. Thumma and Travis, *Beyond Megachurch Myths*, 7.

75. See Warren Bird and Scott Thumma, *Megachurch 2020*, The Hartford Institute for Religious Research, http://hirr.hartsem.edu/megachurch/2020_megachurch _report.pdf.

76. Thumma and Travis, *Beyond Megachurch Myths*, 49.

77. Hybels and Hybels, *Rediscovering Church*, 178.

78. Hybels, *Just Walk Across*, 69.

79. Sargeant, *Seeker Churches*, 23.

80. Sargeant, *Seeker Churches*, 13.

81. Michael Hirsley, "Church's 1-2 Punch a Knockout," *Chicago Tribune*, May 21, 1989.

82. Hybels and Hybels, *Rediscovering Church*, 123.

83. Gustav Niebuhr, "The Minister as Marketer: Learning from Business," *New York Times*, April 18, 1995.

84. Charles Truehart, "The Next Church," *Atlantic*, August 1996.

85. Hybels and Hybels, *Rediscovering Church*, 167–168.

86. Paul Goldberger, "The Gospel of Church Architecture, Revised," *New York Times*, April 20, 1995.

87. Wuthnow, *Crisis in the Churches*, 236.

88. Hybels and Hybels, *Rediscovering Church*, 212–213.

89. William Neikirk, "Scandal Mine Alone, Clinton Says," *Chicago Tribune*, August 11, 2000.

90. Hybels, *Holy Discontent*, 108–9.

91. Hybels, *Holy Discontent*, 110–12.

92. Leon Lagerstam, "Bringing Leaders to a Summit and a Summit to the Leaders," *Rock Island Argus*, August 2, 2014.

93. Manya Brachear Pashman and Jeff Coen, "After Years of Inquiries, Pastor Denies Allegations," *Chicago Tribune*, March 25, 2018.

94. Manya Brachear Pashman, "Willow Creek Members Show Support for Pastor," *Chicago Tribune*, March 26, 2018.

95. Manya Brachear Pashman and Jeff Coen, "Willow Creek's Hybels Resigns," *Chicago Tribune*, April 11, 2018.

96. Jeff Coen, "Report: Claims against Church Founder Credible," *Chicago Tribune*, March 1, 2019.

97. I visited the 9 a.m. service on July 11, 2021.

98. Diane Morgan, "A Few Words from Rick Warren," *Press Democrat*, November 17, 1971.

99. Morgan, "A Few Words from Rick Warren."

100. Sheler, *Prophet of Purpose*, 37–38.

101. Sheler, *Prophet of Purpose*, 47.

102. Sheler, *Prophet of Purpose*, 59–60.

103. Sheler, *Prophet of Purpose*, 75.

104. Warren, *Purpose Driven Church*, 25.

105. Warren, *Purpose Driven Church*, 26.

106. Warren, *Purpose Driven Church*, 26–27.

107. Quoted in Sheler, *Prophet of Purpose*, 95.

108. Warren, *Purpose Driven Church*, 33.

109. Warren, *Purpose Driven Church*, 34.

110. Warren, *Purpose Driven Church*, 36–37.

111. Warren, *Purpose Driven Church*, 39.

112. Warren, *Purpose Driven Church*, 191–192.

113. Warren, *Purpose Driven Church*, 199.

114. Warren, *Purpose Driven Church*, 194.

115. Warren, *Purpose Driven Church*, 194.

116. Warren, *Purpose Driven Church*, 42–43.

117. Warren, *Purpose Driven Church*, 45.

118. Warren, *Purpose Driven Church*, 169–71.

119. Warren, *Purpose Driven Church*, 234.

120. Warren, *Purpose Driven Church*, 18.

121. Warren, *Purpose Driven Church*, 107.

122. Warren, *Purpose Driven Church*, 325.

123. Drucker, *Management*, 28.

124. Drucker, *Management*, 29.

125. Drucker, *Management*.

126. Drucker, *Management*, 177.

127. Krames, *Inside Drucker's Brain*, 196–197.

128. Drucker, *Management*, 74.

129. Warren, *Purpose Driven Church*, 77, 87.

130. Gustav Niebuhr, "The Minister as Marketer: Learning from Business," *New York Times*, April 18, 1995. The reporter noted a poster outside Hybels's office that read, "What is our business? Who is our customer? What does the customer consider value?" The questions came directly from Peter Drucker.

131. Sheler, *Prophet of Purpose*, 137.

132. Sheler, *Prophet of Purpose*, 149.

133. Sheler, *Prophet of Purpose*, 153–54.

134. Sheler, *Prophet of Purpose*, 166.

135. Sheler, *Prophet of Purpose*, 180–81.

136. Sheler, *Prophet of Purpose*, 181.

137. Warren, *Purpose Driven Life*, 17.

138. Warren, *Purpose Driven Life*, 18.

139. Sheler, *Prophet of Purpose*, 181.

140. Malcolm Gladwell, "The Cellular Church," *New Yorker*, September 12, 2005.

141. Marc Gunther, "Will Success Spoil Rick Warren?" *Fortune*, October 31, 2005.

142. Gladwell, "The Cellular Church."

143. Sheler, *Prophet of Purpose*, 258.

144. Sheler, *Prophet of Purpose*, 187.

145. Marcia Z. Nelson, "Purpose Driven Life Gets a 10th Anniversary Makeover," *Publishers Weekly*, November 28, 2012. For the 2020 figure, see Simon & Schuster's author page for Warren at https://www.simonandschuster.com/authors/Rick-Warren/39904606ink.

146. Joseph Liu, "The Future of Evangelicals: A Conversation with Pastor Rick Warren," Pew Forum on Religion and Public Life, November 13, 2009, https://www.pewforum.org/2009/11/13/the-future-of-evangelicals-a-conversation-with-pastor-rick-warren/#12.

147. I visited the 4 p.m. Saturday service on August 28, 2021.

CHAPTER 9

1. Osteen, *Your Best Life*, 5.

2. Abbott at a news conference on Hurricane Harvey preparation on August 25, 2017, https://www.c-span.org/video/?433119-1/texas-governor-briefs-reporters-hurricane-harvey-preparations.

3. Dakin Andone, "Houston Knew It Was at Risk of Flooding, So Why Didn't the City Evacuate?" CNN, August 29, 2017.

4. Michael Graczyk and David Phillip, "More Rain, More Dead: Harvey Floods Keep Houston Paralyzed," Associated Press, August 28, 2017.

5. Katherine Blunt, "Joel Osteen and the Making of a Megachurch," *Houston Chronicle*, May 31, 2018.

6. Blunt, "Joel Osteen and the Making of a Megachurch."

7. Jason Dearen, "Joel Osteen's Houston Megachurch Opens Doors as Shelter," Associated Press, August 29, 2017.

8. Tom Dart, "Why Did America's Biggest Megachurch Take So Long to Shelter Harvey Victims?" *Guardian*, August 30, 2017.

9. Osteen on ABC's *Good Morning America* on August 30, 2017, https://www.youtube.com/watch?v=KlR0giHWYUs.

10. Alex Davies, "Harvey Wrecks Up to a Million Cars in Car-Dependent Houston," *Wired*, September 3, 2017.

11. Sinitiere, *Salvation*, 21–22.

12. Sinitiere, *Salvation*, 25.

13. Osteen, *Becoming a Man*, 14–15.

14. Sinitiere, *Salvation*, 25–26.

15. Sinitiere, *Salvation*, 28–29.

16. FitzGerald, *Evangelicals*, 221–23.

17. "Businessmen to Form Full Gospel Fellowship," *Irving Daily News*, September 5, 1969.

18. Nicholas C. Chriss, "Praying in Unknown Tongues Gains in South," *Los Angeles Times*, January 17, 1971.

19. Sinitiere, *Salvation*, 43.

20. Sinitiere, *Salvation*, 43.

21. Harrell, *Oral Roberts*, 202–3.

22. Martin, *Prophet with Honor*, 588.

23. Harrell, *Oral Roberts*, 299.

24. Harrell, *Oral Roberts*, 266.

25. Harrell, *Oral Roberts*, 267.

26. Harrell, *Oral Roberts*, 269.

27. Harrell, *Oral Roberts*, 269.

28. Harrell, *Oral Roberts*, 269.

29. D'Antonio, *Fall from Grace*, 7.

30. Harrell, *Oral Roberts*, 269.

31. Allen Spraggett, "Miracle Man," *Ottawa Citizen*, August 13, 1966.

32. "Fresno Churches, Clergy Are Hit by Evangelist," *Fresno Bee*, February 25, 1956.

33. Advertisement in *News & Observer*, September 7, 1963.

34. Advertisement in *Miami Herald*, November 9, 1963.

35. Advertisement in *Miami Herald*, November 16, 1963.

36. Advertisement in *Tampa Times*, February 17, 1968.

37. FitzGerald, *Evangelicals*, 215.

38. Charles T. Powers, "Rev. A. A. Allen: He Shakes, Sways, Hallelujah Trail," *Los Angeles Times*, March 8, 1970.

39. Powers, "Rev. A. A. Allen."

40. "Mystery Death of Faith Healer Here," *San Francisco Examiner*, June 12, 1970.

41. "Alcohol Blamed in Healer Death," *San Francisco Examiner*, June 24, 1970.

42. See "Blood Alcohol Level: Let's Put It on the Table," https://www.notredame college.edu/sites/default/files/-Blood-Alcohol-Chart.pdf.

43. Harrell, *Oral Roberts*, 362.

44. Harrell, *Oral Roberts*, 362–63.

45. Harrell, *Oral Roberts*, 250–51.

46. Harrell, *Oral Roberts*, 130.

47. Roberts, *Expect a Miracle*, 126–27.

48. Roberts, *Miracle of Seed-Faith*, 8.

49. Roberts, *Miracle of Seed-Faith*, 21.

50. Roberts, *Miracle of Seed-Faith*, 82–85.

51. Harrell, *Oral Roberts*, 462.

52. Harrell, *Oral Roberts*, 423.

53. Harrell, *Oral Roberts*, 423–24.

54. Eleanor Blau, "Harlem Preacher Stresses Power of Money and Prayer," *New York Times*, July 26, 1972.

55. Clayton Riley, "The Golden Gospel of Reverend Ike," *New York Times*, March 9, 1975.

56. Christopher Lehmann-Haupt, "Reverend Ike, Who Preached Riches, Dies at 74," *New York Times*, July 29, 2009.

57. Riley, "Golden Gospel."

58. Harrell, *Oral Roberts*, 424–25.

59. Harrell, *Oral Roberts*, 425–27.

60. Harrell, *Oral Roberts*, 426.

61. "Oral Roberts Tells of Talking to a 900-foot Jesus," *Tulsa World*, October 16, 1980.

62. See Atlas Obscura post, https://www.atlasobscura.com/places/praying-hands.

63. Harrell, *Oral Roberts*, 413.

64. Harrell, *Oral Roberts*, 435.

65. "Oral Roberts Pleads for Money to Help Him Live Past March," *Daily Oklahoman*, January 6, 1987. Also see Roberts, *Expect a Miracle*, 289–93.

66. Oral Roberts University Library, Holy Spirit Research Center, "Fundraising for City of Faith from the Prayer Tower," Oral Roberts, March 22, 1987. See https://digitalshowcase.oru.edu/cof/24.

67. Oral Roberts University Library, Holy Spirit Research Center, "Fundraising for City of Faith"; "Announcement of 8 Million Goal Reached," Richard Roberts TV show, April 1, 1987. See https://digitalshowcase.oru.edu/cof/27.

68. Scott McCartney, "Empire Crumbling under Weight of Hospital," *Odessa American*, April 4, 1987.

69. Harrell, *Oral Roberts*, 355.

70. Harrell, *Oral Roberts*, 227–28, 306–7.

71. Harrell, *Oral Roberts*, 306.

72. Keith Schneider, "Oral Roberts, Fiery Preacher, Dies at 91," *New York Times*, December 15, 2009.

73. Shepard, *Forgiven*, 85.

74. Bowler, *Blessed*, 109.

75. Shepard, *Forgiven*, xv.

76. For more on the case, see David Brand, "God and Money," *Time*, August 3, 1987; and Peter Applebome, "Bakker Sentenced to 45 Years for Fraud in His TV Ministry," *New York Times*, October 25, 1989.

77. "Televangelists Take a Slice as Churches Accept Billions in US Coronavirus Aid," *Guardian*, July 9, 2020.

78. Charles Duncan, "Televangelist Who Sold Fake COVID-19 Cure Asks Viewers for Cash to Avoid Bankruptcy," *Kansas City Star*, April 23, 2020.

79. Sinitiere, *Salvation*, 45.

80. Sinitiere, *Salvation*, 50–51.

81. Sinitiere, *Salvation*, 64.

82. For example, see John Osteen's final televised sermon in 1998: https://www.youtube.com/watch?v=KYfxkcZUpS8.

83. Osteen, *Becoming a Man*, 40.

84. See https://www.youtube.com/watch?v=BWQ60wowD_M.

85. Katherine Blunt, "How Joel Osteen Made Himself the Smiling Embodiment of a Guilt-Free Gospel," *Houston Chronicle*, June 4, 2018.

86. William Martin, "Prime Minister," *Texas Monthly*, August 2005.

87. Blunt, "How Joel Osteen Made Himself."

88. Martin, "Prime Minister."

89. Blunt, "How Joel Osteen Made Himself."

90. Blunt, "Joel Osteen and the Making of a Megachurch."

91. Osteen, *Your Best Life*, 33.

92. Osteen, *Your Best Life*, 86.

93. Osteen, *Your Best Life*, 7–8.

94. Osteen, *Your Best Life*, 257.

95. Osteen, *Your Best Life*, 250.

96. Douthat, *Bad Religion*, 189.

97. Diana B. Henriques, "Religion-Based Tax Breaks: Housing to Paychecks to Books," *New York Times*, October 11, 2006.

98. Blunt, "Joel Osteen and the Making of a Megachurch."

99. "The Future of Evangelicals: A Conversation with Pastor Rick Warren," Pew Research Center: Religion and Public Life, November 13, 2009. A guest speaker at Saddleback Church who preached that God rewards good Christians with material goods was asked to leave immediately after the service. Putnam and Feldstein, *Better Together*, 131.

100. "When the Church Parsonage Looks Like a Mansion," Trinity Foundation, May 29, 2020. See https://trinityfi.org/uncategorized/when-the-church-parsonage-looks-like-a-mansion/.

101. Posner, *God's Profits*, 114.

102. Thumma and Travis, *Beyond Megachurch Myths*, 51.

103. Laurie Goodstein, "Senator Questioning Ministries on Spending," *New York Times*, November 7, 2007.

104. Memo to Grassley dated January 6, 2011, p. 1. See https://www.finance.senate.gov/imo/media/doc/SFC%20Staff%20Memo%20to%20Grassley%20re%20Ministries%2001-06-11%20FINAL.pdf.

105. Memo to Grassley, 30.

106. Memo to Grassley, 28; and Horowitz, *One Simple Idea*, 225.

107. Katherine Blunt, "Books, Bargains and Stuff: The Selling of Joel Osteen," *Houston Chronicle*, June 7, 2018.

108. Lisa Gutierrez, "'Word from the Lord': Televangelist's Ministry Buys Tyler Perry's Gulfstream Jet," *Kansas City Star*, January 21, 2018.

109. The segment, which aired August 16, 2015, has more than thirty-five million views on YouTube. See https://www.youtube.com/watch?v=7y1xJAVZxXg.

110. Posner, *God's Profits*, 87.

111. Posner, *God's Profits*, 87–88.

112. Burkhard Bilger, "The Antichrist of East Dallas," *New Yorker*, December 6, 2004.

113. Posner, *God's Profits*, 115.

114. Gutierrez, "'Word from the Lord.'"

115. Video dated January 17, 2018, on Kenneth Copeland Ministries' YouTube channel. See https://www.youtube.com/watch?v=pxmQmDEytdo.

116. Video of full interview dated May 20, 2019, on *Inside Edition*'s YouTube channel. See https://www.youtube.com/watch?v=9LtF34MrsfI.

117. Abe Hardesty, "Megachurch Pastor Receives Rousing Support from Congregation after Giving $200K Lamborghini to Wife," *Greenville News*, December 17, 2018.

118. Daniel J. Gross, "This South Carolina Megachurch Bought Its Pastor a $1.8M House. Here's Why," *Greenville News*, January 20, 2019.

119. Rick Rojas, "Let He Who Is without Yeezys Cast the First Stone," *New York Times*, April 17, 2019.

120. Laura M. Holson, "This Preacher Would Be Happy to Share Your Bowl of *Açaí*," *New York Times*, March 17, 2018. In another echo of evangelical history, Veach is the son of a Foursquare Church administrator.

CHAPTER 10

1. Top epigraph from Falwell's 1965 "Ministers and Marches" sermon, distributed in pamphlet form, p. 7. See https://liberty.contentdm.oclc.org/digital/collection /p17184coll4/id/4691. Bottom epigraph from Falwell, *Listen, America!*, 255.

2. Falwell, *Strength for the Journey*, 15.

3. Falwell, *Strength for the Journey*, 36.

4. Falwell, *Strength for the Journey*, 48–49.

5. Falwell, *Strength for the Journey*, 49–50.

6. Falwell, *Strength for the Journey*, 92–93.

7. Falwell, *Strength for the Journey*, 94. An earlier autobiography says the rat was dead. Falwell's books were typically ghostwritten, so there are many odd differences in details among his books.

8. Falwell, *Strength for the Journey*, 102–3.

9. Falwell, *Strength for the Journey*, 176–77.

10. Falwell, *Strength for the Journey*, 192–94.

11. Falwell, *Strength for the Journey*, 206.

12. Falwell, *Strength for the Journey*, 221.

13. FitzGerald, *Evangelicals*, 284.

14. See https://www.africa.upenn.edu/Articles_Gen/Letter_Birmingham.html.

15. Meacham, *American Gospel*, 192.

16. Falwell, "Ministers and Marches," 3.

17. Falwell, "Ministers and Marches," 17.

18. R. J. Reinhard, "Protests Seen as Harming Civil Rights Movement in the '60s," Gallup, January 21, 2019. https://news.gallup.com/vault/246167/protests -seen-harming-civil-rights-movement-60s.aspx. A Gallup poll in June 1963 taken before the March on Washington asked the same question. Sixty percent said the demonstrations would help and 27 percent said they would hurt.

19. Falwell, "Ministers and Marches," 2.

20. Falwell, "Ministers and Marches," 15.

21. Falwell, *Strength for the Journey*, 290.

22. Falwell, *Strength for the Journey*, 291.

23. Perlstein, *Reaganland*, 348.

24. Falwell, *Strength for the Journey*, 298.

25. Meacham, *American Gospel*, 189. See Engel v. Vitale, 370 U.S. 431 (1962); School District of Abington Township, Pennsylvania v. Schempp, 374 U.S. 209 (1963).

26. Linda Lyons, "The Gallup Brain: Prayer in Public Schools," December 10, 2002. See https://news.gallup.com/poll/7393/gallup-brain-prayer-public-schools.aspx.

27. FitzGerald, *Evangelicals*, 295.

28. Wills, *Head and Heart*, 487.

29. Falwell, *Strength for the Journey*, 302.

30. Falwell and Towns, *Church Aflame*, 40–41.

31. "Lynchburg Church to Sponsor Liberal Arts College," *Danville Register*, March 21, 1971.

32. Falwell, *Strength for the Journey*, 318–20.

33. Falwell, *Strength for the Journey*, 327–30.

34. Falwell, *Strength for the Journey*, 333.

35. *Roe v. Wade*, 410 U.S. 113 (1973).

36. Sheila Wolfe and Richard Philbrick, "Cody to Continue Abortion Fight," *Chicago Tribune*, January 24, 1973.

37. "Statements by 2 Cardinals," *New York Times*, January 23, 1973.

38. FitzGerald, *Evangelicals*, 255.

39. FitzGerald, *Evangelicals*, 255–56.

40. Falwell, *Strength for the Journey*, 340.

41. Falwell, *Strength for the Journey*, 345–46.

42. "Poll Finds 34% Share 'Born Again" Feeling," *New York Times*, September 26, 1976.

43. Democratic Party Platforms, 1976 Democratic Party Platform Online by Gerhard Peters and John T. Woolley, The American Presidency Project, https://www.presidency.ucsb.edu/node/273251.

44. Republican Party Platform of 1976, August 18, 1976, The American Presidency Project, https://www.presidency.ucsb.edu/node/273415.

45. Robert Scheer, "The *Playboy* Interview with Jimmy Carter," *Playboy*, November 1976.

46. "Carter Accused of Threats," *Daily Oklahoman*, October 19, 1976.

47. "Rev. Falwell Deletes Criticism of Carter," *Daily Press*, Newport News, VA, October 14, 1976.

48. "Carter Accused of Threats," *Daily Oklahoman*, October 19, 1976.

49. Perlstein, *Reaganland*, 110–11.

50. Perlstein, *Reaganland*, 111.

51. Strober and Tomczak, *Jerry Falwell*, 182.

52. Strober and Tomczak, *Jerry Falwell*, 183–85. Milk and Moscone were killed November 27, 1978; Falwell's quotation is from his *The Old Time Gospel Hour* sermon on December 3, 1978.

53. For example, see advertisement in *Johnson City Press*, May 12, 1978.

54. Strober and Tomczak, *Jerry Falwell*, 120.

55. Perlstein, *Reaganland*, 354.

56. Perlstein, *Reaganland*, 354–55.

57. Perlstein, *Reaganland*, 472.

58. Perlstein, *Reaganland*, 483–84.

59. Balmer, *Thy Kingdom Come*, 16.

60. Perlstein, *Reaganland*, 492.

61. Kara Rogge, "'Freedom to Preach' Rally for Evangelist Packs Center," *Fort Worth Star-Telegram*, June 6, 1979.

62. Gilgoff, *Jesus Machine*, 80–81.

63. Steve Hill, "Falwell Seeking Moral Majority," *Tampa Tribune*, August 25, 1979.

64. Cole C. Campbell and Daniel C. Hoover, "TV Evangelist Calls His Flock to Politics," *News & Observer*, November 3, 1979.

65. Campbell and Hoover, "TV Evangelist Calls."

66. FitzGerald, *Evangelicals*, 354–55. Koop served as surgeon general during the Reagan administration.

67. FitzGerald, *Evangelicals*, 362–63.

68. Wills, *Head and Heart*, 491.

69. Eileen Ogintz, "Evangelists Seek Political Clout," *Chicago Tribune*, January 13, 1980.

70. Ogintz, "Evangelists."

71. Ogintz, "Evangelists."

72. Lichtman, *White Protestant Nation*, 344.

73. Ogintz, "Evangelists."

74. FitzGerald, *Evangelicals*, 291–92.

75. Falwell, *Listen, America!*, 11.

76. Falwell, *Listen, America!*, 12.

77. Falwell, *Listen, America!*, 13.

78. Falwell, *Listen, America!*, 22–23.

79. Falwell, *Listen, America!*, 183.

80. Perlstein, *Reaganland*, 626–27. Reagan also discussed Armageddon with Falwell before the 1980 election.

81. Republican Party Platform of 1980, July 15, 1980, The American Presidency Project https://www.presidency.ucsb.edu/node/273420.

82. Republican Party Platform of 1980.

83. 1980 Democratic Party Platform, August 11, 1980, The American Presidency Project https://www.presidency.ucsb.edu/node/273253.

84. See video at https://www.americanrhetoric.com/speeches/ronaldreagan religiousliberty.htm.

85. Reagan, National Affairs Campaign Address; see video at American Rhetoric Online Speech Bank, https://www.americanrhetoric.com/speeches/ronaldreagan religiousliberty.htm.

86. Reagan, National Affairs Campaign Address.

87. FitzGerald, *Evangelicals*, 317.

88. Cannon, *President Reagan*, 805.

89. Camilla Warrick, "Falwell Proposes Plan to Halt Spread of AIDS," *Cincinnati Enquirer*, July 5, 1983.

90. Don Lattin, "Abortion Ruling Was Genesis of Falwell's Activism," *San Francisco Examiner*, July 13, 1984.

91. Falwell, *Strength for the Journey*, 388.

92. Frye Gaillard, "The Faces of Jerry Falwell," *Charlotte Observer*, June 14, 1987.

93. Wills, *Head and Heart*, 481.

94. Harrell, *Pat Robertson*, 26–28.

95. Harrell, *Pat Robertson*, 30.

96. Gilgoff, *Jesus Machine*, 90.

97. Harrell, *Pat Robertson*, 79–80.

98. Robertson, *New World Order*, 104–5.

99. Harrell, *Pat Robertson*, 88–89.

100. Harrell, *Pat Robertson*, 91–92.

101. Ralph Reed, phone interview with author, October 19, 2021.

102. Reed, interview.

103. Gilgoff, *Jesus Machine*, 96.

104. Reed, *Politically Incorrect*, 200.

105. Lichtman, *White Protestant Nation*, 399.

106. Lichtman, *White Protestant Nation*, 399.

107. Harrell, *Pat Robertson*, 138.

108. Harrell, *Pat Robertson*, 150.

109. "Religion and the Presidential Vote," Pew Research Center, December 6, 2004. For exit poll data for the 2000 and 2004 elections, see https://www.pew research.org/politics/2004/12/06/religion-and-the-presidential-vote/.

110. Harrell, *Pat Robertson*, 274.

111. Robertson, *New World Order*, 6.

112. Robertson, *Secret Kingdom*, 19.

113. Laurie Goodstein, "After the Attacks: Finding Fault," *New York Times*, September 15, 2001.

114. Harrell, *Pat Robertson*, 303–4.

CHAPTER 11

1. From remarks at a White House dinner on August 27, 2018. Robert Jeffress and Franklin Graham were among the attendees. Paula White presented Donald Trump with a Bible signed by evangelical leaders and offered a prayer before the meal. See video at https://www.c-span.org/video/?450757-1/president-trump -remarks-evangelical-leadership-dinner.

2. "June 1, 2020: Statement on Protests against Police Brutality," Miller Center, University of Virginia, https://millercenter.org/the-presidency/presidential -speeches/june-1-2020-statement-protests-against-police-brutality.

3. "June 1, 2020: Statement on Protests against Police Brutality."

4. See "Ivanka Trump Carried the Bible Donald Trump Posed with in her $1,540 Max Mara Handbag in Infamous Photo-Op 'Masterminded by Hope Hicks,'" *Daily Mail*, June 2, 2020, https://www.dailymail.co.uk/news/article -8381977/Ivanka-Trump-carried-Bible-Donald-Trump-posed-1-540-Max -Mara-handbag.html.

5. Michelle Boorstein and Sarah Pulliam Bailey, "Episcopal Bishop on President Trump: 'Everything He Has Said and Done Is to Inflame Violence," *Washington Post*, June 1, 2020.

6. Boorstein and Bailey, "Episcopal Bishop on President Trump"; Donald and Melania Trump's visit to a Catholic shrine on the following day drew a rebuke from Washington's archbishop for similar reasons.

7. McKay Coppins, "The Christians Who Loved Trump's Stunt," *Atlantic*, June 2, 2020.

8. Coppins, "The Christians Who Loved Trump's Stunt."

9. Gwenda Blair, "How Norman Vincent Peale Taught Donald Trump to Worship Himself," *Politico*, October 6, 2015.

10. Todd S. Purdum, "Trump Pledge: In This Plaza, I Thee Wed," *New York Times*, December 18, 1993.

11. Trump, *Crippled America*, 130.

12. Peale, *Power of Positive Thinking*, 11.

13. Marylin Bender, "The Empire and Ego of Donald Trump," *New York Times*, August 7, 1983.

14. Peale, *Autobiography*, 220–21. Peale's autobiography shoehorns his praise of Trump between Dr. Smiley Blanton—who merits only one and a half pages despite the importance of their partnership—and religious leaders he knew personally, such as Billy Graham.

15. "Donald Trump on Failure," *Psychology Today*, May 19, 2009.

16. See *Meet the Press*, https://www.nbcnews.com/meet-the-press/video /trump-in-1999-i-am-very-pro-choice-480297539914.

17. Lee and Sinitiere, *Holy Mavericks*, 114.

18. Lee and Sinitiere, *Holy Mavericks*, 117.

19. Newspaper advertisement, *Tampa Tribune*, January 15, 1994.

20. Walt Belcher, "Trump Gets Spiritual on Show Hosted by Area Minister," *Tampa Tribune*, October 20, 2006.

21. Lee and Sinitiere, *Holy Mavericks*, 111.

22. Michelle Bearden, "Power Pastors Give, Get a Lot," *Tampa Tribune*, August 14, 2002.

23. Bearden, "Power Pastors Give, Get a Lot."

24. Bearden, "Power Pastors Give, Get a Lot."

25. Michelle Bearden and Baird Helegson, "Of Faith, Fame and Fortune," *Tampa Tribune*, May 20, 2007.

26. Bearden and Helegson, "Without Walls Founders Divorcing," *Tampa Tribune*, August 24, 2007.

27. Bearden and Helegson, "Of Faith, Fame and Fortune."

28. Bearden and Helegson, "Without Walls Founders Divorcing."

29. Memo to Grassley dated January 6, 2011, 31. See https://www.finance
.senate.gov/imo/media/doc/SFC%20Staff%20Memo%20to%20Grassley%20re%20
Ministries%2001-06-11%20FINAL.pdf.

30. Senate Finance Committee, minority staff review of Without Walls International Church and Paula White Ministries dated January 5, 2011, 6.

31. Senate Finance Committee, minority staff review of Without Walls, 1.

32. Senate Finance Committee, minority staff review of Without Walls, 1–13.

33. Senate Finance Committee, minority staff review of Without Walls, 8.

34. Senate Finance Committee, minority staff review of Without Walls, 6, 8.

35. Emily McFarlan Miller, "Controversial Inauguration Pastor Answers Her
Critics," *Kansas City Star*, January 21, 2017.

36. Jeremy W. Peters and Elizabeth Dias, "Paula White, Newest White House
Aide, Is a Uniquely Trumpian Pastor," *New York Times*, November 2, 2019.

37. Trump was interviewed by John Heilemann and Mark Halperin in the
Trump Tower atrium on August 26, 2015. See "Trump Talks Bush Bible and
White Supremacist Backers," Bloomberg, https://www.bloomberg.com/news
/videos/2015-08-26/trump-talks-bush-bible-and-white-supremacist-backers.

38. Matt Viser, "Donald Trump Relies on a Simple Phrase: 'Believe Me,'"
Boston Globe, May 24, 2016.

39. Viser, "Donald Trump Relies on a Simple Phrase."

40. Wehner, *Death of Politics*, 78.

41. Bethany Rodgers, "Apopka Pastor Close to Trump," *Orlando Sentinel*, July
23, 2016.

42. Robert Jeffress, phone interview with author, September 23, 2021.

43. Interview dated June 1, 2016. See https://www.youtube.com/watch?v
=G42VEGGmliQ.

44. Shane Goldmacher, "A Tabloid Publisher Will Pay a $187,500 FEC Penalty
for Its Trump Hush-Money Payment," *New York Times*, June 1, 2021. It was not
the only disbursement of hush-money funds during the 2016 presidential campaign.
Michael Cohen, Trump's former personal lawyer and fixer, arranged a $130,000
payment to pornographic film actress Stormy Daniels to conceal an alleged affair
between her and Trump. Falwell also called on Cohen for assistance to suppress the
release of compromising personal photographs.

45. See https://www.youtube.com/watch?v=FSC8Q-kR44o.

46. Interview with Reed on *Atlantic* podcast published May 13, 2021. See
https://www.theatlantic.com/podcasts/archive/2021/05/evangelicals-republican
-voters/618845/.

47. "Backing Trump, White Evangelicals Flip Flop on Importance of Candidate
Character: PPRI/Brookings Survey," Public Religion Research Institute, October
19, 2016. See https://www.prri.org/research/prri-brookings-oct-19-poll-politics
-election-clinton-double-digit-lead-trump/.

48. "Backing Trump, White Evangelicals Flip Flop."

49. Michael J. Mooney, "Trump's Apostle," *Texas Monthly*, August 2019.

50. See Jessica Martínez and Gregory A. Smith, "How the Faithful Voted: A Preliminary 2016 Analysis," Pew Research Center, November 2016, https://www.pewresearch.org/fact-tank/2016/11/09/how-the-faithful-voted-a-preliminary-2016-analysis/.

51. Martínez and Smith, "How the Faithful Voted."

52. Julia Duin, "She Led Trump to Christ: The Rise of the Televangelist Who Advises the White House," *Washington Post Magazine*, November 14, 2017.

53. Russell Moore, phone interview with author, September 14, 2021.

54. Fea, *Believe Me*, 141–42.

55. Jeffress interview.

56. Reed interview.

57. David Crary, "Trump's Prayer Breakfast Jibes Jolt Many Faith Leaders," Associated Press, February 6, 2020.

58. Cohen, *Disloyal*, 133.

59. McKay Coppins, "Trump Secretary Mocks His Christian Supporters," *Atlantic*, September 29, 2020.

60. Brian Slodysko, Jill Colvin, and Will Weissert, "Trump, Biden Go on Offense in States They're Trying to Flip," Associated Press, October 18, 2020.

61. Elana Schor, "Trump's Faith Outreach Aims to Cast Democrats as Enemy," *News-Star*, Monroe, Louisiana, August 3, 2020.

62. Anita Snow, David Goldman, and Lisa Marie Pane, "Trump's Base Refuses to Accept Loss," *Spokesman-Review*, November 8, 2020.

63. Frank Newport, "Religious Group Voting and the 2020 Election," Gallup, November 13, 2020.

64. See https://www.youtube.com/watch?v=Nu96Fhl1Gjo.

65. Brian Naylor, "Read Trump's Jan. 6 Speech, a Key Part of Impeachment Trial," NPR, February 10, 2021. See https://www.npr.org/2021/02/10/966396848/read-trumps-jan-6-speech-a-key-part-of-impeachment-trial.

66. Trump made the remark during his September 29 debate with Joe Biden.

67. See the post dated January 7, 2021, on his personal website: https://albertmohler.com/2021/01/07/briefing-1-7-21.

68. Moore interview.

69. "A Majority of Americans View Biden Favorably as Trump Hits Historic Low," Public Religion Research Institute, January 20, 2021. See https://www.prri.org/research/more-than-half-of-americans-view-biden-favorably-as-trump-hits-historic-lows/.

70. "Dramatic Partisan Differences on Blame for January 6 Riots," Public Religion Research Institute, September 15, 2021. https://www.prri.org/research/dramatic-partisan-differences-on-blame-for-january-6-riots/.

71. "Dramatic Partisan Differences on Blame for January 6 Riots."

EPILOGUE

1. Gibbs and Duffy, *Preacher and the Presidents*, xi.

2. The designation of "lying in state" is reserved for government officials—such as members of Congress and presidents—and military leaders.

3. Frank Newport, "In the News: Billy Graham on 'Most Admired' List 61 Times," Gallup, February 21, 2018. See https://news.gallup.com/poll/228089/news-billy-graham-admired-list-times.aspx.

4. George Dugan, "Graham's Impact Termed Fleeting," *New York Times*, January 26, 1958.

5. "Reverend Billy Graham Funeral Service," March 2, 2018, C-SPAN. See https://www.c-span.org/video/?441940-1/reverend-billy-graham-funeral-service.

6. Richard Nixon memo to H. R. Haldeman, November 30, 1970. Billy Graham Center Archives, Wheaton College, collection 74, box 3, folder 7.

7. Billy Graham letter to H. R. Haldeman dated October 21, 1972. Nixon memo to Haldeman.

8. White House Tapes, February 1, 1972, conversation 662-004. The meeting included detailed discussion about the upcoming 1972 election and how Graham could help Nixon's cause. Graham offered his shrewd appraisal of figures such as John Connally, sounding much more like a political insider than a clergyman. See https://www.nixonlibrary.gov/white-house-tapes/662/conversation-662-004.

9. Frost, *Billy Graham*, 144, 163.

10. Frost, *Billy Graham*, 151.

11. Martin, *Prophet with Honor*, 594.

12. Martin, *Prophet with Honor*, 594.

13. Martin, *Prophet with Honor*, 596.

14. Eliza Griswold, "Franklin Graham's Uneasy Alliance with Donald Trump," *New Yorker*, September 11, 2018.

15. "Interview with the Reverend Franklin Graham," ABC News, April 24, 2011. See https://www.youtube.com/watch?v=lx2E286GAcE.

16. Martin, *Prophet with Honor*, 694.

17. Martin, *Prophet with Honor*, 694.

18. "Reverend Franklin Graham Offers a Prayer at Inauguration Day 2017," January 20, 2017, PBS NewsHour. See https://www.youtube.com/watch?v=l8CHxAoIcl4.

19. Liam Stack and Sheri Fink, "Franklin Graham Is Taking Down His N.Y. Hospital, But Not Going Quietly," *New York Times*, May 10, 2020.

20. Stack and Fink, "Franklin Graham Is Taking Down His N.Y. Hospital."

21. "Reverend Billy Graham Funeral Service."

22. FitzGerald, *Evangelicals*, 169.

23. Gushee, *After Evangelicalism*, 15.

24. Gushee, *After Evangelicalism*, 15–16.

25. Rebecca Ngu, "Princeton Christian Fellowship Ditches the Term 'Evangelical,'" *Daily Princetonian*, October 1, 2017.

26. Ngu, "Princeton Christian Fellowship."

27. Moore interview.

28. Moore interview.

29. Du Mez, *Jesus and John Wayne*, 297–98.

30. Du Mez, *Jesus and John Wayne*, 3.

31. Miles McPherson, email interview with author, October 18, 2021.

32. Walter Kim, phone interview with author, November 3, 2021.

33. Kim interview.

34. Barna interview.

35. Barna interview.

BIBLIOGRAPHY

This listing consists of books consulted as research for this book. They are identified by the author's name when used as citations in the notes. Newspapers, magazines, interviews, and websites referenced are cited in full in the notes.

Ahlstrom, Sydney E., ed. *Theology in America: The Major Protestant Voices from Puritanism to Neo-orthodoxy.* Indianapolis, IN: Bobbs-Merrill, 1967.

Albanese, Catherine L. *Sons of the Fathers: The Civil Religion of the American Revolution.* Philadelphia, PA: Temple University Press, 1976.

Balmer, Randall. *Thy Kingdom Come: How the Religious Right Distorts the Faith and Threatens America.* New York: Basic Books, 2006.

———. *The Making of Evangelicalism: From Revivalism to Politics and Beyond.* Waco, TX: Baylor University Press, 2010.

Balmer, Randall, and Lauren F. Winner. *Protestantism in America.* New York: Columbia University Press, 2002.

Barna, George. *A Step-by-Step Guide to Church Marketing: Breaking Ground for the Harvest.* Ventura, CA: Regal Books, 1992.

Barton, Bruce. *The Man Nobody Knows: A Discovery of the Real Jesus.* Indianapolis, IN: Bobbs-Merrill, 1925.

Bass, Diana Butler. *Christianity for the Rest of Us: How the Neighborhood Church Is Transforming the Faith.* New York: Harper San Francisco, 2006.

Bellah, Robert N. *Beyond Belief: Essays on Religion in a Post-Traditional World.* New York: Harper & Row, 1970.

———. *The Broken Covenant: American Civil Religion in Time of Trial.* New York: Seabury Press, 1975.

Belmonte, Kevin. *D. L. Moody: A Life, Innovator, Evangelist, World Changer.* Chicago: Moody Publishers, 2014.

Berger, Peter L. *The Noise of Solemn Assemblies: Christian Commitment and the Religious Establishment in America.* Garden City, NY: Doubleday, 1961.

————. *The Sacred Canopy: Elements of a Sociological Theory of Religion*. Garden City, NY: Anchor Books, 1969.

Bettger, Frank. *How I Raised Myself from Failure to Success in Selling*. Englewood Cliffs, NJ: Prentice-Hall, 1949.

Birmingham, Stephen. *The Golden Dream: Suburbia in the Seventies*. New York: Harper & Row, 1978.

Bloesch, Donald G. *The Evangelical Renaissance*. Grand Rapids, MI: William B. Eerdmans, 1973.

Blumhofer, Edith L. *Aimee Semple McPherson: Everybody's Sister*. Grand Rapids, MI: William B. Eerdmans, 1993.

Bonomi, Patricia U. *Under the Cope of Heaven: Religion, Society, and Politics in Colonial America*. New York: Oxford University Press, 1986.

Bowler, Kate. *Blessed: A History of the American Prosperity Gospel*. New York: Oxford University Press, 2013.

Bruce, Steve. *The Rise and Fall of the New Christian Right: Conservative Protestant Politics in America, 1978–1988*. New York: Oxford University Press, 2009.

Bruns, Roger A. *Preacher: Billy Sunday and Big-Time American Evangelism*. New York: W.W. Norton, 1992.

Burgess, Stanley M., and Gary B. McGee, eds. *Dictionary of Pentecostal and Charismatic Movements*. Grand Rapids, MI: Regency Reference Library, 1988.

Cannon, Lou. *President Reagan: The Role of a Lifetime*. New York: Touchstone, 1991.

Carpenter, Joel A. *Revive Us Again: The Reawakening of American Fundamentalism*. New York: Oxford University Press, 1997.

Cohen, Michael. *Disloyal: A Memoir*. New York: Skyhorse, 2020.

Conwell, Russell H. *Health, Healing, and Faith*. New York: Harper & Brothers, 1921.

Cousins, Norman, ed. *In God We Trust: The Religious Beliefs and Ideas of the American Founding Fathers*. New York: Harper & Brothers, 1958.

Curry, Thomas J. *Farewell to Christendom: The Future of Church and State in America*. New York: Oxford University Press, 2001.

D'Antonio, Michael. *Fall from Grace: The Failed Crusade of the Christian Right*. New York: Farrar, Straus and Giroux, 1989.

Dochuk, Darren. *From Bible Belt to Sunbelt: Plain-Folk Religion, Grassroots Politics, and the Rise of Evangelical Conservatism*. New York: W. W. Norton, 2011.

Douthat, Ross. *Bad Religion: How We Became a Nation of Heretics*. New York: Free Press, 2012.

Dow, Lorenzo. *The Life, Travels, Labors, and Writings of Lorenzo Dow*. New York: C. M. Saxton, 1859.

Drucker, Peter F. *Management Challenges for the 21st Century*. New York: Harper-Collins, 1999.

Du Mez, Kristin Kobes. *Jesus and John Wayne: How White Evangelicals Corrupted a Faith and Fractured a Nation*. New York: Liveright, 2020.

Eastland, Terry, ed. *Religious Liberty in the Supreme Court: The Cases That Define the Debate over Church and State.* Washington, DC: Ethics and Public Policy Center, 1993.

Eckardt, A. Roy. *The Surge of Piety in America: An Appraisal.* New York: Association Press, 1958.

Ehrenreich, Barbara. *Bright-Sided: How the Relentless Promotion of Positive Thinking Has Undermined America.* New York: Metropolitan Books, 2009.

Einstein, Mara. *Brands of Faith: Marketing Religion in a Commercial Age.* New York: Routledge, 2008.

El-Faizy, Monique. *God and Country: How Evangelicals Have Become America's New Mainstream.* New York: Bloomsbury, 2006.

Ellingson, Stephen. *The Megachurch and the Mainline: Remaking Religious Tradition in the Twenty-First Century.* Chicago: University of Chicago Press, 2007.

Ellis, William T. *Billy Sunday: The Man and His Message.* Philadelphia: John C. Winston Company, 1914.

Emerson, Michael O., and Christian Smith. *Divided by Faith: Evangelical Religion and the Problem of Race in America.* New York: Oxford University Press, 2000.

Enroth, Ronald M., Edward E. Ericson Jr., and C. Breckinridge Peters. *The Jesus People: Old-Time Religion in the Age of Aquarius.* Grand Rapids, MI: William B. Eerdmans, 1972.

Evans, Harold. *They Made America: Two Centuries of Innovators from the Steam Engine to the Search Engine.* New York: Little, Brown, 2004.

Evensen, Bruce J. *God's Man for the Gilded Age: D. L. Moody and the Rise of Modern Mass Evangelism.* New York: Oxford University Press, 2003.

Falwell, Jerry. *Listen, America!* Garden City, NY: Doubleday, 1980.

———. *Strength for the Journey: An Autobiography.* New York: Simon & Schuster, 1987.

Falwell, Jerry, and Elmer Towns. *Church Aflame.* Nashville, TN: Impact Books, 1971.

Farrell, John A. *Clarence Darrow: Attorney for the Damned.* New York: Doubleday, 2011.

Fea, John. *Believe Me: The Evangelical Road to Donald Trump.* Grand Rapids, MI: William B. Eerdmans, 2018.

Feldman, Noah. *Divided by God: America's Church-State Problem—and What We Should Do About It.* New York: Farrar, Straus and Giroux, 2005.

Finke, Roger, and Rodney Stark. *The Churching of America, 1776–2005: Winners and Losers in Our Religious Economy.* New Brunswick, NJ: Rutgers University Press, 2005.

Finney, Charles Grandison. *Lectures on Revivals of Religion.* Cambridge, MA: Belknap Press of Harvard University Press, 1960.

FitzGerald, Frances. *The Evangelicals: The Struggle to Shape America.* New York: Simon & Schuster, 2017.

Foster, Charles I. *An Errand of Mercy: The Evangelical United Front, 1790–1837*. Chapel Hill: University of North Carolina Press, 1960.

Frady, Marshall. *Billy Graham: A Parable of American Righteousness*. Boston: Little, Brown, 1979.

Friedman, Benjamin M. *Religion and the Rise of Capitalism*. New York: Knopf, 2021.

Frost, David. *Billy Graham: Personal Thoughts of a Public Man*. Colorado Springs: ChariotVictor, 1997.

George, Carol V. R. *God's Salesman: Norman Vincent Peale and the Power of Positive Thinking*. New York: Oxford University Press, 1993.

Gibbs, Nancy, and Michael Duffy. *The Preacher and the Presidents: Billy Graham in the White House*. New York: Center Street, 2008.

Gilgoff, Dan. *The Jesus Machine: How James Dobson, Focus on the Family, and Evangelical America Are Winning the Culture War*. New York: St. Martin's Press, 2007.

Goldberg, Michelle. *Kingdom Coming: The Rise of Christian Nationalism*. New York: W. W. Norton, 2006.

Gordon, Arthur. *Norman Vincent Peale: Minister to Millions*. Englewood Cliffs, NJ: Prentice-Hall, 1958.

Gorham, B. W. *Camp Meeting Manual: A Practical Book for the Campground*. Boston: H. V. Degen, 1854.

Graham, Billy. *Just as I Am: The Autobiography of Billy Graham*. New York: Harper-Collins, 1999.

Gushee, David P. *After Evangelicalism: The Path to a New Christianity*. Louisville, KY: Westminster/John Knox Press, 2020.

Hall, Clarence W., and Desider Holisher. *Protestant Panorama: A Story of the Faith That Made America Free*. New York: Farrar, Straus and Young, 1951.

Hangen, Tona J. *Redeeming the Dial: Radio, Religion, and Popular Culture in America*. Chapel Hill: University of North Carolina Press, 2002.

Hankins, Barry. *American Evangelicals: A Contemporary History of a Mainstream Religious Movement*. Lanham, MD: Rowman & Littlefield, 2009.

Harding, Susan Friend. *The Book of Jerry Falwell: Fundamentalist Language and Politics*. Princeton, NJ: Princeton University Press, 2001.

Harrell, David Edwin Jr. *Oral Roberts: An American Life*. San Francisco, CA: Harper & Row, 1987.

———. *Pat Robertson: A Life and Legacy*. Grand Rapids, MI: William B. Eerdmans, 2010.

Hart, D. G. *That Old-Time Religion in Modern America: Evangelical Protestantism in the Twentieth Century*. Chicago: Ivan R. Dee, 2002.

Harvey, Paul, and Philip Goff, eds. *The Columbia Documentary History of Religion in America Since 1945*. New York: Columbia University Press, 2005.

Hatch, Nathan O. *The Democratization of American Christianity*. New Haven, CT: Yale University Press, 1989.

Hayford, Jack W., and S. David Moore. *The Charismatic Century: The Enduring Impact of the Azusa Street Revival*. New York: Warner Faith, 2006.

Henry, Carl F. H. *The Uneasy Conscience of Modern Fundamentalism*. 1947. Reprint. Grand Rapids, MI: William B. Eerdmans, 2003.

Herberg, Will. *Protestant-Catholic-Jew: An Essay in American Religious Sociology*. New York: Anchor Books, 1960.

Hill, Samuel S. *Southern Churches in Crisis Revisited*. Tuscaloosa: University of Alabama Press, 1999.

Hitchcock, William I. *The Age of Eisenhower: American and the World in the 1950s*. New York: Simon & Schuster, 2018.

Hoge, Dean R., Benton Johnson, and Donald A. Luidens. *Vanishing Boundaries: The Religion of Mainline Protestant Baby Boomers*. Louisville, KY: Westminster/ John Knox Press, 1994.

Holmes, David L. *The Faiths of the Postwar President: From Truman to Obama*. Athens: University of Georgia Press, 2012.

Horowitz, Mitch. *One Simple Idea: How Positive Thinking Reshaped Modern Life*. New York: Crown, 2014.

Howe, Ben. *The Immoral Majority: Why Evangelicals Chose Political Power over Christian Values*. New York: Broadside Books, 2019.

Hunter, James Davison. *American Evangelicalism: Conservative Religion and the Quandary of Modernity*. New Brunswick, NJ: Rutgers University Press, 1983.

Hutson, James H. *The Founders on Religion: A Book of Quotations*. Princeton, NJ: Princeton University Press, 2005.

Hybels, Bill. *Holy Discontent: Fueling the Fire That Ignites Personal Vision*. Grand Rapids, MI: Zondervan, 2007.

———. *Just Walk across the Room: Simple Steps Pointing People to Faith*. Grand Rapids, MI: Zondervan, 2006.

Hybels, Lynne, and Bill Hybels. *Rediscovering Church: The Story and Vision of Willow Creek Community Church*. Grand Rapids, MI: Zondervan, 1995.

Inboden, William. *Religion and American Foreign Policy, 1945–1960*. New York: Cambridge University Press, 2008.

Irons, Peter. *A People's History of the Supreme Court*. New York: Penguin, 2006.

Jones, Robert P. *White Too Long: The Legacy of White Supremacy in American Christianity*. New York: Simon & Schuster, 2020.

Kelley, Dean M. *Why Conservative Churches Are Growing: A Study in Sociology of Religion*. San Francisco, CA: Harper & Row, 1977.

Kidd, Thomas S. *Who Is an Evangelical? The History of a Movement in Crisis*. New Haven, CT: Yale University Press, 2019.

Koch, Adrienne, and William Peden, eds. *The Life and Selected Writings of Thomas Jefferson*. New York: Random House, 1993.

Krames, Jeffrey A. *Inside Drucker's Brain*. New York: Portfolio, 2008.

Kruse, Kevin M. *One Nation Under God: How Corporate America Invented Christian America*. New York: Basic Books, 2015.

Lacey, Michael J., ed. *Religion and Twentieth-Century American Intellectual Life*. New York: Cambridge University Press, 1989.

Lambert, Frank. *Pedlar in Divinity: George Whitefield and the Transatlantic Revivals, 1737–1770*. Princeton, NJ: Princeton University Press, 1994.

Lane, Christopher. *Surge of Piety: Norman Vincent Peale and the Remaking of American Religious Life*. New Haven, CT: Yale University Press, 2016.

Lawrence, William. *Memories of a Happy Life*. Cambridge, MA: Riverside Press, 1926.

Lee, Shayne, and Phillip Luke Sinitiere. *Holy Mavericks: Evangelical Innovators and the Spiritual Marketplace*. New York: New York University Press, 2009.

Lehmann, Chris. *The Money Cult: Capitalism, Christianity, and the Unmaking of the American Dream*. Brooklyn, NY: Melville House, 2017.

Leonnig, Carol, and Philip Rucker. *I Alone Can Fix It: Donald J. Trump's Catastrophic Final Year*. New York: Penguin, 2021.

Lichtman, Allan J. *White Protestant Nation: The Rise of the American Conservative Movement*. New York: Atlantic Monthly Press, 2008.

Lindsay, Michael D. *Faith in the Halls of Power: How Evangelicals Joined the American Elite*. New York: Oxford University Press, 2007.

Lindsey, Hal. *The Late Great Planet Earth*. Grand Rapids, MI: Zondervan, 1970.

Loveland, Anne C., and Otis B. Wheeler. *Meetinghouse to Megachurch: A Material and Cultural History*. Columbia: University of Missouri Press, 2003.

Luhrmann, T. M. *When God Talks Back: Understanding the American Evangelical Relationship with God*. New York: Vintage Books, 2012.

Marsden, George M. *Religion and American Culture*. San Diego: Harcourt Brace Jovanovich, 1990.

———. *Understanding Fundamentalism and Evangelicalism*. Grand Rapids, MI: William B. Eerdmans, 1991.

Martin, Robert F. *Hero of the Heartland: Billy Sunday and the Transformation of American Society, 1862–1935*. Bloomington: Indiana University Press, 2002.

Martin, William. *A Prophet with Honor: The Billy Graham Story*. 1991. Reprint. Grand Rapids, MI: Zondervan, 2018.

Martinson, Tom. *American Dreamscape: The Pursuit of Happiness in Postwar Suburbia*. New York: Carroll & Graf Publishers, 2000.

Marty, Martin E. *Modern American Religion: Vol. 3. Under God, Indivisible, 1941–1960*. Chicago: University of Chicago Press, 1996.

———. *Righteous Empire: The Protestant Experience in America*. New York: Dial Press, 1970.

McGavran, Donald A., revised and edited by C. Peter Wagner. *Understanding Church Growth*. Third ed. Grand Rapids, MI: William B. Eerdmans, 1990.

McGavran, Donald A., and George G. Hunter III. *Church Growth: Strategies That Work*. Nashville, TN: Abingdon, 1981.

McGirr, Lisa. *Suburban Warriors: The Origins of the New American Right*. Princeton, NJ: Princeton University Press, 2001.

McLoughlin, William G. Jr. *Billy Graham: Revivalist in a Secular Age.* New York: Ronald Press, 1960.

———. *Modern Revivalism: Charles Grandison Finney to Billy Graham.* New York: Ronald Press, 1959.

McPherson, Aimee Semple. *This Is That: Personal Experiences, Sermons and Writings.* Los Angeles: Bridal Call Publishing House, 1919.

Meacham, Jon. *American Gospel: God, the Founding Fathers, and the Making of a Nation.* New York: Random House, 2007.

Meyer, Donald. *The Positive Thinkers: A Study of the American Quest for Health, Wealth and Personal Power from Mary Baker Eddy to Norman Vincent Peale.* Garden City, NY: Doubleday, 1965.

Miller, Donald E. *Reinventing American Protestantism: Christianity in the New Millennium.* Berkeley: University of California Press, 1997.

Miller, Steven P. *The Age of Evangelicalism: America's Born-Again Years.* New York: Oxford University Press, 2014.

———. *Billy Graham and the Rise of the Republican South.* Philadelphia: University of Pennsylvania Press, 2009.

Miller, William Lee. *Piety along the Potomac: Notes on Politics and Morals in the Fifties.* Boston: Houghton Mifflin, 1964.

Moody, Dwight L. *Moody's Latest Sermons.* Chicago: Bible Institute Colportage Association, 1900.

———. *Moody's Stories.* Chicago: Bible Institute Colportage Association, 1899.

———. *The New Sermons of Dwight Lyman Moody.* New York: Henry S. Goodspeed, 1880.

———. *Secret Power: The Secret of Success in Christian Life and Christian Work.* Chicago: Fleming H. Revell Company, 1881.

Moody, William R. *The Life of Dwight L. Moody.* New York: Fleming H. Revell Company, 1900.

Moore, R. Laurence. *Selling God: American Religion in the Marketplace of Culture.* New York: Oxford University Press, 1994.

———. *Touchdown Jesus: The Mixing of Sacred and Secular in American History.* Louisville, KY: Westminster/John Knox Press, 2003.

Moreton, Bethany. *To Serve God and Wal-Mart: The Making of Christian Free Enterprise.* Cambridge, MA: Harvard University Press, 2009.

Morgan, Edmund S. *Benjamin Franklin.* New Haven, CT: Yale University Press, 2002.

Morrison, Charles Clayton. *Can Protestantism Win America?* New York: Harper & Brothers, 1948.

Murch, James DeForest. *The Protestant Revolt: Road to Freedom for American Churches.* Arlington, VA: Crestwood, 1967.

Neuhaus, Richard John. *The Naked Public Square: Religion and Democracy in America.* Grand Rapids, MI: William B. Eerdmans, 1984.

Neuhaus, Richard John, and Michael Cromartie, eds. *Piety and Politics: Evangelicals and Fundamentalists Confront the World*. Washington, DC: Ethics and Public Policy Center, 1987.

Niebuhr, Reinhold. *The Irony of American History*. Chicago: University of Chicago Press, 2008.

Noll, Mark A. *America's God: From Jonathan Edwards to Abraham Lincoln*. New York: Oxford University Press, 2002.

———. *The Scandal of the Evangelical Mind*. Grand Rapids, MI: William B. Eerdmans, 1994.

Okrent, Daniel. *Last Call: The Rise and Fall of Prohibition*. New York: Scribner, 2010.

Osteen, Joel. *Your Best Life Now: 7 Steps to Living at Your Full Potential*. New York: Warner Faith, 2004.

Osteen, John. *Becoming a Man of Unwavering Faith*. New York: Faith Words, 2011.

Pally, Marcia. *The New Evangelicals: Expanding the Vision of the Common Good*. Grand Rapids, MI: William B. Eerdmans, 2011.

Parker, Everett C. *Religious Television: What to Do and How*. New York: Harper & Brothers, 1961.

Peale, Norman Vincent. *The Power of Positive Thinking*. New York: Touchstone, 1952, 2008 edition.

———. *Stay Alive All Your Life*. Englewood Cliffs, NJ: Prentice-Hall, 1957.

———. *The True Joy of Positive Living: An Autobiography*. Pawling, NY: Foundation for Christian Living, 1984.

Perlstein, Rick. *Reaganland: America's Right Turn, 1976–1980*. New York: Simon & Schuster, 2020.

Pollock, John. *Billy Graham: The Authorized Biography*. New York: McGraw-Hill, 1966.

Posner, Sarah. *God's Profits: Faith, Fraud, and the Republican Crusade for Values Voters*. Sausalito, CA: PoliPoint Press, 2008.

———. *Unholy: Why White Evangelicals Worship at the Altar of Donald Trump*. New York: Random House, 2020.

Preston, Andrew. *Sword of the Spirit, Shield of Faith: Religion in American War and Diplomacy*. New York: Knopf, 2012.

Putnam, Robert D., and David E. Campbell. *American Grace: How Religion Divides and Unites Us*. New York: Simon & Schuster, 2010.

Putnam, Robert D., and Lewis M. Feldstein. *Better Together: Restoring the American Community*. New York: Simon & Schuster, 2004.

Reed, Ralph. *Politically Incorrect: The Emerging Faith Factor in American Politics*. Dallas, TX: Word Publishing, 1994.

Richey, Russell E., and Donald G. Jones, eds. *American Civil Religion*. New York: Harper & Row, 1974.

Roberts, Oral. *Deliverance from Fear and from Sickness*. Tulsa, OK: Oral Roberts, 1954.

————. *Expect a Miracle: My Life and Ministry*. Nashville, TN: Thomas Nelson Publishers, 1995.

————. *Miracle of Seed-Faith*. Tulsa, OK: Oral Roberts, 1970.

Roberts, Oral, and G. H. Montgomery, eds. *God's Formula for Success and Prosperity*. Tulsa, OK: Oral Roberts, 1956.

Robertson, Pat. *The New World Order: It Will Change the Way You Live*. Dallas, TX: Word Publishing, 1991.

————. *The Secret Kingdom: Your Path to Peace, Love, and Financial Security*. Dallas, TX: Word Publishing, 1992.

Robins, R. G. *Pentecostalism in America*. Santa Barbara, CA: Praeger, 2010.

Roof, Wade Clark. *Spiritual Marketplace: Baby Boomers and the Remaking of American Religion*. Princeton, NJ: Princeton University Press, 1999.

Sargeant, Kimon Howland. *Seeker Churches: Promoting Traditional Religion in a Nontraditional Way*. New Brunswick, NJ: Rutgers University Press, 2000.

Scarlett, William, ed. *Phillips Brooks: Selected Sermons*. New York: Dutton, 1949.

Schaller, Lyle E. *Effective Church Planning*. Nashville, TN: Abingdon, 1981.

Schneider, Louis, and Sanford M. Dornbusch. *Popular Religion: Inspirational Books in America*. Chicago: University of Chicago Press, 1958.

Schuller, Robert H. *God's Way to the Good Life*. New Canaan, CT: Keats Publishing, 1963, 1974 edition.

————. *My Journey: From an Iowa Farm to a Cathedral of Dreams*. New York: HarperSanFrancisco, 2001.

————. *Tough Times Never Last, But Tough People Do!* Nashville, TN: Thomas Nelson, 1983.

————. *Your Church Has Real Possibilities!* Glendale, CA: G/L Regal Books, 1974.

Sehat, David. *The Myth of American Religious Freedom*. New York: Oxford University Press, 2011.

Sexton, Jared Yates. *American Rule: How a Nation Conquered the World but Failed Its People*. New York: Dutton, 2020.

Sharlet, Jeff. *The Family: The Secret Fundamentalism at the Heart of American Power*. New York: Harper Perennial, 2009.

Sheler, Jeffery L. *Believers: A Journey into Evangelical America*. New York: Viking, 2006.

————. *Prophet of Purpose: The Life of Rick Warren*. New York: Doubleday, 2009.

Shepard, Charles E. *Forgiven: The Rise and Fall of Jim Bakker and the PTL Ministry*. New York: Atlantic Monthly Press, 1989.

Shibley, Mark A. *Resurgent Evangelicalism in the United States: Mapping Cultural Change Since 1970*. Columbia: University of South Carolina Press, 1996.

Silk, Mark. *Spiritual Politics: Religion and America Since World War II*. New York: Simon & Schuster, 1988.

Sinitiere, Phillip Luke. *Salvation with a Smile: Joel Osteen, Lakewood Church, and American Christianity*. New York: New York University Press, 2015.

Smidt, Corwin E. *American Evangelicals Today*. Lanham, MD: Rowman & Little-field, 2015.

Smith, Christian. *American Evangelicalism: Embattled and Thriving*. Chicago: University of Chicago Press, 1998.

Smith, Chuck Jr. *Chuck Smith: A Memoir of Grace*. Costa Mesa, CA: Word for Today, 2009.

Smith, Chuck, and Tal Brooke. *Harvest*. Costa Mesa, CA: Word for Today, 1993.

Starr, Kevin. *Golden Dreams: California in an Age of Abundance, 1950–1963*. New York: Oxford University Press, 2009.

Stewart, Katherine. *The Power Worshippers: Inside the Dangerous Rise of Religious Nationalism*. New York: Bloomsbury, 2019.

Stout, Harry S. *The Divine Dramatist: George Whitefield and the Rise of Modern Evangelicalism*. Grand Rapids, MI: William B. Eerdmans, 1991.

Strobel, Lee. *Inside the Mind of Unchurched Harry and Mary*. Grand Rapids, MI: Zondervan, 1993.

Strober, Jerry, and Ruth Tomczak. *Jerry Falwell: Aflame for God*. Nashville, TN: Thomas Nelson, 1979.

Sunday, Billy, and Karen Gullen, ed. *Billy Sunday Speaks*. New York: Chelsea House, 1970.

Sutton, Matthew Avery. *American Apocalypse: A History of Modern Evangelicalism*. Cambridge, MA: Belknap Press of Harvard University Press, 2017.

Thumma, Scott, and Dave Travis. *Beyond Megachurch Myths: What We Can Learn from America's Largest Churches*. San Francisco, CA: Jossey-Bass, 2007.

Tocqueville, Alexis de. *Democracy in America*. New York: Library of America, 2004.

Trump, Donald J. *Crippled America: How to Make America Great Again*. New York: Threshold Editions, 2015.

Turner, John G. *Bill Bright and Campus Crusade for Christ: The Renewal of Evangelicalism in Postwar America*. Chapel Hill: University of North Carolina Press, 2008.

Twitchell, James B. *Branded Nation: The Marketing of Megachurch, College, Inc., and Museumworld*. New York: Simon & Schuster, 2004.

Veach, Chad. *Faith Forward Future: Moving Past Your Disappointments, Delays, and Destructive Thinking*. Nashville, TN: Nelson Books, 2017.

Wacker, Grant. *America's Pastor: Billy Graham and the Shaping of a Nation*. Cambridge, MA: Harvard University Press, 2014.

———. *Heaven Below: Early Pentecostals and American Culture*. Cambridge, MA: Harvard University Press, 2001.

Warner, Michael, ed. *American Sermons: The Pilgrims to Martin Luther King Jr*. New York: Library of America, 1999.

Warner, R. Stephen. *A Church of Our Own: Disestablishment and Diversity in American Religion*. New Brunswick, NJ: Rutgers University Press, 2005.

Warren, Rick. *The Purpose Driven Church: Growth without Compromising Your Message and Mission*. Grand Rapids, MI: Zondervan, 1995.

———. *The Purpose Driven Life*. Grand Rapids, MI: Zondervan, 2002.

Wehner, Peter. *The Death of Politics: How to Heal Our Frayed Republic after Trump.* New York: HarperOne, 2019.

Wells, David F., and John D. Woodbridge, eds. *The Evangelicals: What They Believe, Who They Are, Where They Are Changing.* Nashville, TN: Abingdon Press, 1975.

Wilcox, Clyde, and Carin Robinson. *Onward Christian Soldiers? The Religious Right in American Politics.* Philadelphia, PA: Westview Press, 2011.

Wilkerson, David. *The Cross and the Switchblade.* New York: Bernard Geis Associates, 1963.

Williams, Daniel K. *God's Own Party: The Making of the Christian Right.* New York: Oxford University Press, 2010.

Wills, Garry. *Head and Heart: American Christianities.* New York: Penguin, 2007.

———. *Under God: Religion and American Politics.* New York: Simon & Schuster, 1990.

Wilson, John F. *Public Religion in American Culture.* Philadelphia, PA: Temple University Press, 1979.

Winter, Gibson. *The Suburban Captivity of the Churches: An Analysis of Protestant Responsibility in the Expanding Metropolis.* New York: Macmillan, 1962.

Winters, Michael Sean. *God's Right Hand: How Jerry Falwell Made God a Republican and Baptized the American Right.* New York: HarperOne, 2012.

Wolfe, Alan. *The Transformation of American Religion: How We Actually Live Our Faith.* Chicago: University of Chicago Press, 2003.

Worthen, Molly. *Apostles of Reason: The Crisis of Authority in American Evangelicalism.* New York: Oxford University Press, 2014.

Wright, Lawrence. *God Save Texas: A Journey into the Soul of the Lone Star State.* New York: Knopf, 2018.

Wuthnow, Robert. *The Crisis in the Churches: Spiritual Malaise, Fiscal Woe.* New York: Oxford University Press, 1997.

———. *God and Mammon in America.* New York: Free Press, 1994.

ABOUT THE AUTHOR

David Clary is a news editor at the *San Diego Union-Tribune* and has been a journalist for more than twenty-five years. His previous book, *Gangsters to Governors: The New Bosses of Gambling in America*, earned medals from the Independent Publisher Book Awards and the Next Generation Indie Book Awards in 2018. For more, go to www.davidclaryauthor.com.